...LLEGE

WITHDRAWN FROM
THE LIBRARY

UNIVERSITY OF
WINCHESTER

D1334433

GOMBRICH ON
ART AND PSYCHOLOGY

E. H. Gombrich (photo: Mary Robert).

Contents

List of figures

For Lynn

Preface

I T has been thirty-five years since E. H. Gombrich's *Art and Illusion* was first published. The most recent reprint, of 1986, contains four additional prefaces and a reference to a collection of material published in *The Image and the Eye*. This is just the very large tip of the enormous iceberg of his work on art and perception. Besides *Meditations on a Hobby Horse* there is *The Sense of Order* and a host of articles and lectures uncollected in Gombrich's Phaidon volumes. The time has come to take stock, albeit in a limited and provisional way, since he is still busy, refining past ideas and working on his next book *The Preference for the Primitive*.

I am grateful to my fellow contributors for sharing in the enterprise of coming to terms with Gombrich's work and to Professor Sir Ernst Gombrich for agreeing to make an offering himself. I have also included two of his responses to the papers in this volume (all of which had been sent to him for his comments). I am delighted that Manchester University Press has agreed to publish the results of this project.

For practical assistance I am indebted to The Nottingham Trent University, its Department of Visual and Performing Arts and Carolyn Welling, my boss, not only for giving moral and financial support but also for the most valuable of all commodities, the time to reflect and write. My colleagues on the photography course team have provided an ideal working environment and Linda Dickinson deserves special mention for her very able help with proofreading. I am also grateful to Rebecca Archer for her early assistance with word-processing.

My project was interrupted by a spell in hospital for major heart surgery and I am indebted to Dr Keith Morris, my consultant, Mr Richard Firmin, my surgeon, and the medical and support staffs of the Queen's Medical Centre, Nottingham, and the Nuffield Hospital, Leicester for my life.

I owe a special word of thanks to Sir Ernst Gombrich, who has over the years patiently tolerated my questions.

Finally, this book is dedicated to Lynn, who has been a constant source of encouragement and support.

Richard Woodfield   Nottingham 1995

Short titles

Art and Illusion	E. H. Gombrich, *Art and Illusion: A study in the psychology of pictorial representation*, fifth edition, Oxford 1986.
Eribon	E. H. Gombrich, *A Lifelong Interest: Conversations on art and science with Didier Eribon*, London 1993.
Heritage	E. H. Gombrich, *The Heritage of Apelles: Studies in the art of the Renaissance III*, Oxford 1976.
Ideals	E. H. Gombrich, *Ideals and Idols: Essays on values in history and in art*, Oxford 1979.
Illusion	E. H. Gombrich, 'Illusion and art' in R. L. Gregory and E. H. Gombrich (eds.) *Illusion in Nature and Art*, London 1973.
Image and Eye	E. H. Gombrich, *The Image and the Eye: Further studies in the psychology of pictorial representation*, Oxford 1982.
New Light	E. H. Gombrich, *New Light on Old Masters: Studies in the art of the Renaissance IV*, Oxford 1986.
Norm and Form	E. H. Gombrich, *Norm and Form: Studies in the art of the Renaissance I*, fourth edition, London 1985.
Reflections	E. H. Gombrich, *Reflections on the History of Art* (edited by Richard Woodfield), Oxford 1987.
Symbolic Images	E. H. Gombrich, *Symbolic Images: Studies in the art of the Renaissance II*, third edition, Oxford 1985.
The Story of Art	E. H. Gombrich, *The Story of Art*, fifteenth edition, Oxford 1989.
The Sense of Order	E. H. Gombrich, *The Sense of Order*, second edition, London 1992.
Topics	E. H. Gombrich, *Topics of our Time: Twentieth-century issues in learning and in art*, London 1991.
Tributes	E. H. Gombrich, *Tributes: Interpreters of our cultural tradition*, Oxford 1984.

Introduction:
mapping the ground

Richard Woodfield

A MONG the books that Gombrich read while he was still at school was
Max Dvořák's *Kunstgeschichte als Geistesgeschichte*, soon after its publication.
Gombrich later remarked that it had convinced him that 'the art of the past
offered an immediate and exciting access to the mind of bygone ages'.[1] Ten
years after reading Dvořák he took a different view: the idea that art reflected
the mind of the past accounted for the 'social success of art history today,
its receptivity to the art of all times and all peoples'.[2] Gombrich granted that
its author had offered a persuasive case for studying art, but that his views
on mannerism failed the test of critical analysis.

His change of mind had been brought about by his studentship, under
Schlosser, at the University of Vienna's second institute of art history. Schlosser
had been sceptical of the *Geistesgeschichte* approach and insisted on rigorous
work in the archives, which could be the only point of entry into history:
art was a separate matter and the 'language' of construction of visual imagery,
Kunstsprache, something yet again. In preparing his doctoral dissertation for
Schlosser on the architecture of Giulio Romano in the archives of Mantua,
Gombrich qualified his earlier assessment of his hero's achievement.

But it wasn't just a matter of the archives proving that Dvořák's assessment
of mannerism was wrong, it was that Gombrich had entered into a completely
different arena for understanding the history of art. This was due to the
prevalence of an interest in the methodological problems of art-historical
explanation, encouraged in Schlosser's special seminar. Explanation, as opposed to chronology, was an integral part of the grand tradition of the Vienna
School of Art History, of which Schlosser was the lineal descendent. Perhaps
its interest in the psychology of perception has been overemphasised to the
exclusion of other matters, but it was psychology which was to gain Gombrich's everlasting fascination: 'we all imbibed psychology with the milk of
our Viennese *Alma Mater*'. He has told that particular story himself in his
article 'Art history and psychology in Vienna fifty years ago'.[3] Riegl's work

had just been republished; Schlosser had an interest in the area; Loewy was testimony to the continuity of a particular kind of psychology and Sedlmayr had just published a book on Borromini's architecture using the new approach of gestalt psychology. Ernst Kris, one of Schlosser's ex-students, was both a curator at the Kunsthistorische Museum and a practising psychoanalyst, a member of Freud's circle. It was more or less inevitable, then, that Gombrich should turn his attention to the work of Karl Bühler, who held the chair in psychology, follow his lectures and associate with his students. Bühler and Kris together were to have a profound effect on Gombrich's attitude to the history of art.[4] In his Bodonyi review, written while he was still a student in the summer of 1932, Gombrich argued that any art-historical analysis which used psychology should make its assumptions plain for detailed scrutiny; they could not simply be taken for granted.

The Bodonyi review was Gombrich's first published theoretical essay and entrance into methodological debate.[5] It was on the use of the golden ground in late antique art, a subject raised by Riegl's *Spätrömische Kunstindustrie* (1901). He argued that Riegl's interpretation of late antique art was open to criticism: Riegl treated its imagery as having naturalistic ambitions. The idea that visual imagery resulted from a naturalistic impulse in front of nature, though sweeping from a haptic to an optic pole of perception, failed to recognise the exceptional nature of the Greek revolution in artistic production.[6] Egyptian and late antique art were fundamentally different in terms of their cultural roles and the demands they made upon the visual responses of their spectators.

Gombrich took exception to the view shared by Riegl and Dvořák that *Art* was an unchanging absolute. The stimulus to art's production was a historical variable,[7] not a constant *Kunstwollen*, and the language of visual imagery, its *Kunstsprache*, was just as historically and culturally specific as verbal language.[8] There was a crucial difference between the classical artist's ambition to capture life and the late antique artist's creation of a pictograph; the same modes of visual analysis could not be applied to the two different forms of imagery.[9]

Both Riegl and Dvořák used outdated psychological theories in their analysis of late antique art. Both committed what Gombrich was later to call the physiognomic fallacy, seeing the style of a period as reflecting its *Geist*.[10] He argued that expression was only achievable within a language and that a language could not have an expressive character of its own. At any given moment, the style in which a visual image was produced (that is, its overall characteristics which made it identifiable as being the product of a moment of culture and history) were the mechanics of its actual production. Style was not an abstract mirror to thought. Later, in his work in the Mantuan archives, Gombrich realised that a unified, and abstract, *Geist* did not lie behind the production of mannerist works of art; history was populated by people, with individual minds, inclinations and habits of work, not by abstractions.[11]

Gombrich cited Bühler's work in the Bodonyi review and Bühler's own concerns with expression had been fed from a number of different sources. Besides having close contacts with the gestalt school of psychology he was also very involved with linguistics. This resulted in what could be called a concern with the mind's products rather than with the mind *per se*. In his fundamental work *Sprachtheorie* (1934), anticipated by an earlier article 'Die Axiomatik der Sprachwissenschaften' (1933), he was concerned to 'clarify the capacities of language by glancing at other sign systems':

> Bühler . . . starts from the insight that there exists a spectrum, ranging from the extreme fidelity to nature exhibited by a waxwork, which (even so) resembles the model only relatively, to, for instance, a temperature chart, which merely records certain relationships in a given field. In between we find (if I may simplify and supplement his account a little), for instance, the notes of a musical score, the map, the landscape painting, and the illusionist backdrop of the stage as different but equally valid systems of signs. As you notice, this analysis no longer speaks of the question of the notion of the 'conceptual image', because first we have to get our logic right before psychology can come into its own again. What is at stake is the notion of 'relational fidelity', which is brilliantly explained in connection with black and white photography.[12]

Gombrich was to pick up the strands from Bühler's work after the war, when working on *Art and Illusion*, but on leaving university he joined forces with Ernst Kris on two projects, first on expression and then on caricature.

As Freud's disciple, Kris was keen to write a book on visual humour, an equivalent to *Der Witz und seine Beziehung zum Unbewussten* (1905). Besides addressing itself to the mechanics of visual satire, drollery, the grotesque, the cartoon and the caricature, the study was concerned with the question of why portrait caricature had emerged at such a late state (*c.* 1600) in the development of visual art. Kris, accepting Freud's Lamarckian account of the growth of civilisation, argued that it was not possible until humankind was civilised enough to have left the irrational fear of magic. The advent of the Second World War prevented the publication of the book[13] and the Holocaust put paid to ideas concerning the growth of human civilisation. But the project left Gombrich with a deeper interest in the mechanics of visual imagery, including the problem of likeness, which Kris had not addressed. How could it be possible that a few lines could bear such a striking resemblance to an individual to a point where one could see that individual in terms of those lines?

Before the war, and as a result of Schlosser's insights, Gombrich had been struck by the recurrent use of the formula in artistic creativity: not just the medieval simile but also the schematic image in post-Renaissance art. The war also increased his interest in the role of projection in perception, a subject which had already been explored by gestalt psychologists.[14]

After the war, he honoured his promise to write *The Story of Art*. Building on his earlier theoretical work, he argued that different social functions demanded different kinds of imagery. The majority of the world's artistic production was dominated by the need to produce magical substitutes for the figure:

> We remember how the primitive artist used to build up, say, a face out of simple forms rather than copy a real face; we have often looked back to the Egyptians and their method of representing in a picture all they knew rather than all they saw. Greek and Roman art breathed life into these schematic forms; medieval art used them in turn for telling the sacred story, Chinese art for contemplation. Neither was urging the artist to 'paint what he saw'. This idea dawned only during the age of the Renaissance. At first all seemed to go well. Scientific perspective, '*sfumato*', Venetian colours, movement and expression, were added to the artist's means of representing the world around him; but every generation discovered 'pockets of resistance', strongholds of conventions which made artists apply forms they had learned rather than paint what they really saw. The nineteenth-century rebels proposed to make a clean sweep of all these conventions; one after another was tackled, till the Impressionists pro-claimed that their methods allowed them to render on canvas the act of vision with 'scientific accuracy'.[15]

Modern art, by contrast, rejected that ideal. The artist was no longer concerned to produce naturalistic imagery because that function had been usurped by photography; other values came to the fore. It is a mistake to think that the Cubists simply extended a line of development inaugurated by the Impressionists, their artistic concerns were entirely different.

We need to separate out two phenomena: on the one hand, the development of visual imagery, and on the other, conspicuous success in the use of that imagery. This is analogous to our drawing a distinction beween the development of languages and conspicuous literary success in those languages.[16] Our own visual world is dominated by photography, and we are aware of developments towards the creation of virtual reality.[17] It is not inappropriate to see ourselves as inheriting the classical concern with the production of the naturalistic image, but that is a different matter from art. It should be remembered that the account of the development of the arts of working with pigment, bronze and marble found in Pliny's *Natural History* was orientated towards techniques rather than aesthetic values.[18]

The two great periods of visual discoveries about the world and its representation, classical antiquity and the Italian Renaissance, formed the focus of Gombrich's post-war project which ultimately led to *Art and Illusion*. Naturalistic imagery was a problem worth addressing, particularly in the light of its rejection by contemporary artists. Gombrich's strong sense of problem made him ask why its development was such a major human achievement if a child today could draw better than Giotto.

In a proposal sent to Walter Neurath on 9 March 1947, Gombrich wrote:

Any number of books have been written on pictorial art as a mode of expression, as creative activity or aesthetic experience. Without necessarily questioning the fruitfulness of this approach, it may be asked whether the time has not come to investigate the realm of the image as such, much in the way modern linguists have studied the functions of speech. The studies of Richards in Cambridge and the development of the Semantic approach, notably in the USA, seem to hold out the promise that ultimately even the analysis of aesthetic values can but benefit from a clarification of these primary matters. It should perhaps be said from the outset that the development of Modern Art facilitates and stimulates such a fresh approach, for the various symbolic aspects of art are, of course, much more manifest in Picasso than they were, say, in Manet.[19]

He mentioned Picasso, who, of all artists, demonstrated that style was a visual construction. But in *The Story of Art* Gombrich had also shown himself to be intrigued by Salvador Dali, whose painting

brings it home to us for the last time why it is that modern artists are not satisfied in simply representing 'what they see'. They have become too aware of the many problems which are hidden in this demand . . . Dali's way of letting each form represent several things at the same time may focus our attention on the many possible meanings of each colour and form – much in the way in which a successful pun may make us aware of the function of words and their meaning.[20]

Dali's work had also intrigued Freud, who expressed an interest in exploring 'the origins of a painting by him analytically', i.e. through free association and memories like a dream.[21] But Gombrich chose a different approach: it could be analysed at the level of a joke. Dali's paintings played with visual puns, and, like puns, which are real linguistic discoveries, they render conspicuous the generative potential of visual configurations.[22] Dali had hit on the phenomenon later explored by Adelbert Ames: the fundamental ambiguity of the monocular view of a spatial configuration.

It was with the problems of the visual image in mind that Gombrich wrote his Morris review of 1949.[23] There he found Morris's theories fundamentally flawed on a number of counts, not least of which was his explanation of iconicity. If the iconic sign is defined as a symbol which looks like its subject, then how that likeness occurs still needs to be explained; it might, after all, be just by habituation. Is it just a matter of convention, for example, that a patch of paint in one of Guardi's paintings comes to look like a gondolier? Is there ever an image which is purely iconic, that just looks like what it is? Guardi depended upon projection for completion of the image:

> Guardi relies on the beholder's capacity to read 'iconicity' *into* his sign. The contextual, emotional, or formal means by which this interpretation is evoked or facilitated – in other words, the relation between objective 'iconicity' and psychological projection – would have to form one of the main fields of study of a descriptive semiotic of the image. Perhaps it will show that what has been called the history of 'seeing' is really the history of a learning process through which a socially coherent public was trained by the artist to respond in a given manner to certain abbreviated signs.[24]

This idea is close to the suggestion, and could have been taken as meaning, that naturalistic imagery could be purely conventional. It is not surprising that some commentators, Nelson Goodman in particular, should have come to understand *Art and Illusion* in these terms.

Two years after the Morris review, in 'Meditations on a hobby horse', Gombrich argued that the representational function of the image *originated* in substitution, not visual similarity, and that the child's hobby-horse extended the class of 'horse' by offering an object that was treatable as a horse. The hobby-horse had two interesting distinct features: it was a viable substitute for a horse, because it afforded riding, and it only became desirable to ride because of the social prestige of the rider on horseback. The biological substitute of the cat's ball for a mouse can be translated, in more general terms, as the later Gibsonian idea of the object's offering visual information for use. It is both a product of nature, a stimulus to 'see *as*', and culture, a social pressure for use. Given the fact that a hobby-horse affords riding, or that a manikin may become the centre of ritual,[25] the way is open to the user to increase the information offered by the stick or manikin to enhance its simulative capacities. Where would a horse be without its mane, or Athena without her garments? Naturalistic imagery is, needless to say, even more complex than the primitive substitute.

'Meditations on a hobby horse' originated the idea that 'making comes before matching', and it also considered the way in which conventions, and the perception of pictures as visually constructed objects, come to play a role in picture perception. The extension of a class does not imply that the member of a class refers to a reality beyond itself;[26] that is a new step in the representational process. The so-called 'illusionist style' took that step; it not only suggested the possibility of creating an extension of the viewer's space, but also created the possibility that an element within the picture field must signify a presence. The idea that a picture offers a window on to an imagined nature demands that

> we cannot conceive of any spot on the panel which is not 'significant', which does not represent something. The empty patch thus easily comes to signify light, air, and atmosphere, and the vague form is interpreted as enveloped by air. It is this confidence in the representational context which is given by the very context of the frame, which makes the development of impressionist methods possible.[27]

Guardi's patch is interpretable as a gondolier as a result of a complicity of understanding between the artist and his public over how his painted imagery actually works.

In 1955 Gombrich presented his germinating ideas to the Durham conference of the British Psychological Society.[28] He emphasised the nature of depiction as a sorting and classifying process, using the example of the mosaic as a constructed relational model. The idea of prototypes emerged to explain the use of the known to explore the unknown. While Gombrich was deeply interested in the Whorf–Sapir hypothesis that language decisively shapes our conception of the world, he stressed that the artist's visual vocabulary can also produce mismatches which offer the possibility of correcting drawings. The ultimately correct drawing is one which offers as many different interpretations as its model; such a drawing is possible when it is a drawing of a drawing, such as a Rorschach blot. Even so, Gombrich emphasised the importance of feedback. The artist's depictions offer models for construing the visual world: a landscape can be seen as a Constable, and a fingerprint, as in a humorous drawing by Steinberg, can be seen as a Van Gogh.

The choice of the title *Art and Illusion* for his Mellon Lectures 'The visible world and the language of art' did Gombrich a profound disservice. It invited two mistaken views: that the book was about art and an exercise in aesthetics, and that illusion was the criterion of successful art. In fact, as Gombrich has often said, visual imagery needs a linguistics prior to its poetics. Furthermore, anyone with a smattering of knowledge of the history of art criticism will know that 'sparrow aesthetics' has never been regarded as the criterion of a successful work of art.[29] Gilpin, writing in the eighteenth century, echoed general feelings about illusion when he wrote:

> But it is not under the idea of deception, that the *real* artist paints. He does not mean to *impose* upon us, by making us believe that a picture of a foot long is an extended landscape. All he wishes is to give such *characteristic touches* to his picture as may be able to rouse the imagination of the beholder. The picture is not so much the *ultimate end*, as it is the *medium*, through which the ravishing scenes of nature are excited in the imagination.[30]

Art and Illusion offers a series of theses about the mechanics of the construction of visual imagery rooted in the view that they constitute objective discoveries about the way in which the world's appearance may be simulated.

While it may be a convention to want to depict the world naturalistically, and has had a minority appeal in the past until photography swept the face of the earth, operations within that convention are not, of themselves, necessarily conventions.[31] It is not a matter of convention that one cannot see around corners, it is a matter of fact. If the cubists decide to represent what can be seen around corners, it is a matter of fact that they are not representing what can be seen from a stationary point of view. Picasso's cubist paintings will never represent the way in which we see the world at a momentary point of time.

Much of the misunderstanding of *Art and Illusion* has arisen from a failure to grasp the relationships between natural effects and conventional constraints in the perception of images. The question of whether illusionistic imagery is natural or conventional is a product of a habit of thinking in terms of polarities, of black and white, when it should be recognised that there is a range of grey in between: 'What we observe is rather a continuum between skills which come naturally to us and skills which may be next to impossible for anyone to acquire.'[32] It might be thought, for example, that the outline figure is a matter of convention, because outlines do not exist in nature:

> yet it turns out that the traditional view of the contour as a convention is based on an oversimplification. Things in our environment are indeed separated from their background; at least they so detach themselves as soon as we move. The contour is the equivalent of this experience . . .
>
> So important are these boundaries indicating what psychologists call 'common fate' in features of the immediate environment that it has been shown that animals too respond to objects in outline as they do to their three-dimensional prototypes. The equivalence is so obvious that no special learning appears to be required.[33]

Does 'no special learning' imply any learning at all? Does it not indicate an inbuilt disposition to respond to such outlines? Are there not inbuilt dispositions, like the disposition of a baby to recognise a smiling face, or to pick up a language? What are the limits of dispositional behaviour?

Gombrich solved his early problem of projection by bringing into his account the new discoveries of ethology: the importance of trigger mechanisms in animal behaviour. Seeing faces in clouds, for example, is not like learning a language, but is a product of biological conditioning. On the other hand, seeing the Indian in the white chalk drawing of a typically Indian profile (Philostratus' example), is a product of the cultivation of seeing what one can see in an image, which is a product of culture.[34] The naturalistic artist's use of increasingly sophisticated visual effects depends upon a culture of appreciation.

A successful naturalistic image depends upon a range of perceptual triggers to gain the spectator's visual assent. It could be argued that Pliny's *Natural History* described the development of one particular series that he was able to identify, such as the use of three colours to generate the illusion of relief.[35] The ability to depict a knee under a drapery is another such skill:

> At least from the sixth century onwards Greek art appeals to our imagination, by implying more than it can show. Every genuinely narrative

illustration must be thus supplemented by us along several dimensions – by extending that of time we can see the figures move, by supplying that of space we can relate them to each other, and by projecting life into them we give their gestures and expressions meaning . . .

It was at the same time that the sculptors' statues were seen to 'come to life'. We sense the tension of the muscles under the surface, we see the play of the body under the garment, we feel the presence of a mind behind the smile. In discussing the illusions created by art, art historians (including this writer) have concentrated too much on the pictorial inventions of foreshortening, perspective, or light and shade, and failed to analyse the illusion of life that a Greek statue can give.[36]

This question of illusion, and the relationship between stimulation and simulation, was one which Gombrich explored further in *Illusion*.

Gombrich had already raised the question of whether perceptual triggers were natural or a product of habituation in his Morris review. His conclusion was that *both* elements entered into the production of illusionistic images. There are effects which compel visual reaction and there are also those which come into play once one has joined the game, like Guardi's patch.[37] Triggers may stimulate, though they need not simulate. The phenomenon of imprinting in ducks 'shows how far objective likeness can be dispensed with in certain circumstances'.[38] The concern of the naturalistic artist is to invent triggers, or keys, to unlock sensory responses: foreshortening for depth, tonal contrast for modelling, highlights for texture, 'or the clues to expression discovered by humorous art'.[39] In *Illusion* Gombrich considered the depiction of eyes. The artist's problem is 'not necessarily to fashion a facsimile eye. It is to find a way of stimulating the response to a living gaze.'[40] A variety of different conventions of depicting the eye have been invented to achieve this effect, Houdon's probably being the most remarkable. The difficult question concerns what we are actually seeing when we see a successful effect; we are certainly not seeing the object, but are we seeing a phantom? This question opens up an enormous area for debate among perceptual psychologists, in which Gombrich comes out against the empiricists, on the one hand, and J. J. Gibson on the other.

In the course of his career, Gibson had found it increasingly intolerable that there could be a distinction between appearance and reality, and denied that we could actually experience visual fields. In so far as we move around the world, our perception of it is self-correcting, enabling us to perceive its invariant structures; but we may not do this with pictures. Confronted by

Gombrich's criticisms, Gibson had to admit that appearances may be seen in the world as they may in pictures: witness the Vault of Heaven. These, according to Gombrich, 'form the limit of our visual world'.[41] The ambiguities of the world's appearance may be removed by movement, but in painting the ambiguities potentially in an image have to be removed by the intro-duction of reinforcing cues: witness the modifications which are necessary to support a purely geometrical construction of perspective as unambiguously representing a particular natural space. True to Popper's falsificationism, Gombrich believes that there is always the possibility of error in perception, but that error may be removed by further tests. The artist's process of making and matching reflects the process of testing and correcting.

This 'searchlight' theory of perception does not turn Gombrich into a constructivist, however; that represents a massive oversimplification of the problems involved. Monkeys do not make guesses when they leap from tree to tree, and humans do not make inferences based upon their experiences; the classical distinction between sensation and perception is too crude to handle what happens. Psychology lacks an adequate concept of feedback, tied, as it is, to an eighteenth-century language of experience and causality and, as I understand it, the computer modelling approach, introduced by Marr, is also very primitive, tied as it is to a picture theory of processing; it assumes what it tries to explain. In so far as pictures are used in experiments to test visual processes, and as they necessarily contain less information than objects in the real world, the role of conjecture is bound to play a greater role in their perception.

Humans are propelled through a world of objects, not sensations, by a search for meaning which can, itself, condition the experience of pictures and other visual notations. The major discovery of *Art and Illusion* was that

the human imagination is a powerful thing when expertly manipulated . . . the less information is given, the more what I would call 'the beholder's share' comes into play, provided of course the search for meaning is suitably guided. The visual information the painter can stimulate may never actually duplicate the information we pick up from solid objects close by. But is it not possible that he can mobilize the system to produce the same phantom sensations which come into play in those processes of search or probing for simplicity precisely in situations of inadequate information? If that is true, our perception of pictures would indeed differ from the perception of the visible world, but the right stimulation from the canvas may still engender a reaction similar to that which we experience in front of nature. A fine landscape or seascape by one of the Dutch masters certainly does not give me the illusion that the museum wall opens into parts of Holland. But I would claim that in getting absorbed in such a painting my search for meaning between and behind its brush-strokes weaves on its surface a rich fabric of uncontradicted sensations.[42]

Gombrich's attitude to Gregory's kind of contructivism stems from his aversion to relativistic interpretations of perception.[43] If one accepts the idea that all pictures offer insights into visual experience of the world or, as the philosophers put it, criteria of perception,[44] it would have to be accepted that the world was seen differently in the twelfth century from the way it is now. The difference in perception is then taken to account for the difference between pictures then and pictures now. But this is to make the same mistake as Riegl and Dvořák, remarked on before, which is to assume a unity of pictorial purpose. Once it is recognised that pictures can serve a variety of purposes besides depicting a world, a new type of analysis can emerge.

Gombrich's work, then, is a form of historical psychology; it asks what may be thought of as being possible at a particular moment of art-historical time. The historian has to ask what the devices were that were available to makers of visual imagery, and the range of their possible applications. A fundamental example of this is the potentialities of the painted and drawn mark, explored in *Art and Illusion* and then developed in 'Light and highlights' in *Heritage* and 'Watching artists at work: commitment and improvisation in the history of drawing' in *Topics*. A further example is the use of the frame, used in connection with the painted mark in 'Meditations' and then later, in connection with the development of narrative, in *Means and Ends: Reflections on the History of Fresco Painting.*[45] Of course, the idea of the device is inseparable from that of the receptive viewer, and this is a topic which is still foremost in his mind.

'Mental set', or the beholder's share, plays a very important role in the perceptual process. As Gombrich suggested in a recent lecture at the Warburg Institute, 'I believe that the difference between signs and images rests in the different mental sets we have to adopt for their understanding.'[46] At this point we may return to a remark made by Gombrich in his Durham lecture of 1955: 'One of the things I believe to have learned is that it makes very little sense to speak of "seeing the world" or any such generality. We can study perception only through actions or reactions in given situations.'[47] In *Art and Illusion* he reformulated this idea as: 'The test of the image is not its lifelikeness but its efficacy within a context of action.'[48] One is invited to consider what spectators would have made of the images that were produced for them; what purposes they fulfilled. By recognising the role of 'mental set' in picture perception we realise that not all pictures of things are intended to be seen as records of visual experiences of those things.

There are important differences between looking at naturalistic pictures and looking at objects in the world, but there are dangers in going too far in asserting the extent to which naturalistic pictures are governed by conventions.[49] In a very real sense we look into a Leonardo drawing of a face and we look at a typographic symbol for one (☺); we recognise them both as faces, but expect animation from the first and not from the second.[50] How, then, do we look at this symbol (☻) in relation to this one (𝕮)? We look *into* a photograph of a city and *at* a map;[51] a photograph invites a point of view, a map doesn't. We gain an impression, right or wrong, of what a city is like from a photograph, but not from a map. The information potentials all vary in character depending on the requirements placed upon the constructed image. This idea of visual processing goes back to Bühler's principle of abstractive relevance;[52] features of a configuration become meaningful in terms of their information potential within a given situation. One may wonder what the information potential of a given situation is. In a world of objects, it is their availability for use. In a world of visual imagery, it is again their availability for use. But life gets very difficult when one tries to specify what those uses might be.

One looks for different significant features in the sculptures of the founders at Naumburg Cathedral,[53] armorial bearings,[54] confraternity decorations[55] and paintings like Masaccio's *Holy Trinity*,[56] Raphael's *Madonna della Sedia*[57] and Dutch landscapes.[58] Most obvious of all, one is not expected to look at flowers in wallpaper as one looks at them in a still life.[59]

The question which Gombrich started to address in '*Icones Symbolicae*. The visual image in neo-Platonic thought'[60] concerned the status of what had hitherto been regarded as symbols in Baroque art: what is the difference between looking at peace personified and the personification of peace? From my own experience, I would suggest that it is the kind of attention that one gives to the various aspects of the image.[61]

While Rudolph Arnheim, following Picasso's dealer Daniel Kahnweiler, predicted that the works of Picasso, Braque or Klee would begin to 'look exactly like the things they represent',[62] the same kind of point can be made again. It is a mistake to think that Picasso intended to offer pictures of reality in his analytic cubist images; they were intended to disrupt normal perceptual processes in front of the object by offering conflicting spatial clues in the depicted object. Synthetic cubist constructions, on the other hand, played with the differences between pictorial ground (the 'invisible' primed surface), real space (the actual occupied space of a newspaper or piece of veneer) and pictorial space (a depicted guitar, for example). These subtleties of pictorial appeal were appreciated by Picasso's patrons as part of an avant-garde game which was being played by a small number of artists, centred in Paris.[63] If the world actually did look like cubist paintings, we would have enormous difficulty in getting around it, and if the world looked as if it was depicted in twelfth-century pictures, archers would have had no difficulty in shooting their prey around corners. If naturalistic art is concerned with a *moment* of vision, it must involve itself with movement as well as space:

> While the problem of space and its representation in art has occupied the attention of art historians to an almost exaggerated degree, the corresponding problem of time and the representation of movement has been strangely neglected.[64]

Following Hildebrand's concern with the representation of movement, Wickhoff's interest in narrative and his own early explorations of gesture and expression, Gombrich has turned this into another of his major areas of exploration. Actions take place through time, and a naturalistic visual image captures only a moment. Two obvious questions follow: whether the moment is necessarily a slice of time like a film frame, and whether a slice of an expressive gesture forms the foundation of representation of states of mind. To the first question, the answer is that the staged moment, like a film still, could well stray beyond the slice of time to embody a full sense of the action; thus there is something suspect about Lessing's characterisation of visual imagery as simply an art of space.[65] In answer to the second question, Gombrich suggests that one might look in the direction of 'ritualised gesture' to find a repertoire for the expression of mental states.[66]

The idea of a repertoire highlights a confusion in understanding Gombrich's views on expression; one which he set out to redress in 'Four theories of artistic expression'.[67] The idea of a repertoire may characterise either the range of expressions depicted by an artist in an image or an artist's own expressive range. The idea that it is artists' business to express themselves is a legacy of the Romantic view of art. It is significant that while Gombrich has developed a psychological approach to understanding visual imagery, his own approach, despite his work with Ernst Kris, has never been psychologistic.[68] His own work has never been directed towards the artist's personal psychology, and he is unconcerned with the artist's inner states in giving accounts of intentions.[69] He is preoccupied by the problem of how visual imagery may be seen to work, and this critical stance in relation to psychologism comes out most clearly in his essays on Freud.[70]

In a letter to Hermann Struck, Freud declared that his essay on Leonardo 'does not in the least aim at making the great man's achievements intelligible'.[71] Freud's essay on Leonardo[72] is well known as an attempt to explore the mentality of the man through his imagery; but he described it himself as 'half novelistic fiction [*Romandichtung*]'.[73] The historian's business is to ask how Leonardo's imagery would have been understood by his contemporaries; at least one had a problem with his *St Anne*.[74] The first step towards clarification is to determine the representational status of the image: 'The traditional group . . . [of the Virgin and Child with St Anne] had never been conceived as a realistic representation', let alone an expression of Leonardo's state of mind. Leonardo, unlike contemporary artists, wasn't paid to paint his states of mind, and no one had the slightest interest in them.[75] The image is simply a reworking of a traditional motif rendered more complex by Leonardo's interest in naturalistic depiction.

While other commentators on Freud have had recourse to his work on dreaming, Gombrich regards his ideas on jokes as more appropriate to an analysis of the workings of visual imagery.[76] A joke depends for its effectiveness on the resources of language as such; creativity in image-making is, in turn, based upon the resources which emerge out of the traditions of image-making. As language is generative and can operate by way of feedback, so too may the visual image.

The problem of feedback is a mighty one. Once a work of art has been created it may serve a variety of different functions,[77] which may compete with each other in terms of the appreciation and future development of the work. Nowhere is this problem better illustrated than in Gombrich's hugely complex and ambitious study *The Sense of Order*.

The creation of substitutes is only one dimension of image-making activity; the desire to ornament is another. Ornament is generative and plays on the human interest in enriching and extending the visual field. It has quite different characteristics from picturing:

> Painting, like speaking, implicitly demands attention whether or not it receives it. Decoration cannot make this demand. It normally depends for

its effect on the fluctuating attention we can spare while we scan our surroundings.[78]

While we might enjoy examining a Persian carpet, we don't believe that it is necessary to examine its every detail. The mechanism which facilitates this response is our sense of order.[79] If a key idea behind *Art and Illusion* was 'making before matching', the one behind this book is 'groping comes before grasping or seeking before seeing'.[80] While the picture offers us the delight of recognition, the Persian carpet cultivates the pleasures of 'anticipation and memory' which 'may largely be subliminal, but they are none the less real'.[81] Gombrich had thought of calling his book *The Unregarded Art*.

It is central to his theory of perception, however, that the search for meaning plays a key role. Now meaning is one of those multifaceted phenomena which can spill into imagery in a variety of different ways: one has only to remember gold as a visual metaphor of value to realise how complex the situation might be. Colours and shapes may possess more than formal values. It is for this reason that *The Sense of Order* is a polyphonic text, including such chapters as 'Ornament as art', 'Towards an analysis of effects', 'The psychology of styles', 'Designs as signs' and 'The edge of chaos', the latter chapter concerned the dissolution of figurative images and the play of grotesques and the fantastic. The art of ornament may reach the heights of control, as in the Alhambra or the Book of Kells, or regress into fantasy.

The tendency to regression forms a focus for another of Gombrich's central interests, which is now, after a lifetime's gestation, emerging as a book on the preference for the primitive. Like other members of the Vienna School, Gombrich has been deeply interested in so-called artistic 'declines'; this was marked both by the Bodonyi review and his doctoral dissertation on Giulio Romano's architecture. In the following Garger review he maintained that a decline of interest in naturalism had

> facilitated the emancipation of formal values . . . in as far as the recogniz-
> ability of symbols is not compromised and the sign remains a sign, primitive
> predelictions may be allowed free rein. This applies to the pure use of
> precious colours in medieval illumination as much as to that ornamental
> elaboration of the whole work which leads to such high decorative
> achievement.[82]

In his later essay 'Visual metaphors of value in art' he returned to the theme of the golden ground. What had been taken for a valuable addition to the artist's armoury in late antiquity had become a problem for Alberti in the fifteenth century. Not only did he see it as an obstacle to a managed depiction of space, disrupting the carefully wrought devices of one-point linear perspective, its use posed moral problems as well; it was felt to have a different moral significance. In his Ernest Jones lecture 'Psychoanalysis and the history of art' he argued that contemporary primitivism was a product of forms of sophistication and refinement:

> a compensation, a redistribution of psychological gratifications, must also take place during the post-Bougereau period . . . Impressionism succeeded in excluding literary association and in confining the give and take to the reading of the scrambled colour-patches. But in return for this effort of shared activity, it yields a wonderful premium of regressive pleasure.

Impressionism stood between the pursuit of appearances and 'an openly regressive art, of primitivism'.[83]

It was Cicero who had remarked:

> For it is hard to say why exactly it is that the things which most strongly gratify our senses and excite them most vigorously at their first appearance, are the ones from which we are most speedily estranged by a feeling of disgust and satiety.[84]

Gombrich's reading of ancient rhetorical theory convinced him that there was there a model for the explanation of the development of a primitivising style.[85] It was a theory of literary effects which could be applied with equal validity to the visual arts. He subsequently made use of that model in accounting for the distinctive nature of Giulio Romano's deployment of the rustic style of architecture.[86] His 1971 lectures 'Ideas of progress and their impact on art'[87] focused particularly on changes which occurred in the eighteenth century, in the rejection of Rococo. Blake, for example, objected to Reynolds's admiration of works by painterly artists; clean lines can come to have a moral significance superior to decadent conspicuous brush-strokes. It is obvious that this was a matter to be explained not by changes in perception, but in the values placed upon perceived features of visual imagery; a matter for the social or cultural, as opposed to the perceptual, psychologist. At this point there is an obvious link into his work on 'The logic of Vanity Fair'[88] and his account of the historical development of ornament, which in turn harks back to his fascination with the golden ground and visual metaphors of value in art.

Social, or cultural, psychology also found an outlet in his important essay

'Botticelli's mythologies. A study in the neo-Platonic symbolism of his circle'.[89] But in this book it would be appropriate to turn to the matter of the relationship between image and text as yet another application of the idea of mental set.

Earlier interpreters of Botticelli's *Primavera* read into the appearance of the central figure features corresponding to their anticipations of what the painting depicted[90] and the occasion of its use. The important methodological point is that context dictates the expressive possibilities of the image, not just in terms of the expressions of the individual figures, but the expressive effect of the image as a whole. Thus it is important to grasp the connection between the image and its predecessors in courtly tapestries and celebratory religious images to see its novelty as an image.[91]

The theatre-goer who thinks that *King Lear* is a comedy would rather miss the point of the play; recognition of its genre enables the spectator to appreciate its subtleties. Gombrich argues that genre plays a similar role in imagery: getting the genre wrong is the first step to misunderstanding the image.

In his unpublished book on secular iconography Gombrich wrote: 'H. Wölfflin's carefully balanced formula of historical approach to art "Not everything is possible in every period" applies to iconographical no less than to stylistic questions.' Raphael would not have illustrated Shakespeare and Simone Martini would not have painted a beggar-boy; 'To tell a story like the supposed "paternal advice" was simply "not possible" in Terboch's day and could therefore not be the true interpretation of the picture.'[92]

A book on the history of genres could be written out of Gombrich's published essays. It could start with the legacy of medieval imagery in Raphael's *Stanza della Segnatura* and *Tobias and the Angel* by a follower of Verrocchio. It could look at the rise of the portrait,[93] the landscape,[94] and the emergence of mythological painting.[95] Some serious thought could be given to the emergence of the programme in Renaissance art.[96] It could consider the idea of imagery as environment and illustration in the Middle Ages and also the emergence of anecdotal imagery in the nineteenth century which witnessed a reverse in the relation of image to text; from text to image to image to text.[97] It could also consider the way in which a particular theme within traditional art gains its manifold resonances in the same way as different performances of the same piece of music.[98]

All of this has taken us a very long way from the issues raised in *Art and Illusion*, but it does raise a very important point for the perceptual psychologist.

Traditional psychology worked upon the false assumption that looking at things was like looking at pictures, so pictures could be used unproblematically in experiments on perception. The assumption was compounded by the belief that looking at things in the world was simply a product of processing retinal images, again like looking at pictures. But, as Gombrich pointed out, there are fundamental differences between looking at objects and looking at pictures of them – and there are also fundamental differences between looking at different kinds of pictures.

Psychologists are still exploring the perceptual issues which Gombrich raised. But it seems to me that the area between psychology and linguistics, whose subject is the visual image, needs something better than contemporary popular semiotics to deal with it. Gombrich's critique of Morris still stands, and his use of Bühler has resulted in great gains, but, as he has frequently said, it is not method which offers a way forward, but a sense of the problems which need to be solved.[99] In his review of *Art and Illusion*, Gibson concluded:

> The discoveries of painters have been far more elaborate than the discoveries of psychologists, if less rational, and Gombrich shows that they are at least potentially investigable. The student of perception is tempted to limit his research to what he can control by the methods he has been taught. This book will widen his horizon and stimulate his ambition.[100]

I think that Gibson's forecast was correct.

Notes

1. 'Focus on arts and the humanities', *Tributes*, p. 14.
2. 'Wertprobleme und mittelalterliche Kunst', *Kritische Berichte*, 1937, translated as 'Achievement in medieval art' in *Meditations*, p. 84.
3. *Art Journal*, 1984, pp. 162–4.
4. On Gombrich's work with Bühler see 'Art history and psychology in Vienna' and Klaus Lepsky's contribution to this volume. On his work with Kris see 'The study of art and the study of man: reminiscences of collaboration with Ernst Kris (1908–1975)' in *Tributes*.
5. 'J. Bodonyi, *Entstehung und Bedeutung des Goldgrundes in der spätantiken Bildkomposition (Archaeologiai Értesitë, 46, 1932/3)*', *Kritische Berichte zur Kunstgeschichtlichen Literatur*, 5, 1932/33 (published in 1935), pp. 65–75.
6. The exceptional nature of Greek art had been pointed out by Heinrich Schäfer in his *Von ägyptischer Kunst*, third edition, Leipzig 1930.

7. He explored this idea further in his subsequent Garger review, republished in *Meditations* as 'Achievement in medieval art'.

8. On this subject see J. von Schlosser, '"Stilgeschichte" und "Sprachgeschichte" der bildenden Kunst. Ein Rückblick' *Sitzungsberichte der phil.-hist. Abteilung der Bayerischen Akademie der Wissenschaften 1935*, München 1935, Heft 1.

9. For a further discussion of this article see Richard Woodfield, 'Gombrich, formalism and the description of works of art', *British Journal of Aesthetics*, 34 (1994).

10. For the fallacy see 'Art and scholarship' and 'On physiognomic perception' in *Meditations*. Gombrich revisited the subject in *Sense of Order* where he says that, ultimately, anything may be made to fit with anything else. A friend's habitual expressions identify her even when she might change her clothes in an atypical way; they become assimilated into one's thoughts about her identity (pp. 199–200).

    It should be observed in relation to what used to be called the new art history and is now called the new art criticism, that any argument based simply on appearance, rather than hard historical evidence, is bound to be psychologically compelling at the same time as having null explanatory value. This may be termed the '*Cicerone* syndrome'.

11. 'Focus on the arts and humanities' in *Tributes*, p. 14.

12. 'Art history and psychology in Vienna fifty years ago', *Art Journal*, 1984, p. 164.

13. With Ernst Kris, Gombrich published 'The principles of caricature', *British Journal of Medical Psychology*, 17 (1938) and *Caricature*, Harmondsworth 1940. His latest statement on the subject is 'Magic, myth and metaphor: reflections on pictorial satire', to be republished in my forthcoming collection of his essays.

14. See O. Renier and V. Rubinstein, *Assigned to Listen*, London 1986, which includes an extract from a memorandum concerning 'listening' from Gombrich to his fellow listeners.

15. *The Story of Art*, first edition, London 1961, pp. 421–2. It was disingenuous of M. A. Hagen to argue 'Gombrich explicitly denies that his theory depicts art history as a development towards realism, but his treatment both of that history and of perception leads to that interpretation' ('A new theory of the psychology of representational art' in C. F. Nodine and D. F. Fisher (eds), *Perception and Pictorial Representation*, New York 1979).

16. One of the drawbacks of the use of the word 'art' is that it can be used as a blanket term to refer to all visual imagery; thus child art, chimpanzee art etc. There is no word which stands to art, in that blanket sense, as literature stands to language; 'children's literature' refers, of course, to literature written *for* children, not *by* children.

17. Gombrich included photography in the fifteenth edition of *The Story of Art*, Oxford 1989. When he was asked why he had not included film, he replied that he had not earlier included drama. Whether there have been any significant artistic achievements in holography is an interesting issue; there seems to be more potential for virtual reality.

18. I sympathise strongly with Göran Sörbom's point of view in 'The theory of

imitation is not a theory of art: some stages in a conceptual tradition', in J. Emt and G. Hermerén (eds.), *Understanding the Arts: Contemporary Scandinavian Aesthetics*, Lund 1992. I would not, however, want to encumber Gombrich with Schlosser's Crocean views on the subject.

19. Manuscript in the possession of Sir Ernst Gombrich, to whom I am indebted for its use.

20. *The Story of Art*, p. 443.

21. Quotation and elaboration from E. H. Gombrich, 'Verbal wit as a paradigm of art: the aesthetic theories of Sigmund Freud (1856–1939)' in *Tributes*, p. 104.

22. This idea is developed at greater length in 'The necessity of tradition: an interpretation of the poetics of I. A. Richards (1893–1979)' in *Tributes*.

23. Reprinted in *Reflections*.

24. *Ibid.*, p. 248.

25. The allusion here is to the account of the emergence of Greek statuary offered by Jane Harrison in *Ancient Art and Ritual*, London 1913.

26. An idol of a god is not a representation of that god, it is the god; hence the rejection of idols in terms of their material characteristics: 'That is not an idol, it is only wood'; wood not having the powers of the idol. There could be some interesting anthropological reflection on the difference between powers and affordances in this context, along the lines offered by D. Sperber, *Rethinking Symbolism*, Cambridge 1975.

27. 'Meditations on a hobby horse', p. 10. There is an important exception to this: an inscription written across, say, a view of London, is not taken to be an object hovering over London, but simply read as an inscription. This exercise of a mental set also conspicuously applies to comics; although the frame indicates spatial action, it is also filled with script – two different mental sets come into play.

28. 'Art history and the psychology of perception', unpublished manuscript.

29. On the subject of 'sparrow aesthetics' see now Goethe, 'On realism in art' (1798) in *Goethe: The collected works*, edited by J. Gearey; vol. 3, Princeton 1986, pp. 74–8.

30. William Gilpin, *Observations on the Western Parts of England*, London 1798, p. 176 (Gilpin's emphasis).

31. The best philosophical discussion of this matter is Hilary Putnam, 'Convention: a theme in philosophy', *New Literary History*, 13 (1981), pp. 1–14.

32. 'Image and code: scope and limits of conventionalism in pictorial representation', *Image and Eye*, p. 283.

33. *Ibid.*

34. In the context of talking about expectation Gombrich writes:

> Once more the effect experienced by the trained observer can be most conveniently imitated in the perception of images. It has been found in a well-known experiment that a familiar shape will induce the expected colour; if we cut out the shape of a leaf and of a donkey from identical material and ask observers to match their exact shade from a colour wheel, they will tend to select a greener shade of felt for the leaf and a greyer one for the

donkey. We remember that the result of this experiment was anticipated by
our ancient author Philostratus: 'even if we drew one of these Indians with
white chalk', Apollonius concludes, 'he would seem black, for there would
be his flat nose and stiff curly locks and prominent jaw . . . to make the
picture black for all who can use their eyes.' He was right. Interpreting,
classing a shape affects the way we see its colour. *Art and Illusion*, pp. 189–90.

This is a specialised skill which is the product of a habit of reading images for
their potential information content. It is, however, a skill developed from the
fact that one looks at a coloured world. I believe it would be true to say that
when one misrecognises an object one misperceives its precise colour; recognition results in the correct colour perception – one perceives the colour of
the bus as opposed to the colour of the robin.

The subject in the psychological test and Apollonius's complicit spectator are
both invited to form judgements about aspects of images which may simply
not have crossed their minds.

35. Discussed by Gombrich in 'The heritage of Apelles' in *Heritage*. On modelling
and highlights see 'Light, form and texture in fifteenth-century painting north
and south of the Alps' in the same volume.

36. 'The art of the Greeks' in *Reflections*, p. 16.

37. This subject is discussed in chapter seven of *Art and Illusion*, 'Conditions of
illusion'.

38. *Illusion*, p. 200.

39. *Ibid.*, p. 201.

40. *Ibid.*, p. 205.

41. 'The sky is the limit', *Image and Eye*, p. 167.

42. *Ibid.*, p. 171.

43. This opens a complex argument, as many of Gombrich's comments do. The
relativism remark was made in conversation with Richard Gregory on a radio
programme 'Seeing and knowing' made to celebrate Sir Ernst's 85th birthday.
It can be pursued in the difference of opinion aired in *Illusion*: 'I am not quite
happy with the suggestion made by Gregory that representations should be
classified as "impossible objects" – objects, that is, which give us contradictory
impressions at the same time . . . what we see is not a tuning fork of impossible
shape but a very possible drawing on paper' (pp. 236–7). This leads into the
question of differences in mental set that are invited by different kinds of
drawings, which takes us back to the difference between illusionist and non-
illusionist imagery.

44. Wittgenstein's remarks have caused a great deal of debate in this context: 'What
is the criterion of the visual experience? – The criterion? What do you suppose?
The representation of "what is seen".' (*Philosophical Investigations*, Oxford 1963,
198e). Among others, this has been picked up by R. Wollheim in 'On drawing
an object', in *On Art and the Mind*, Harvard 1974, and M. Wartofsky in *Models:
Representation and the Scientific Understanding*, Dordrecht 1979.

45. London 1976.

46. 'Signs and images', manuscript of a lecture given at the Warburg Institute on

8 June 1994, pp. 10–11, courtesy of Sir Ernst Gombrich. The interest in mental set runs throughout his work and is to be found in *Art and Illusion*, *Illusion* and *Image and Eye*.

47. Unpublished manuscript, p. 5.

48. *Art and Illusion*, p. 94.

49. This theme is handled in much greater depth by other contributors to this volume.

50. In this context 'The image family' in J.-P. Sartre, *The Psychology of Imagination*, London 1978, pp. 17–62 repays reading.

51. Gombrich's example, *Illusion*, pp. 225–8. For an extended discussion of the difference between images and maps see 'Mirror and map: theories of pictorial representation' in *Image and Eye*.

52. Discussed by Gombrich in 'The use of art for the study of symbols', *American Psychologist*, 20 (1965), pp. 34–50.

53. As Gombrich and Kris discovered in their work on the sculptures at Naumburg Cathedral, it was sufficient that they should be seen as lifelike; their expressive features were actually indeterminate, open to a wide variety of readings (*Tributes*, pp. 226–7).

54. One does not attribute deep spiritual states to an armorial bearer:

> The eyes gaze into the distance, they stand in a face that bears the marks of hard experience. This man is no longer a wild adventurer, he is sensitive to the sufferings destiny has laid upon him; it is with sorrow that he awaits the next test, though he is sure that he will win through in the end. ('The priority of context over expression' in C. S. Singleton (ed.) *Interpretation. Theory and practice*, Baltimore 1969, p. 71).

55. See 'Tobias and the angel' in *Symbolic Images*: not a narrative, or an illustration of a biblical story, but an image of the Archangel Raphael with his attribute Tobias. On the difference between *imagini* and *storie* see C. Hope, 'Religious narrative in Renaissance art', *Journal of the Royal Society of Arts*, 134 (1986), pp. 804–18.

56. *Means and Ends: Reflections on the History of Fresco Painting*, London 1976:

> what it represents within this highly convincing religious chapel is not an imagined reality but a purely symbolic image, a reminder of a doctrine which cannot be visualised at all. The real presence in art of the First Person of the Trinity in so tangible a form is not easy to reconcile with the Decalogue, but it does not seem to have disturbed Masaccio's contemporaries (p. 41).

57. 'Raphael's *Madonna della Sedia*' in *Norm and Form*, pp. 66–7: 'If we were really meant to relate it to an image of everyday life, we might feel this relationship is false and prettified. It is this feeling which presents the greatest obstacle in our day to the understanding of Raphael's achievement.'

58. See 'Mapping and painting in the Netherlands in the seventeenth century' in *Reflections*, pp. 121–2.

59. *Sense of Order*, pp. 34–5. The history of mural painting can be seen in terms of the tensions between decoration and illusion; on which, see *Means and Ends*.

60. Extended in its republication in *Symbolic Images*.

61. This is another case of 'mental set'. A point of entry may be found in considering one's responses to a 'documentary' which turns out to be a fiction. A few years ago, on April Fools' Day, British television broadcast a hoax about astronauts' discoveries on the other side of the moon. The film had my absolute attention until I realised that it was a hoax; what was different was the *kind* of attention which I paid to detail. This is rather different from what Roland Barthes described in 'The reality effect', reprinted in T. Todorov (ed.), *French Literary Theory Today*, Cambridge 1982. Sartre's *Psychology of Imagination* might offer some point of entry here as well. More work needs to be done on this; I have started to address the issue in 'L'effet du réel: an alternative account' in a special issue of the Polish philosophy journal *Dialectics and Humanism*, 15 (1988), pp. 63–73.

62. *Art and Illusion*, p. 22.

63. In this respect their point was completely missed both by R. Arnheim (*Art and Visual Perception*, London 1956) and M. Hagen (*Varieties of Realism*, Cambridge 1986) who followed him.

64. 'Moment and movement in art', in *Image and Eye*, p. 40. This applies as much to still life as it does to the portrayal of events; the 'play' of light is, after all, time based.

65. 'Moment and movement in art', 'The mask and the face: the perception of physiognomic likeness in life and in art' and 'Action and expression in Western art' in *Image and Eye*.

66. 'Ritualized gesture and expression in art' in *Image and Eye*.

67. *Architectural Quarterly*, 12 (1980), pp. 14–19.

68. It must at the same time be said that he has never subscribed to behaviourism; indeed, this is one of the issues that he raises in the Morris review. This is not the place to concern myself with Norman Bryson's extraordinary and perverse misrepresentation of Gombrich's views.

69. On this subject Gombrich's remarks are scattered through his writing. See, in particular, 'The psycho-analytic approach' in 'Aims and limits of iconology' in *Symbolic Images*, pp. 17–18.

70. Though see also his important Ernest Jones Lecture 'Psycho-analysis and the history of art' reprinted in *Meditations on a Hobby Horse*.

71. Quoted by Gombrich in 'Seeking a key to Leonardo' in *Reflections*, p. 66.

72. See volume 14 of the Pelican Freud Library, *Art and Literature*, Harmondsworth 1985.

73. In the letter to Struck, again, as cited by Gombrich in 'Seeking a key to Leonardo'.

74. Fra Pietro da Novellara; see 'Aims and limits of iconology' in *Symbolic Images*, p. 16.

75. On this subject see *A Lifelong Interest*, pp. 157–9.

76. See 'Verbal wit as a paradigm of art: the aesthetic theories of Sigmund Freud' in *Tributes*.

77. In replying to Peter Burke's suggestion that art history should concern itself with the social functions of images, Gombrich argued that

> one of the things we have learnt from psychoanalysis is that what is successful in society will have many functions at the same time . . . Most things in society . . . fulfil many functions. The number of specialised tools is very small, and art certainly belongs to those institutions which meet many demands at the same time ('Ernst Gombrich discusses the concept of cultural history with Peter Burke', *The Listener*, 27th December 1973, pp. 881–3 (p. 883)).

78. *The Sense of Order*, p. 116.

79. Gombrich didn't feel that the central thesis of *The Sense of Order* had been sufficiently appreciated, and so he offered a résumé in his preface to the second edition (1992).

80. *Ibid.*, p. 5.

81. *Ibid.*, p. 103.

82. 'Wertprobleme und mittelalterliche Kunst', *Kritische Berichte*, 1937, translated as 'Achievement in medieval art' in *Meditations*, p. 74.

83. 'Psychoanalysis and the history of art', *Meditations*, p. 41.

84. *De Oratore*, III, xxv. 98, translated by H. Rackham, London 1948.

85. 'The debate on primitivism in ancient rhetoric', *Journal of the Warburg and Courtauld Institutes*, 29 (1966), pp. 24–37.

86. 'Architecture and rhetoric in Giulio Romano's Palazzo del Tè', reprinted in *New Light*.

87. 'I. From Classicism to Primitivism', 'II. From Romanticism to Modernism' (privately circulated); these have not yet been made publicly available in English.

88. Reprinted in *Ideals*.

89. Reprinted in *Symbolic Images*.

90. Footnote 23 of the article offers a fascinating microstudy of the varieties of readings, from pensiveness to laughter, with pregnancy and consumption *en route*.

91. See the discussion of innovation and refinement in 'The necessity of tradition' in *Tributes*, pp. 206–7 and the prior discussion of Michelangelo's *Moses*, pp. 200–2.

    Is novelty something that one may *see* or does one simply see that something is novel, or see something novel in some thing? How would a psychologist respond to the question?

92. *Secular Iconography*, MS. dated 26 November 1941 and held at the Warburg Institute; I am indebted to Sir Ernst Gombrich for its use.

93. 'Giotto's portrait of Dante?', reprinted in *New Light*.

94. 'The Renaissance theory of art and the rise of landscape', reprinted in *Norm and Form*.

95. 'Botticelli's mythologies: a study in the neo-Platonic symbolism of his circle', republished in *Symbolic Images*.

96. It would start with the Introduction to *Symbolic Images* and then consider the issue in the light of 'Botticelli's mythologies' and 'Raphael's *Stanza della Segnatura*'.

97. The transitions involved are discussed in 'Action and expression in Western art', reprinted in *Image and Eye*.
98. This idea was mentioned first in 'Achievement in medieval art', and then reiterated much later in 'Painted anecdotes', reprinted in *Reflections*.
99. See, for example, 'Approaches to the history of art: three points for discussion', reprinted in *Topics*.
100. *American Journal of Psychology*, 73 (1960), pp. 653–4 (p. 654).

Art and Language:
Ernst H. Gombrich and Karl Bühler's theory of language

Klaus Lepsky

THERE is no reference to Karl Bühler either in the bibliographies or the index of *Art and Illusion* and *The Sense of Order*. Even in his numerous articles Gombrich hardly mentions Karl Bühler's work, and when he does, usually when he deals with expression in the broadest sense, he only gives it a brief mention. So it seems a little bold to connect Bühler with Gombrich's work.

On the other hand it is well known that when he was studying the history of art in the Vienna of the early thirties Gombrich soon came into contact with psychology. His close relationship to Ernst Kris, who changed from art historian to psychoanalyst, led Gombrich to the two most important trends in psychology at the time: psychoanalysis and gestalt psychology, the former represented by its founder, Sigmund Freud, the latter by the young Karl Bühler. 'Bühler's lectures were visited by a lot of students and his seminar was the ground for new ideas',[1] notes Gombrich, and furthermore we may assume that the ideas formed there left their mark on Gombrich's work.

Karl Bühler and the theory of language

But who was this Karl Bühler, 'whose influence on us was very important',[2] as Gombrich affirms in the recollection of his time in Vienna? Karl Bühler was born on 27 May 1879 in Meckenheim, Baden, and died in 1963 in Los Angeles. Professionally his most successful years were in Vienna during the twenties and thirties, where he worked as a professor of psychology until 1938. His emigration to the United States brought a premature end to his scientific career and also to his wife's, who was also a psychologist. Gombrich offers a penetrating description of the events of 1938:

> Karl Bühler lost his job since his wife Charlotte was not a so-called Aryan

and perhaps both were too old to come to terms with America. Even the younger of us, with whom fate dealt more graciously, will never know what thoughts and insights were nipped in the bud.[3]

Indeed, this fateful year marks a break in Bühler's scientific work, and its future possible development can only be guessed at from what had been achieved to that point. Bühler had been a student of the famous psychologist Oswald Külpe (1862–1915), the founder of the Würzburger Schule. Külpe's teacher was no less than Wilhelm Wundt (1832–1929), who laid the foundation of modern experimental psychology with his Leipziger Schule.[4]

The two schools placed a different emphasis on their experimental psychology. While the main focus of Wundt's research was on perception, the Würzburger Schule centred on cognitive psychology. And despite a similar method – both schools started with self-reflection – they came to a bitter methodological dispute. Consequently the young Karl Bühler and his important works on cognition[5] received strong criticism from Wundt.

In addition, however, Bühler found a stimulus to his psychological thinking in the recent trend of gestalt psychology. From 1912 the Berliner Gruppe with Wertheimer, Köhler and Koffka had developed this direction in psychological theory on the basis of the concept of the 'Gestalt' coined by von Ehrenfels. In 1913 Bühler published a preliminary work on the gestalt psychology of thinking.[6] gestalt psychology became well known above all for its experimental research in perception which later influenced the theory of art through the work of Rudolf Arnheim.[7]

Bühler's interest in gestalt psychology was never dogmatic because he always preserved his intellectual independence, and his range of interests extended beyond those of the gestalt psychologists. Above all this is evident in his work on the psychology of language, especially in his monumental *Sprachtheorie* of 1934.

While Bühler's concerns were, on the whole, within the sphere of cognitive psychology, it was his work on language, even before the *Sprachtheorie*, which gave his thought its distinctive character. Bühler and his wife Charlotte conducted a large number of studies on the psychology of the child, especially on the problems of early language learning and expression, which eventually resulted in a more comprehensive theory of language and expression.

When Bühler first published his *Ausdruckstheorie* of 1933, with the indicative subtitle 'Das System an der Geschichte aufgezeigt' (The system outlined on a historical basis) he was already concerned with the expressive function of

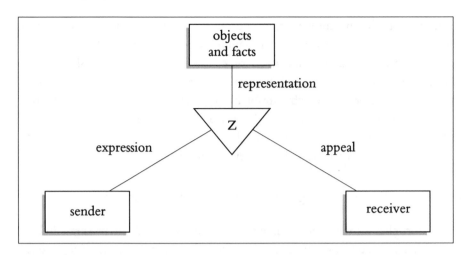

Figure 1.1 Bühler's model of communication. The lines symbolise the semantic functions of the (complex) linguistic sign. It is a *symbol* through its association with objects and states of affairs, a *symptom* (sign, indicium) through its dependance on the sender whose feelings are expressed and a *signal* through its appeal to the listener, whose outer and inner behaviour it guides as do other signs during social intercourse.[8]

language from a historical point of view. One year later this function became one of the three central functions of his 'Organonmodell der Sprache'.

This now famous model of communication (Figure 1) which Bühler presents in the second paragraph of the first chapter of his *Sprachtheorie* examines language within a functional network of object, sender, and receiver. This requires closer analysis, since what Bühler expresses in his very dense style seems to be a remarkably modern concept of human (and non-human) communication.[9] Against the background of the three basic functions of language, representation, expression and appeal, Bühler's linguistic sign takes on various semantic functions. As a symbol it acts as a substitute for objects, as a symptom it is able to transmit the emotions, moods and intentions of the sender, and as a signal it is able to arouse specific reactions in the receiver. Bühler compares language with a tool that is in his words 'ein geformter Mittler' (an articulated intermediary).[10] Today we would say, 'language is a medium of communication.'

Bühler chooses the subtitle of his *Sprachtheorie* very carefully, *Die Darstellungsfunktion der Sprache* (The representative function of language), because despite the helpful distinction between three separate functions of language, the representative function has a special place.[11] For example, if a theoretical distinction between representation and appeal seems possible, the separation of representation and expression is much more problematic, because there is such a thing as a representation of expression. This clearly shows that Bühler's *Organonmodell* is an abstraction, the vast philosophical and psychological implications of which cannot be discussed here. With regard to the current theme, representation in the visual arts, we must be permitted to take the subtitle of *Sprachtheorie* literally, and restrict this study to a consideration of the representational function of language.

Theory of language and theory of representation

In a short chapter with the complex title 'Symbolfelder in nicht-sprachlichen Darstellungsgeräten' (Symbolic fields in non-linguistic methods of representation) Bühler writes on the role of the representational function beyond language. For Gombrich this chapter is of special interest:

> It is Bühler's express aim to illustrate only the representative means of language by looking at other sign systems, but the eleven pages he dedicated to this question constitute the most fundamental material which to my knowledge has been written on the problem of representation.[12]

It is therefore worth taking a closer look at Bühler's thoughts.[13]

Bühler's concept of the *Symbolfeld* (symbolic field) is of special significance for his conception of the problem of representation. He recognises that the symbolic function is only possible when the particular symbol is seen against the background of a specific context. Bühler gives two examples: the geographic map and a sheet of music. The musical symbol and the cartographic symbol both derive their meaning, their *Feldwert* (field value), when located in an appropriate symbolic field. A musical note on a map makes no sense or leads to the misinterpretation 'here is a music-hall'. Conversely the cartographic symbol 'church', set on a stave, cannot be read by a musician.

With this example Bühler points out that the meaning of symbols depends on conventions, but these conventions are not necessarily arbitrary – a point which is often overlooked. Rather, the capacity of the symbol to represent certain states of affairs depends on the fact that it is within an appropriate symbolic field; it is only there that it is *feldfähig* (field-operative, or capable of functioning in a field). Notes are *feldfähig* on the stave, the symbol for a church is *feldfähig* on the map.

It is only a short step from Bühler's gratifyingly clear definition of the concept of the symbol, indicated above, to the problem of pictorial representation. Bühler sees that there is a close relationship between the two notions, and he tries to clarify this relationship. He separated two possible forms of representation: one more symbolic, the other more image-like. Bühler shows that there is a spectrum of ways of representation, and that the symbolic marks the one end and the image-like the other. One extreme could be represented by the language and the other by completely realistic representation, which can never be achieved. For Bühler there is no doubt 'that all known means of representation use the moment of representation in conjunction with that of "arbitrary" (empty) assignment, each predominating at differing times.'[14]

But what exactly is the meaning of the term 'image-like'? Bühler also speaks about the 'höchst denkbaren Grade der Bildhaftigkeit' (highest conceivable level of image-likeness)[15] or about 'Gradabstufungen der Erscheinungstreue' (gradations of verisimilitude)[16] and this probably means nothing more than the fact that certain forms of representation correspond more closely to the represented object than others. Again Bühler's conceptual sharpness is exceptionally helpful, for he distinguishes between *Erscheinungstreue* (verisimilitude), *Materialtreue* (fidelity to material) and *Relationstreue* (truth of relation). This makes it easy to understand that language as a pure symbol system attaches no value to material fidelity (Napoleon's name is no illustration of his characteristics); on the other hand, it is impossible to make a portrait of Napoleon without the representation of certain material characteristics, e.g. by reproducing the colour of his face through corresponding colour values on the canvas.

Let us first discuss Bühler's concept of *Relationstreue* (truth of relations), which avoids the philosophical problems of the terms *Erscheinungstreue* (truth of appearance) or *Materialtreue* (truth of material). This concept can be used to cast the problem of representation in a new light. Bühler clarifies *Relationstreue* with the example of musical notes: 'The musical note is located higher or lower on the stave according to whether the note symbolized is higher or lower on the tonal scale.'[17] Characteristics of the represented object, the object of symbolisation, are transposed into a system that is primarily suited for the adequate reproduction of relationships rather than material characteristics. There is no doubt that exact pictorial representation is possible by using a high material fidelity, every copy of a work of art shows this, but for what we tend to call illustration *Relationstreue* is of equal importance. Hence Bühler finds a definition of illustration that sounds, seen against the background of the previous considerations, stunningly simple: 'Illustration means nothing else here than the "reproduction of field values".'[18] In this extended sense the term illustration includes both the system of musical notation and the portrait of Napoleon, although Bühler knows that there is also a definition of illustration that corresponds much more to the one in use in art history: 'There is also in use another concept of the image, that demands the graphic identity of the image and the object or (in other words) truth to appearance, of course in degrees, which must not be excluded.'[19]

Later we have to come back to the relationship of these two definitions. For the moment let us summarize: with the introduction of the concept of the *Relationstreue* Bühler succeeds in clarifying the complex situation governing the conditions of illustration. This is especially true for the case of pictorial representation. As Gombrich says, this can be shown very clearly by looking at Bühler's application of his theory to black-and-white photography. Bühler impressively demonstrates that the reproduction of objects by transposition into black and white is only accepted as 'vivid' when the relation of the grey tones of the photograph correspond to relations in the represented object. Naturally there exist numerous representational variants, for example because of different exposure or processing of the photograph, but besides these differences it is true that these pictures are 'correct representations of the objects in the sense we have determined: whenever one point on the picture is more white than another the same is true for the albedo values (grey values) of the object (but not with the same steps)'.[20] Of course, Karl Bühler did not intend to design a theory of pictorial representation with his marginalia – he was too well aware of the complexity of the problem. But what he does achieve is to indicate the close relationship between the principles of linguistic and pictorial expression. It therefore required even greater efforts to adapt Bühler's basic ideas to the history of art, and it is no exaggeration to give that credit to E. H. Gombrich.

The beholder's share

This is not the place to give a short summary of the most important ideas from *Art and Illusion*, even if it were possible to do so. Therefore we are limited to a small area of Gombrich's thought, specifically his concept of the image and its capacity to represent objects realistically. Above all he is concerned in his 'psychology of pictorial representation' with giving an answer to the widely debated question of how it is possible for the artist to produce in the beholder the impression of reality, an illusion. Essentially there are two aspects: on the one hand there is the artist's role of attempting to produce a realistic representation; on the other the beholder who has to read the painting. The first depends on 'schema and correction', while the latter is only possible through the contribution of the beholder. However, both sides are inseparably bound to the aim of correction and the basis in the beholder's share, that is, the image and its ability to represent reality.

Gombrich's argument in *Art and Illusion* led to a whole series of misunderstandings, caused mainly by his efforts to keep theory in the background.[21] This gave room for a variety of interpretations of Gombrich's concept of the realistic representation of nature in pictures. It is this phenomenon that plays an important role in art history and which, at the same time, is one of the most controversial ideas in the theory of art in the twentieth century. In short, there is a group of scholars who have rejected strictly every concept of *Erscheinungstreue*, to use Bühler's term, to explain the phenomenon of representation.[22] One of the most prominent members of this group is the philosopher Nelson Goodman, who in his famous book *Languages of Art* argues vehemently for the strictly symbolic character of representation. Once again it is not only Karl Bühler who stands for the opposite tendency, but also E. H. Gombrich, who is critical of Goodman's ideas.

Let us first turn to Goodman's theory: for him, a realistic representation depends only on the use of certain conventions:

> The plain fact is that a picture, to represent an object, must be a symbol for it, stand for it, refer to it; and that no degree of resemblance is sufficient to establish the requisite relationship of reference. Nor is resemblance *necessary* for reference; almost anything may stand for almost anything else. A picture that represents – like a passage that describes – an object refers to and, more particularly, *denotes* it. Denotation is the core of representation and is independent of resemblance.[23]

For Goodman a symbol is a sign established by conventions, which stands in fixed relation to what it symbolises. Within this theory a picture is only a system of symbols. And the degree of realism of a representation only gives information on the qualities of the symbol or the power of the convention.

In the context of Bühler's theory we emphasised the helpful parallel between language and pictorial representation. Now we see that Goodman's equation of picture and language is of no help. Goodman labours under the misapprehension that there is no difference between the word 'tree' and the picture of a tree, because both denote the real tree in their own way. By doing this Goodman ignores the important fact, which is of course seen by Bühler, that in so-called *nicht-sprachlichen Darstellungsgeräten* (non-linguistic methods of representation) there are rules or principles which are not based on an arbitrary allocation of the symbol and the symbolised. One of these principles is the *Relationstreue* (truth of relation), others are *Erscheinungstreue* (verisimilitude) and *Materialtreue* (fidelity to material), which together give substance to Bühler's *engeren Bildbegriff* (narrower concept of the image).

It is this *engere Bildbegriff* with the aim of *Erscheinungstreue* which forms the basis of Gombrich's argument in *Art and Illusion*. He has no doubt that the assimilation of nature/reality and picture is possible. This can be shown by his famous example of the comparison between Constable's *Wivenhoe Park* and a copy of this picture made by a child: 'Granted . . . that Constable's painting of Wivenhoe Park is not a mere transcript of nature but a trans-position of light into paint, it still remains true that it is a closer rendering of the motif than is that of the child.'[24] Goodman would say that Constable's picture is seen as more realistic because Constable used a system of symbols that is better known than the child's representational language. On the other hand, Bühler would have told us that Constable's picture is, of course, more realistic than the child's because Constable was able to include more *Material-treue* – light to oil colour – and more *Relationstreue* – gradation of colour and brightness – in his picture. Perhaps he would even add that on the range of the possible illustrations Constable's picture lies nearer to the ideal of complete 'verisimilitude', but that ultimately this ideal can neither be desired nor attained.

This is what Gombrich in *Art and Illusion* calls the 'Limits of likeness' under which he includes all restrictions on the artist's activity: the limits of the medium, the means and the technology.[25] The perfect representation of reality cannot be successful because these limits prevent the artist from including completely the complex optical information of the reality in his or her picture. Therefore Gombrich's argument is that for the artist, the representation of reality is mainly a question of attaining an approximate adaptation to the ideal of complete *Erscheinungstreue* by using the artistic means available to him or her and adapting them, step by step, to reality. It is this process of assimilation which forms the central component of Gom-brich's notion of schema and correction.

There is another consequence resulting from this natural incompleteness of 'realistic' representation: the fact that in the interpretation of the representations, the artist can and has to rely on the co-operation of the beholder. It is this which Gombrich summarises in the formula of 'the beholder's share': 'Any picture, by its very nature, remains an appeal to the visual imagination; it must be supplemented in order to be understood.'[26] It is an interesting fact that Gombrich consciously uses Bühler's terminology, for, as we remember, the 'appeal' was one of the three important features of his *Organonmodell*. The natural incompleteness of all pictures leads to an appeal to our capacity for visual supplementation, and this then leads to an illusion of a realistic representation of nature, without there being a risk of confusing image and reality with each other. Gombrich's illusion is not a deception, because we are conscious of the pictorial character of the representation. Here again we see a close relationship to Bühler's idea of 'language as an articulated intermediary' in the context of his Organonmodell: 'We can read the image because we recognise it as an imitation of reality within the medium.'[27] In retrospect it is hard to understand that the views formulated in *Art and Illusion* became the occasion for almost endless discussions about the truth to reality of art, especially since Gombrich was able to show the validity and logical strength of these ideas for the history of style and art. Given the long theoretical debate on the validity of perspectival representation – here again Nelson Goodman appears as a defender of his symbolic theory – one might have wished that some of those scholars involved had read Bühler's chapter 'Symbolfelder in nicht-sprachlichen Darstellungsgeräten' as carefully as Gombrich had done.

Art and expression

As we have learned from Gombrich, the representation of reality in images is a genuine artistic and art-historical problem. Artists attempting to solve this problem developed specifically artistic means, e.g. perspective, to this end. Art history is in the position of looking back on developments within art as occurring in a field of tensions between ends and means. Through this theoretical framework, demonstrated perfectly in *Art and Illusion* and *The Sense of Order*, Gombrich reaches a rational treatment of what in art is at times treated in a more irrational manner.

When the problem of realistic artistic representation became less important, because of the invention of photography, a development in art begins which avoids rational judgement. The formulation of new artistic ideas and objectives in the art of the twentieth century – Expressionism, Surrealism, abstract art

– is accompanied by the growth of new ideas in art theory. The confrontation with this fundamentally changed situation is a strong test for the art theory of Gombrich (he would deny having an art theory, but we consider the sum of his ideas an art theory). It fits perfectly well that beside his primary field of interest, the art of the Renaissance, Gombrich also deals with more recent developments in the history of art. Primarily, his work on Expressionism and the expressionist theory of art deserves attention, because it reveals the strength of Bühler's *Organonmodell* of language.

To return to Bühler's language; the artists of the Renaissance were able to communicate objects and states of affairs in pictures because they knew how to employ the representational function of the image, its capacity to symbolise objects and states of affairs, in order to solve their problems. It therefore seems reasonable to bring other functions of the linguistic sign, e.g. the expressionistic function, into the medium of the picture. The art theory of Expressionism asserts nothing else when it places the expression of feelings/emotions as the central point of artistic creation. In his critical examination of the theory, Gombrich shows that this view leads to various problems.

Gombrich takes the basic assumptions of the expressionistic art theory and brings them into the following polarised scheme:

Expression	Communication
Emotion	Information
Symptom	Code
Natural	Conventional [28]

The left-hand side of this opposition characterises what Gombrich likes to call the 'resonance theory', that presupposes 'that expression is somehow rooted in the nature of our minds, and that it therefore stands in no need of conventional signs'.[29] The right-hand side recalls the symbolic theory of Nelson Goodman. In contrast to the 'resonance theory', it is an outline of the pure conventionalistic view, for which communication is always a matter of prior agreement and the learnability of a common symbol system. To answer the question of verisimilitude Gombrich used Bühler's concept of a spectrum of possibilities of representation. A similar spectrum is important for the expressionistic function of art; without this spectrum communication between artist and beholder will not work. Bühler calls this the *Feldcharakter* (field character) of the sign, to describe the dependence of meaning on context. It is the lack of this field which for Gombrich marks the obvious deficiency of the resonance theory applied to art:

From the critic's point of view, surely, its principal weakness lies in its total inability to account for structure. It is no wonder, in fact, that its popularity led to an abandonment of structure and to the increasing cult of the spontaneous 'natural' symptom in abstract expressionism and, beyond, to the uniformly blue canvas that expresses the artist's 'blues'.[30]

It is quite obvious that Gombrich holds these experiments in small regard. His view of artistic problems is closely related to the existence of worthwhile artistic objectives, and therefore the monotone blue canvas is not a serious problem. The representation of reality and the representation of expression are worthwhile problems in this sense, but to reach these aims, the artist has to accept certain rules, which are indispensable for successful communication between artist and beholder. The blue canvas meant to represent the artist's blues disregards these rules of communication, because, as Gombrich said in Bühler's sense, 'we cannot judge expression without an awareness of the choice situation, without a knowledge of the organon'.[31] The blue canvas can only create the intended depressive atmosphere successfully either if the artist had earlier produced only colourful red canvases, or if there exists an artistic tradition that equates the use of the colour blue with depression. This is completely without regard to the question of whether the representation of the artist's depression is a serious objective or not.

What Bühler says about the requirements of correct interpretation also applies to the fine arts: 'To put it simply, situation and context are the two sources on which one draws for the precise interpretation of linguistic utterances in every case.'[32] It is exactly this, the importance of the situation and the context, that Gombrich has in mind when he complains about the renunciation of the 'structure of the work of art' in abstract expressionism. This renunciation is important because it disrupts communication between artist and beholder; the beholder cannot interpret the message of the artist to him because he lacks the context, the Organon.

In his discussion of the theories of Expressionism Gombrich develops a theory of artistic expression which is a perfect complement to his theory of pictorial representation. Beginning with a communication model close to Bühler's theory of language he establishes the conditions for the communication of expression through art. It is not astonishing that once more we meet well-known themes and motives; on the one hand, the importance of artistic tradition and on the other hand, the no less important share of the beholder. The artistic tradition, that is the existence of a history of style with a certain continuity, defines the Organon, the 'playground' for the artist. If the artist refuses this range of conventions of representation, manifested in the history of style, contact with the beholder is lost. The beholder's part of understanding the artist's message is finally just as dependent on the consideration of certain conventions; if these are missing or ignored it will not be possible for the beholder to reconstruct the situation and context of the artist's statement – the work of art will be misunderstood.

Gombrich called this weave of relations and reciprocal dependences on artist, viewer, work of art and history of style a 'centripetal theory of artistic expression' whose outstanding characteristic is that it is a 'theory of feedback', 'a theory which stresses the constant interaction between the feeling and the form, the medium and the message'.[33] In his emphasis on the feedback between artist, medium and beholder Gombrich's theory fundamentally differs from the simplistic views of the resonance theory. The feedback theory is at first sight more complicated, but it places the effect of the work of art in the middle of the discussion, and the attainment of this effect is no trivial matter.

Gombrich's theory of artistic expression naturally conforms with his theory of pictorial representation, for in both models artists have to achieve a certain effect, and to do so in both models they have to work with the beholder's share. In the case of the realistic representation of nature they try to adapt to reality the schemes available to them, a process of feedback with themselves as first beholders. In the case of the representation of emotions, they are also the first beholders studying the effect.

> At every stage of the creative process, he must be his first audience and his first critic. He will explore his medium and observe how any combination of shapes, colours or tones affects himself. In his watchful play with the possibilities of his art, the painter will no less exploit happy accidents, than will the poet who explores the language.[34]

The beholder's share begins with the artist himself and is one of the important moments in the creative process. That sounds simple but is not simple at all. Gombrich's theory makes clear that art is pragmatically seen as a matter of reaching certain objectives with certain means, and that the achievement of these objectives is no question of self-confident declarations of the artist but rather a question of the effect on the beholder.

The relationship of art and language surely ends where it concerns the means that can be used to achieve a communication. Language is, of course, a pure symbolic system and therefore works with other rules than the variety of artistic means in pictorial art. Their development and change before the background of the changing tasks of the arts led to a variety of visual possibilities of expression, which could not be clarified solely with reference to language. However, in both fields, language and art work with the transmission of contents, a fact that Gombrich expresses in a simple sentence: 'We represent or describe *something to someone.*'[35] Seen against this general background it is without doubt useful to look at linguistic communication and its use for the art historian. Gombrich did exactly this, and as so often in his writings, by recourse to Karl Bühler's theory of language he successfully shows the use of important ideas from neighbouring disciplines for the history of art.

Notes

We would like to thank Matthew Rampley for his generous assistance in translating this chapter. R. W. and K. L.

1. 'Bühlers Vorlesungen wurden von vielen besucht, und sein Seminar war eine Pflanzstätte neuer Ideen', 'Kunstwissenschaft und Psychologie vor fünfzig Jahren', in *Wien und die Entwicklung der kunsthistorischen Methode* (XXV. Internationaler Kongreß für Kunstgeschichte, Wien 4–10 September 1983), p. 101.

2. 'dessen Einfluß auf uns alle sehr bedeutend war', Gombrich, 'Kunstwissenschaft und Psychologie vor fünfzig Jahren', p. 101.

3. 'Karl Bühler verlor seine Stelle, da seine Gattin Charlotte keine sogenannte Arierin war, und beide waren vielleicht zu alt, um noch in Amerika so recht Fuß zu fassen. Auch die Jüngeren unter uns, mit denen das Schicksal gnädiger verfuhr, werden nie wissen, was damals alles an Gedanken und Einsichten im Keim erstickt wurde' (Gombrich, 'Kunstwissenschaft und Psychologie vor fünfzig Jahren', p. 103).

4. See also 'Würzburger Schule' and 'Experimentelle Psychologie in Leipzig', in *Geschichte der Psychologie: ein Handbuch in Schlüsselbegriffen*, ed. Helmut E. Lück, Rudolf Miller and Wolfgang Rechtien, Darmstadt 1984.

5. Karl Bühler, 'Tatsachen und Probleme zu einer Psychologie der Denkvorgänge', Teil I in *Archiv für die gesamte Psychologie* 9, 1907, pp. 297–365; Teil II in 12, 1908, pp. 1–23; Teil III in 12, 1908, pp. 24–92.

6. Karl Bühler, *Die Gestaltwahrnehmungen*, Stuttgart 1913.

7. See *Art and Visual Perception: a Psychology of the creative eye*, Berkeley 1954.

8. 'Die Linienscharen symbolisieren die semantischen Funktionen des (komplexen) Sprachzeichens. Es ist *Symbol* kraft seiner Zuordnung zu Gegenständen und Sachverhalten, *Symptom* (Anzeichen, Indicium) kraft seiner Abhängigkeit vom Sender, dessen Innerlichkeit es ausdrückt, und *Signal* kraft seines Appells an den Hörer, dessen äußeres oder inneres Verhalten es steuert wie andere Verkehrszeichen' (Karl Bühler, *Sprachtheorie: Die Darstellungsfunktion der Sprache*, ung. Neudr. d. Ausg. Jena 1934, Stuttgart 1982, p. 28).

9. Bühler laid down the basic concept in an article of 1918; see *Sprachtheorie*, p. 28, and the preface to this edition by F. Kainz.

10. *Sprachtheorie*, p. XXI.

11. F. Kainz missed the fourth function of language, the question; see his 'Geleitwort' to the *Sprachtheorie*.

12. 'Es geht Bühler ausdrücklich nur darum, durch einen Blick auf andere Zeichensysteme die Darstellungsmittel der Sprache zu klären, aber die elf Seiten, die dort diesen Fragen gewidmet sind, gehören zum Grundlegendsten, was meines Wissens jemals über das Darstellungsproblem geschrieben wurde' (Gombrich, 'Kunstwissenschaft und Psychologie vor fünfzig Jahren', p. 103).

13. See *Sprachtheorie*, Kapitel III, §12, pp. 179–95.

14. 'daß *alle* bekannten Darstellungsmittel in wechselnder Dominanz das Abbildungsmoment gepaart mit dem Moment der "willkürlichen" (leeren) Zuordnung verwenden'. (*Sprachtheorie*, p. 188).

15. *Ibid.*

16. *Ibid.*, p. 189.

17. 'Das Notenzeichen steht höher und tiefer in der diskreten Skala der Fünferlinie entsprechend dem Höher und Tiefer des symbolisierten Tones in der Skala der diskreten Tonleiter' (*Ibid.*).

18. 'Abbildung heißt hier nichts anderes als "die Wiedergabe durch Feldwerte"' (*Ibid.*, p. 190).

19. 'Daneben aber ist ein engerer Bildbegriff im Gebrauch, der anschauliche Gleichheit des Bildes mit dem Abgebildeten oder (wie man auch sagen kann) erscheinungstreue Wiedergabe vom Bilde verlangt; in Stufen und Graden natürlich, die nicht ausgeschlossen werden müssen' (*Ibid.*).

20. 'relationstreue Abbildungen des Aufgenommenen in dem Sinne, den wir fixiert haben: wo immer auf dem Bild eine zweite Stelle weißer ist als die erste, da sind auch die Albedowerte [Grauwerte, Anm. d. Verf.] der Objektstellen in demselben Sinn (wenn auch nicht um denselben Treppenschritt) verschieden' (*Ibid.*).

21. *Art and Illusion*, p. 24.

22. See also Klaus Lepsky, 'Bild und Wirklichkeit – Die Wirklichkeit im Bild', *Kunsthistorisches Jahrbuch Graz*, 33, 1987, pp. 166–73.

23. Nelson Goodman, *Languages of Art*, London 1968, p. 5.

24. *Art and Illusion*, p. 252.

25. *Ibid.*, pp. 48–54, 'The limits of likeness'.

26. *Ibid.*, p. 204.

27. 'Image and code: scope and limits of conventionalism in pictorial representation', *Image and Eye*, p. 278.

28. 'Expression and communication', in *Meditations*, p. 57.

29. *Ibid.*, p. 57.

30. *Ibid.*, p. 59.

31. *Art and Illusion*, p. 319.

32. 'Situation and Kontext sind also grob gesagt die zwei Quellen, aus denen in

jedem Fall die präzise Interpretation sprachlicher Äußerungen gespeist wird' (*Sprachtheorie*, p. 149).

33. 'Four theories of artistic expression', in *Architectural Association Quarterly*, 12 (1980), p. 18.

34. *Ibid.*, p. 19.

35. 'Mirror and map: theories of pictorial representation', *Image and Eye*, p. 172.

Art and Illusion and *The Image and the Eye*: philosophical implications

Menahem Brinker

Art *and Illusion* was conceived not as a philosophical treatise on artistic pictorial representation and its illusionistic powers but as a collection of studies in the psychology of pictorial representation. It was intended to shed light on the evolution of Western representational art. The two words in its title, 'art' and 'illusion', were linked in the book to a specific narrative.

True, in order to create a convincing historical narrative on the rise and evolution of illusionistic art some allusions to philosophy had to be made. Plato was quoted as a witness to the Greek revolution and later philosophers as sources for the views of artists. The problems treated in *Art and Illusion* engaged many philosophers in the past; for example, it may be argued that the different views held by Plato and Aristotle on the illusionistic norm itself (e.g. what is entailed, and especially what is not entailed, by the achievement of illusion in art) launched the entire tradition of Western aesthetics.

Yet Gombrich attempted to limit his discussion to his immediate theme. Even the introduction of models from contemporary philosophers, such as Popper's models for progress in scientific knowledge, were completely woven into the texture of a history whose purpose is to explain the development of specific devices and techniques aimed at achieving better illusion. No attempt was made in the book to suggest that a general philosophical lesson could be drawn from it concerning learning or representation or progress in the acquisition of knowledge 'in general', outside the limited area of illusionistic pictorial representation in the West.

Nevertheless, many philosophical readers thought that *Art and Illusion* contains far-reaching philosophical implications. Gombrich's belief in continuous progress in achieving the illusionistic norm, taken completely out of its context, seemed to support the claims of the most 'naive' realists that there is constant progress in our representation of reality. In contrast, his discussion of the dependence of naturalistic pictorial representation on artistic 'vocabularies' seemed (again, when taken completely out of context) to endorse the most extreme claims made by conventionalists and relativists.

I claim that the recruiting of *Art and Illusion* to support various philosophical programmes is based on misinterpretation. These misinterpretations, however, point to certain lacunae or gaps in the book. Since Gombrich's formulations allowed for several basic ambiguities concerning his argument, it is no wonder that the author of *Art and Illusion*, (the subtitle of which is *studies in the psychology of pictorial representation*) was pressed to add significant clarifications of his position in several lectures – the 'further studies in the psychology of pictorial representation' collected in *The Image and the Eye*. In the following pages I (a) describe the argument of *Art and Illusion*; (b) explain why I think the argument cannot be used to support either philosophical realism or its philosophical adversaries, relativism and conventionalism; (c) point to the formulations that gave rise to these mistaken philosophical interpretations of Gombrich's argument; and (d) critically consider some of the revisions and the improved formulations offered in *The Image and the Eye* concerning the main argument of *Art and Illusion*.

I

'Illusionistic art' is a term which Gombrich prefers to 'naturalism' or 'realism', although these very often cover the same ground. This preference makes it clear that the book deals with a specific historical phenomenon that should not be confused with all representational art. There are, in art and outside it, non-illusionistic pictorial representations. Yet illusionism cannot be identified with one specific technique or one local school; it is an aesthetic norm, a conception of the task of artists that encouraged the development of a plurality of styles and techniques. Shared by artists of different times and places, working in different forms or genres of visual representation, illusionism constitutes a tradition. Despite changes in themes, styles and techniques, a noticeable continuity, and even progress, can be found within this tradition.

The tradition of illusionistic painting emerged between the seventh and fifth centuries BC in Greece. Painters and sculptors influenced by the mimetic norm of Greek theatre became interested in depicting concrete 'appearances'. They were no longer satisfied with offering general information concerning their model. Egyptian painting and other traditions demonstrate that this may be accomplished without applying the illusionistic norm. The ambition to capture a momentary scene or the 'look' of a landscape at a specific moment made these artists aspire to turn the spectator into a stationary eyewitness of the represented scene.

The primary factor in illusionistic painting, the base for everything illusionistic, is the creation of pictorial images. Images are projections of three-dimensional objects on a two-dimensional canvas. For Gombrich, the creating of images is a fundamental original human capacity that should not be confused with, or reduced to, any other mental or representational activity. It is the 'wonder', the 'miracle' upon which the peculiar 'paradox' of naturalism rests. There is something 'magical' in all two-dimensional images of three-dimensional objects, and the illusionistic impression of depth created by a flat canvas is the source of all the additional illusions of naturalistic painting. It is here that we must look for the basic unbridgeable gap that separates, in Gombrich's view, a map from a mirror.

Yet the illusion that naturalism deals with is much more specific and much more elaborate than the mere ability to create pictorial images. In contrast to magic, the image in naturalistic art is usually not exploited to create optical delusions. Therefore the sense of the illusionistic norm should be defined in a way that will fit the non-deluded consciousness of the beholder. In a later essay Gombrich makes a very clear distinction between illusion and false belief.[1] Though illusion in itself is not a false belief it may lead the beholder to endorse such belief. None of the specific devices used in illusionistic painting to create specific illusions (of depth, distance, size, light, indistinctness etc.) are aimed to delude us. Therefore none of them are linked to a specific false belief. Yet the holistic artistic intention that is revealed through all of them, i.e. the norm of illusionistic painting, may be defined in terms of a non-deluding false belief. I think we require this false belief in order to understand the peculiar sense the word 'illusion' acquires in defining a progressive evolution from 'less' illusion towards 'more' illusion. Illusionistic painters seek to bring spectators to believe that were they to stand where the painter stood, and look at the object at the time it was painted, they would see it precisely as depicted in the painting.

If we do not want to say that this belief in itself is an illusion we should say that it is based on an illusion. First, in most cases the spectator is unable to test its truth. Many illusionistic paintings 'depict' fictional, though possible, objects.[2] Many others represent objects to which the spectator has no access. Finally, even with familiar, accessible objects, their 'look' or 'appearance' (the object of the illusionistic painter's quest) is transitory. Hence even when viewing a portrait of my best friend or a drawing of the street in which I live, I will be in no position to appreciate its accuracy.

Philosophically the second point is more important. Suppose I am in a rare privileged position from where I can actually judge the painter's achievement. Say I was standing or sitting near the painter at the time he or she produces his or her masterpiece. Thus, like the painter, I am able to shift my gaze from object to painting and be very much impressed. I find a perfect match between the figures in the painting and the represented landscape. Yet on a closer comparison or even upon abstract reflection, I can see that the resemblance which I am witnessing is very limited. I realise that pictorial representations are dependent on their medium and no medium is able to represent appearances precisely as they look. The mere fact that a painting is usually smaller than its object excludes depiction of details that may be seen in the object, simply because they are too small for representation. Even in one-to-one scale paintings there will always be representational gaps because of the limitations of the medium. For example, there is never a perfect match between the painter's available colours and the colour and shades of the object. Though admiring the achievement of the painter, we never really assume a total or complete 'match'. Thus we appreciate as highly 'realistic' drawings in black and white as well as non-coloured sculptures.

These instances show that perhaps in all others, too, we look for the resemblance in particular domains and intentionally ignore as 'irrelevant' other domains. The belief that pictorial representation accurately depicts everything that is seen at a given moment from a particular spot, exactly as it is seen, is, therefore, erroneous. Persisting in the beholder as a general 'overall' impression, even when one knows better, it is an illusion.

Yet it is not a delusion, certainly not in a literal sense, since the painter seeks not a *trompe-l'œil* but an impression of a perfect resemblance between the representation and its object. It is also not a delusion, nor a deluding illusion, in a more refined sense. The audience that the painter intends to appreciate his work is not naive; it is composed of experienced and reflective viewers who are fully aware of the illusionistic nature of the impression of 'complete faithfulness' or 'perfect resemblance', yet for whom this does not cancel the aesthetic experience of a successful match. The audience does not find that this falling short demands the relinquishing of the commonsensical notion that pictorial representations resemble more, or resemble less, the object.

Though erroneous and misleading in its superlative use, resemblance, in its comparative use, is no illusion. One may argue that all comparisons of resemblance are guided by specific interests, but one cannot deny that there is always something there, in the representations themselves, to justify appreciation. Disputes over the relative superiority or inferiority of representations are often settled by demonstration. The clear cases of such superiority are sufficient to indicate that the conviction that some painting (or any other pictorial representation, e.g. photography) is superior to others in resembling the object is not to be dismissed as an illusion. The impression is not wholly subjective. It can be demonstrated that the superior representation includes aspects missing in the inferior one, or that the better representation does not contain mistakes found in worse ones.

I believe that these phenomenological findings are the bases of Gombrich's double claim: first, that a perfect match between a representation and its object is an illusion, and second, that the Western tradition of pictorial representation manifests real progress in evoking that illusion. There is no contradiction between the two claims. Quite the contrary; Gombrich's analysis succeeds, I think, in showing not only how strongly they are linked, but also how much they support and complement each other. The linkage is the idea that the illusionistic impression of a global match is created by a real and conspicuous partial match of aspects in the painting and aspects in the object.[3] It is made possible by the intentional ignoring of non-matching aspects or missing aspects (what I propose to call representational gaps) on the part of the beholder.

The intentional ignoring of non-matching aspects and representational gaps results from training in different modes and genres of artistic mimesis. (This is true not only in the visual arts but also in literature and the theatre.) Seeking a match between a drawing and its object, a trained viewer will not complain about the lack of colours. We are trained to appreciate degrees of suggestiveness and verisimilitude within the confines of the medium, the mode, or the genre. By ignoring those confines and the ensuing necessary gaps we let ourselves to be swept up by the overall impression (i.e. the illusion) of a full match.[4] The 'philosophical' ground for Gombrich's second claim requires, therefore, nothing more than demonstrating that later painters in the tradition achieve greater partial veritable and conspicuous resemblance between representations and their objects. A belief in a real partial match of aspects between the representation and its model is not illusionistic: techniques and devices invented in the evolution of illusionistic art achieve better partial resemblance; they embody more and more 'visual truth'.

This means that artists are able progressively to include in their paintings more weighted aspects of their objects, because they can overcome technical problems connected with the representation of these aspects. At the same time, they develop devices to conceal representational gaps from the beholder. This aspect of the progress depends heavily on the beholder's training and willingness to participate in the aesthetic 'game'. The two names of the game are Indistinctness and Projection.

A greater 'visual truth' or better 'illusion' need not supply more information concerning the object. The correctness which the illusionistic artist aspires to achieve has nothing to do with the object 'as it really is'. It has to do only with the way the object is perceived, or imagined as perceived, at a definite moment from a definite point in space. The relevant comparison between representations of the same object is always carried out within the specifications of the aesthetic illusionistic norm. A representation that represents the model from different perspectives at once, and shows the back as well as the front of the object, is more informative but not more illusionistic.

A significant implication of Gombrich's claim is that progress in the representational arts was not achieved by taking a better look at the objects or by learning more details about them. At certain turning-points this process did not even involve better awareness of the way they appear. Progress occurred when technical obstacles, which prevented artists from rendering appearances as they saw them, were overcome. Artists working within the main tradition of Western art discovered better ways to achieve the match between visual appearances and their pictorial representation by abandoning old, entrenched habits of representation, experimenting with new methods and schemes and introducing new devices for attaining the norm. According to Gombrich this progress may be demonstrated objectively; this, indeed, is the goal of *Art and Illusion*.

II

As far as I know, no philosopher made the mistake of considering Gombrich's history as a defence of fully-fledged philosophical realism. Gombrich was careful enough to block such understanding of his book by repeating that he does not know what to make of the expression 'things as they really are', and that he considers this expression useless for understanding illusionistic (naturalistic) art, or for writing its history. He avoids philosophical disputes on truth and reality that have no direct bearing on his subject; instead he only talks of appearances, illusion and visual truth.

Nevertheless, to identify progress with the addition of more 'visual truth' in the visual arts is to assume a realistic posture, for it requires that the perceived visible world be constant *vis-à-vis* the various changing modes of its pictorial representation. One must assume that our perceptions (i.e. our awareness of the 'look' of things) remain more or less the same, even when our pictorial representations of them change considerably. Since *Art and Illusion* narrates an evolution that lasts for centuries, acknowledgement of progress implies that our visible world did not change as a result of changes in its pictorial representation, but remained more or less the same, even though our understanding (i.e. our verbal and scientific representations) of it did change dramatically. It must assume that sunsets look more or less the same before, and after, the Copernican revolution. Do these assumptions commit Gombrich to a philosophical Naive Realism, at least with regard to perception? Do they make him postulate the continuous existence through the centuries (from classical Greece to the Impressionists at the end of the nineteenth century) of a Great Transcendental Innocent Eye constantly observing the same sky, the same stars, the same sea?

I do not think so. Both *Art and Illusion* and *The Image and the Eye* deal with relative constancies; hence their cautious avoidance of sweeping or absolute philosophical commitments. Though the problem is not mentioned explicitly, I think that what Gombrich tacitly assumes throughout his history is that our perceptions of the models did not change as much, or as significantly, as our modes of pictorial representations of them.[5]

Such an assumption negates extreme anti-realist claims, e.g. the claim that Whistler invented the fog in London. Obviously *Art and Illusion* makes the counter-claim, i.e. that people could appreciate the achievement of Whistler in inventing a suggestive way of rendering London's fog only because they were familiar with the fog before they looked at the paintings. Yet there is no need to deny that the paintings could have enhanced awareness of the way London's fog appears. A forceful representation may teach us new things about the model; it may bring us to notice new aspects. That is why at first innovative representations may look strange to us because of (and not just despite) their realism. But when we come to find them highly convincing, we do so because we perceive, or in other cases imagine, that they ideally match our perceptions of their objects.

This commonsensical realist posture is indeed implicit in Gombrich, and his frequent use of the word 'matching' makes it explicit. Yet this posture does not commit him to fall back either on the Myth of The Given or the Myth of The Innocent Eye. One may admit that our perceptions of the visual world are never 'pure perceptions'.[6] One may admit that they are shaped by expectations and habits derived from our knowledge, including scientific knowledge. One may even admit their indirect dependence on our language and the totality of our form of life. Yet one may insist that, relative to our modes of pictorial representation, there is in general much constancy in our perceptions.

Changes in perception, that is, changes in what we see and are aware that we see, may occur; it may make sense to speak, like Matisse, of the 'history of seeing'. In order to accept Gombrich's narrative and the explanatory paradigm upon which it is based, we do not have to deny these changes. We do not even have to consider them marginal or negligible. However, we do have to assume that, if they exist, changes in the ways of perceiving the world must be smaller and slower in comparison to the changes in our ways of representing pictorially what we see. The extent of realism needed here is that which will allow us to say that the introduction of perspective into painting made a great change in our pictorial representations of the same objects, while these same objects were perceived before, and after, perspective, in (more or less) the same way. This implicit assumption of *Art and Illusion* is made plausible by the thought that if things were otherwise, people sharing the illusionistic norm would not be so excited with this innovation. In that case, not only Gombrich and his readers would be unable to notice progress; painters and their audiences would not be able to celebrate it, either.

I believe that this is the position held by Gombrich, or at the very least, that this is what his position entails. The only philosophical realist who could hope for support from Gombrich's claims is one who presumes an absolute constant and independent identity of the perceptual world; yet, if I am correct, Gombrich's history does not require this strong realistic assumption. Therefore, a philosophical realist cannot use Gombrich to support these claims.

III

I focused on Gombrich's distance from philosophical realism, though no attempt had been made to offer a complete realist reading of *Art and Illusion*. Such a reading is, however, suggested when one realises how far the full argument of the book is from militant anti-realism, i.e. the philosophical relativists or conventionalists who drew upon *Art and Illusion* to support their cause.

This misreading of *Art and Illusion*, exemplified by Nelson Goodman's review of the book and its assessment by Murray Krieger,[7] was highly influential and is still influential today, after all the clarifications offered by Gombrich in at least three of the papers collected in *The Image and the Eye* against the conventionalist interpretation of his view.[8]

I think that what gives this reading of Gombrich a misleading air of a plausible interpretation is the frequent use in *Art and Illusion* of language as a model for the understanding of pictorial representation and its evolution. Stressing that illusionistic representation depends on the artist's vocabularies, Gombrich came very close to a semiotic conception of art. Indeed, he profited from the notion that pictorial representation, like any other system of representation, uses something that may be considered as a vocabulary. One may also attribute to the impact of the semioticians the significant fact that Gombrich never believed in any immediate, transparent or exclusive links between objects and their iconic representations. The hobby-horse had to be invented, and as long as makers of hobby-horses do not subscribe to a specific illusionistic norm, they can invent many kinds of hobby-horses and endow all of them with a minimal extent of iconicity. There may be many relational models to guarantee minimal resemblances between objects and their representations. (The situation changes only when a norm and standards for maximal resemblance are introduced. This is what happens in illusionistic painting and I shall return to it later.)

Despite the emphasis on making (rather than finding) Gombrich still maintained that iconicity defines a specific domain of representation. Even more significant in revealing the distance between his and the semiotic approach is the fact that he adhered to naturalness as an aesthetically and critically valid notion, its disrepute within semiotics and structuralism not-withstanding. Unlike most contemporary historians of art, he was sufficiently bold to outline a history in which there is a growth in the extent of iconicity and naturalness accompanied by a diminishing extent of conventionality.[9]

Of course, if iconicity is not simply and immediately found, naturalness cannot be a gift of nature to the unconscious genius. Both are the result of the conscious pursuit and the indefatigable effort of the artist. Neither can exist in art in a 'pure', complete, or absolute manner, sin conventions that pertain to the artform or the artistic genre as specific modes of pictorial representation are always there. The most illusionistic painting still has a frame, and the relationship between 'iconic' or 'natural' artistic representation and the represented reality is, therefore, not the work of nature that artists simply reproduce.

The achievements of illusionistic art result from artists' patient experiments. They emerge slowly and gradually in the evolution of representational painting, and take place in conformity with established and traditional forms of representation. Therefore, achievements of naturalness or illusion are relative to the possibilities opened by these established forms. Within the confines of these basic forms – the institutions of pictorial representation – resemblance, naturalness and illusion are pursued as desirable aesthetic effects. From this point of view they are ART-ificial: made rather than found.

Common to Gombrich and the semiotic (or structuralist) theorists is the emphasis on the amount of labour needed to achieve naturalness. Both outlooks insist on the elaborate strategies and constructions needed for creating the illusion that paintings are mirrors. Hence the partial agreement between the two outlooks; nevertheless, the agreement ends where, for Gombrich, with the introduction of the illusionistic–naturalistic norm the acquisition of these aesthetic effects cannot follow many different ways. There are many ways of achieving partial resemblances between objects and their represent-ations, but the partial resemblance that will invoke in the beholder the impression (or illusion, or false belief) of a perfect match cannot be achieved in too many ways. For example, it cannot be achieved without the laws of perspective. Therefore those techniques and devices that are indispensable for progress are not reducible to convention, custom or habit. Hence despite the fact that the illusionistic norm is not a universal of representational art but a norm typical of a specific Western tradition, success in achieving it can be measured by objective and universal standards.

Gombrich maintains that seen from the vantage point of the accomplished masterpieces of illusion, the artist's methods are not arbitrary. Through a long process of search and research, after centuries of experimentation by trial and error, certain methods, schemata and formulae are chosen by artists because they serve them in producing the desired effect better than their alternatives. They are indispensable devices rather than conventions; they are part of a teleological context in which they function as means to the achievement of a goal.

Neither the concept of objective standards nor the concept of device (as distinct from convention) is defined in *Art and Illusion*. But as the clarifications in *The Image and the Eye* clearly show, they are a part of Gombrich's full argument. This, I think, is regrettable. Making these two concepts more explicit could prevent the conventionalist misreading of the first book. It would have made clear that semiotic expressions, models and metaphors are used by Gombrich to endorse a view as distant as possible from a semiotic programme and a conventionalistic conception of art.

Let me start with 'vocabulary': by using that word Gombrich indicates that without certain formulae and schemata for drawing objects, illusionistic pictorial representation is impossible. These schemata and formulae make pictorial representation possible just as words make verbal communication possible. This is the full extent of the analogy. Gombrich's discussion of these schemes and formulae itself indicates the limitations of the analogy.

According to any structuralism or semiotics based on Saussure's analysis of the linguistic sign, words are conventional due to the mutual indifference of the signifier (in the case of language, the sound or the graphic form of the word) and the signified, its meaning. This lack of internal relationship between the material of the sign and its meaning inveighs against regarding the linguistic mark as a necessary tool of expression or representation; the semiotic system could use other materials as tools. Although certain developments in the linguistic system may be explained, even by the structuralist, teleologically, e.g. as answering needs felt in the linguistic community, the basic nature of language as a system of signs is a set of arbitrary conventions.

Artists' vocabularies, including all their elements, are taken by Gombrich as goal-directed from the start. Even if a painter's scheme for drawing an object is a sign, there is no sense in distinguishing its material from its meaning as indifferent components linked by a system of conventions. Should we distinguish linguistic signs from pictorial icons or linguistic conventional signs from pictorial iconic signs? Gombrich does not answer this question, which shows how limited the analogy of pictorial representation to language is. What is perfectly clear is that in the artists' 'vocabularies' the connection of specific 'words' to the purpose of representation is given from the beginning. Goal-directedness is not added with evolution, nor through attempts of artists to widen or enrich their vocabularies. The first formula or scheme of pictorial representation is already used by the artist as a tool. Carefully adjusted to the performing of a definite task of representation because of their materiality, their visible form, these schemes or formulae cannot be viewed as conventional signs.[10]

The second point that distinguishes Gombrich from conventionalism is the existence of objective standards for successful realist painting. That point is firmly linked to the non-conventional nature of painters' vocabularies. That what we can say or mean depends on our 'vocabulary' has relativistic implications only if we assume that an alternative vocabulary is potentially at our disposal. Our vocabulary, by setting limits to what we can express, does indeed predetermine what we say. Relativism and conventionalism are therefore connected; since the language we have at our disposal is a set of conventions, all expression and representation are relative to it and cannot be compared to similar achievements in other languages. Illusionistic painting is not a language in this sense; it does not use language to achieve its norm. Any tradition of painting that has the same norm needs to advance along the same lines. It needs to discover the same devices (foreshortening, high-lights, the laws of perspective, etc.) precisely because these are not conventions. Thus, even theoretically, there is no logical room for a plurality of illusionistic traditions.

The analogy of language may be put to a better use in connection with another aspect of the history of art. Gombrich's narrative, like any other sound history of representational art (theatre, fiction or film-making), does refer to conventions, but these are not to be identified with the formulae of the painter, but rather with the traditional existing modes of painting considered as institutions of pictorial representation. Black-and-white drawing and coloured oil painting can be regarded as different 'languages' of pictorial representation. Indeed, there is no point in comparing the degree of illusion achieved by a black-and-white drawing to that achieved by a coloured oil painting of the same object. Of course, the oil painting may impart more information about the object, and in this sense it is more 'realistic', but, as I shall explain later, more information is not necessarily more illusion. As I have indicated, representational gaps, aspects of the object not represented in the work, exist in every mode of representation, and these are ignored by the viewer when looking for illusion.

In this sense the basic forms of representational art are separate 'languages'. Each one of them opens and allows different possibilities of representation. There is a point in limiting all comparisons and gradations of illusionistic achievements to a form, since the achievement is relative to the possibilities of representation it allows. But this form-relativism does not imply a relativistic theory either of perception or of representation. (This goes beyond the theory of painting. For example, I think it also applies to comparisons between novels and films. A film is trivially more 'realistic' than any novel; yet I believe that this is irrelevant to Gombrich's notion of illusion. In the sense of 'illusion' that is of interest to aesthetic theory, a good novel may offer, despite all the famous 'gaps' and 'indeterminacies' of literary (linguistic) representation, a higher illusion than its cinematic counterpart; compare Tolstoy's *Anna Karenina* with any of the movies of the same title.) Thus animal drawings or oil portraits can be compared and graded according to their degree of illusion by the same standards, whether they are Chinese, Egyptian or European. These standards allow Gombrich to describe the history of illusionistic painting as a history of progress, and to supply teleological explanations for crucial turning-points within it. Without assuming these standards, there is no movement towards the achievement of an aesthetic goal, but an accidental plurality of schools and styles, each understood and appreciated by its internal aims.

The explicit discussion of these standards of truth is found only in *The Image and the Eye*. It fills a lacuna in *Art and Illusion*, and as the discussion in the first book requires, these standards of (visual) truth are both general and specific enough to measure the attainment of the norm in the entire tradition of illusionistic painting. Indeed I am sure that 'truth' as in 'standards of truth' and in 'visual truth' – two expressions central to *The Image and the Eye* – is an improvement over 'illusion'. But Gombrich's discussion avoids the risk of another misinterpretation and makes it clear that both 'visual truth' and the 'standards' to which all pictorial representations must conform have very little to do with factual truth (i.e. the amount of information paintings contain concerning their object). Hence the negative standard (Do not Paint What Cannot be Seen From an Imagined Perspective) is so much more important than the positive rule (Paint All That is Seen from an Assumed Perspective). It is more important because it applies to imaginary or fictional objects as well as to those that can be seen; but it is also more important because contradiction will not just diminish illusion. It will destroy it immediately.

The 'truth' we speak of is, therefore, the truth of seeing in general, rather than the truth about a specific object. Even repleteness need not be conducive to realism in rendering the look of real or imagined objects; indistinctness may take its place. In some cases illusion (or visual truth) is served by repleteness and richness of details (as in the case of Constable) while in other cases it is better achieved by indistinctness (as in the case of Turner). Great works of art almost always mix regional repleteness and vividness with regional indistinctness to achieve illusion, (as in the case of Rembrandt). In brief, information and repleteness may be valuable as such, but in the specific tradition which Gombrich studies they are valued only in so far as they advance perfect illusion.

The explanations of visual truth and standards of truth, the notions added in the later essays, are of great help in preventing philosophical misunderstandings or misuses of *Art and Illusion*. Gombrich's historical narrative can encourage relativistic conceptions of realism in art only when information or repleteness are invoked as separate values, distinct form the global experience of illusion. This, I think, is the core of the misinterpretation of *Art and Illusion* by conventionalists and relativists.

IV

Readers familiar with Gombrich's writings, especially those written after *Art and Illusion*, will probably find that an essential component in his theory is missing in my account. I have avoided any discussion of Gombrich's many references to biology and the findings on animal behaviour, despite the fact that in his later presentations of his argument in *Art and Illusion* much is made of these references.

The omission is deliberate. I do not share Gombrich's conviction that these findings can be used to refute the claims of the cultural relativist with regard to pictorial representation. However, I believe that the force of Gombrich's anti-relativist argument does not depend on an interpretation of these findings.

Gombrich is impressed with these findings because they supply us with evidence that resemblances (or, as he prefers to call them, 'equivalences') exist 'in nature' and not solely 'in the human mind'. Indeed, that is demonstrated by the experiments in which animals' behaviour towards certain harmless and useless imitations is exactly what it would be if the latter were the real desirable or the real threatening object. Animals behave towards certain objects rather than others, as if those objects belonged to the same category as the original objects they resemble. This suggests, indeed, the existence of biological constraints on resemblance. If we could prove that this is what makes an illusionistic painting so convincing in suggesting its object, we would make all talk of the role of custom, habit and cultural inculcation redundant. But in this case we will have to redefine the task of the illusionistic painter. If the same powers that govern delusions in animals also govern artistic illusion, if our appreciating x as a perceptual equivalent of y is fully dictated by unconscious biological constraints in painting also, then the task of the painter is to discover the language of nature rather than invent a language of his own. He or she has to find the key to the system of biologically constrained equivalences.

I think that this seductive speculation vitiates rather than strengthens the force of Gombrich's analysis of illusion in painting. The case of deception in animals is partly similar to the self-deception that brought primitive man, in magic and ritual, to classify objects and their representations as belonging to the same category. The two cases are similar at least in that Gombrich tends to think of both as remote origins of artistic illusionism. Yet in both cases we are dealing with perceptual equivalences between two different objects that are indistinguishable for the perceiver. We do not deal with the conscious identification and the conscious enjoyment of a representational equivalence as such, which is for artist and beholder alike the aim of illusionistic painting. Even if we accept the biological or anthropological speculations that trace the ultimate origins of illusionism in art to magic or to animal behaviour, we may still question the validity of the analogy drawn between the three different phenomena. We may still argue that it blurs the distinctive features of artistic illusion as a psychological and aesthetic phenomenon.

In part three of *Art and Illusion* Gombrich offers one of the best analytic descriptions of the experience of illusion in art. He shows that the beholder fully participates in the game of illusion by intentionally ignoring some aspects of the representation and by concentrating on others; he shows how we follow the hints of the painter in our interpretations and projections; he shows not only how active we are but also how conscious we must be, at least in regard to the general meaning of that activity. Hence, while intentionally producing (or co-producing, together with the painter) an illusion, we are very far from falling into a delusional trap. A precondition of that intentional activity is our realising that representation and its object do not belong in the same category. Cognisant of all that, we wish to continue the work of the painter in endowing the painting with powers that will make it into a perfect image of its object. If we succeed, we can see the object through or in the image without blurring the ontological boundaries that separate them one from the other.

There is nothing in Gombrich's analysis to support the contention that the aesthetic experience of illusion is partly an experience of delusion, whatever its remote biological or anthropological origins may be. It is true that we may be misled by tricks played upon us by the painter; for example, we may form mistaken beliefs about what is actually painted and what is merely suggested in the painting, or even projected on it by our own imagination. Gombrich does not confuse these mistaken beliefs with fully-fledged delusions. However, I believe that it is these 'delusive' elements in the experience of illusion that make him suggest, at least on one occasion, a conflict between delusional tendencies and our better knowledge.[11] If such conflict exists, it must take place below the conscious level. Otherwise the conscious struggle between a (delusional) reflex and reflection will destroy the unity of our aesthetic experience.

Here, I think, the theorist of illusion must choose: carrying the analogy with animal behaviour or magic too far makes delusion the ideal limit or the hidden basis of illusion. It vitiates a part of Gombrich's main argument according to which the difference between the two is not quantitative. On the other hand, insisting on the intentional nature of the experience of illusion and on the willing co-operation of the culturally trained beholder leaves the issue of objectivity and universality of visual truth in representation open to different philosophical interpretations.

I do not believe that the anti-relativist stand of Gombrich in the two books needs the findings on animals' mistakes for its completion. Biologists, psychologists and other theorists may differ in their estimates of how essential the role played by biological constraints in visual perceptions is in comparison with factors such as knowledge or acquired habits. Although the result of that debate may influence our views of pictorial representation, the force of the explanatory model used in *Art and Illusion* to explain the evolution of illusionistic painting does not depend on it. Gombrich succeeds in showing that artists' devices and the invention or discovery of new techniques are non-accidental and constitute an advancement by referring us to the satisfaction felt both by painters and viewers with any new discovery or invention. To make the concept of advancement as objective as it can be, all that is required is to assume the relative constancy of human vision, namely that vision and the visible world are relatively more stable than our pictorial representations of them. A theory that gives a dominant role to biological constraints in vision does indeed offer a kind of scientific 'grounding' for the hypothesis of the stability of vision. That is the source of its attraction for Gombrich. Yet the hypothesis of the relative constancy of vision may also be made plausible on simple phenomenological grounds. I am not sure it can be proved 'scientifically', but I do not think that even without a complete biological theory of vision we must surrender to relativism. Another tradition of illusionistic pictorial representation that avoids the devices and techniques of the tradition Gombrich studies (e.g. perspective, foreshortening, highlighting) and yet realises the same illusionistic norm is hardly in the offing.

Notes

1. 'We obviously must distinguish between an accurate imitation, an illusion and a false belief', *Illusion*, p. 196. This obvious distinction has its own problems of course. But by making an attempt to situate illusion in exactly midway between accurate imitation and delusion it clarifies the use of the term in *Art and Illusion*. Illusion accompanied by false beliefs will create (or rather be) a delusion. An accurate imitation will simply evoke reflective appreciation. Illusion proper will be the exact intermediary state where you have 'complex interplay between reflex and reflection' (*Illusion*, p. 242). The reflex is to sense three-dimensional depth in the two-dimensional painting. The reflection is the knowledge that there is no real three-dimensional depth there, but only a two-dimensional image of it. I find the distinction between the three terms instructive. But I think that the term 'reflection' is somewhat misleading. The knowledge of the viewer that what he looks at is a representation or an image of depth is always there. We are not aware of a real struggle between an urge to treat the representation as the real thing and a reflection that overcomes such an urge. Reflex, knowledge and the interplay between them must all exist in the unreflective experience of the beholder. I will return to this issue at the end of this chapter.

2. Gombrich does not discuss fictional objects. His argument assumes the existence of a model, even when this model serves to represent imaginary (e.g. biblical or mythological) objects. Gombrich's analysis makes it clear that usually illusion has to do with figures and objects whose existence the viewer assumes. Nevertheless, one may speculate that the concept 'visual truth', developed in *The Image and the Eye*, may allow fantastic objects. That concept is introduced as an explication of the term 'illusion', which is never defined in *Art and Illusion*. It implies Kantian transcendental notions of visually possible and visually impossible objects that cut across ordinary ontological distinctions. Thus, even the most fantastic dragon can be represented as 'visually true' if shown according to the laws of perspective and if it contains no details that cannot be seen from an imagined stationary point in space, and so on. If this is correct we may have an illusionistic painting of anything or any non-thing we like. Admittedly this speculation perverts Gombrich's view; yet it points to a certain gap in aesthetic explications and theories of illusion, verisimilitude etc., that neglect thematic and ontological considerations.

3. Gombrich's earliest term for the partial match of aspects of two-dimensional pictorial representations and three-dimensional objects represented in them is 'relational models' (*Art and Illusion*, pp. 214–16).

4. Influenced by my reading of Gombrich, I developed the idea that effects of

realism in fiction, the theatre or the cinema should be regarded as non-conventional, despite the fact that they are achieved in art-forms that obey specific sets of conventions. See my papers 'Aesthetic illusion', *The Journal of Aesthetics and Art Criticism*, 36 (1978), pp. 96–107; 'Verisimilitude, conventions and beliefs', *New Literary History*, 13 (1983), pp. 253–267; and 'The discrimination of realisms in the literary work of art', *Journal of Aesthetics and Comparative Literature*, 5 (1985), pp. 10–21.

5. Hesitation concerning the absolute constancy of the perceived world is expressed by Gombrich in a conversation with Didier Eribon:

> I do not think that it is correct to say that people in the twelfth century saw the world differently. They did not. But since there is no innocent eye, we are also influenced by our knowledge. I am not so sure that we can see the moon as we saw it thirty years ago. We are influenced by what we saw on the TV screen and by our knowledge that the surface of the moon is black, like charcoal (*Eribon*, pp. 110–11).

There is no formal contradiction here. However, there is a glaring instability and inconsistency concerning the relationship between perception and knowledge. Nevertheless, I believe that my explication of the tacit assumptions of *Art and Illusion* and *The Image and the Eye* on this issue demonstrates the consistency in Gombrich's overall outlook.

6. In Bergson's sense of this term: a direct exposure to objects uninfluenced by memories and knowledge derived from past experiences.

7. Nelson Goodman, *Languages of Art*, London 1969; Murray Krieger, 'The ambiguities of representation and illusion: an E. H. Gombrich retrospective', *Critical Inquiry*, 11 (1984), pp. 181–94.

8. 'Mirror and map: theories of pictorial representation'; 'Standards of truth: the arrested image and the moving eye' and especially 'Image and code: scope and limits of conventionalism in pictorial representation'.

9. At the end of the last paper mentioned in note eight, Gombrich asserts that in naturalism 'the incorporation in the image of all the features that serve us in real life for the discovery and testing of meaning enabled the artist to do with fewer and fewer conventions' (*Image and Eye*, p. 297).

10. For a different interpretation of this issue see J. Hyman, 'Language and pictorial art', in the *Companion to Aesthetics* (edited by David Cooper), Oxford 1992, pp. 261–8.

11. This is suggested at the end of the essay 'Illusion and Art': 'I believe that no verbal formula can do justice to the complex interplay between reflex and reflection, involvement and detachment that we so inadequately sum up in the word "illusion"' (*Illusion*, p. 242).

From : Gombrich on Art and Psychology,
R. Woodfield (Ed), Manchester U P, 1996

Gombrich and the psychology of visual perception

Ian Gordon

> Nothing could be more familiar than pictures, and yet nothing is
> more strange. Almost any statement about a picture is controversial
> (J. J. Gibson, review of *Art and Illusion*).

A N attempt will be made in this chapter to review some of the areas in
the experimental study of visual perception which have interested
Gombrich and may have influenced his thought. It is of course impossible
to discover all the influences which have operated during the lifetime of a
distinguished scholar, but Gombrich has always been generous in his ac-
knowledgements, and these have suggested a plan for the present chapter.

There seems to be a general rule that when people become aware of
exciting new ideas in fields other than their own, it is the early accounts of
these ideas which are absorbed. Many outsiders experienced the excitement
of Chomsky's radical suggestions concerning the origins of language; few
will have followed the subsequent development of his highly technical work.
There are of course exceptions to this rule; it is likely that the eventual
readership of *The Blind Watchmaker* will exceed that of *The Selfish Gene*, but
these are books by a specialist directed at a lay audience.

Gombrich has written much since *Art and Illusion* appeared in 1960.
However, from my discussions with researchers in visual perception, I am
convinced that for them this is the best-known and most widely admired of
his works. As it would be impossible for a psychologist to discuss all
Gombrich's ideas in a single chapter, I shall abstract from *Art and Illusion*
certain themes which are still of interest in contemporary perceptual research.
In what follows, an account will be given of some of the facts and theories
in the scientific literature which were available to Gombrich earlier in his
career – when he was writing *Art and Illusion*. I shall then attempt to describe
what has happened in various areas since then. In a sense, this will be to ask

the question, 'What would Gombrich have found in contemporary research on visual perception had he been starting now?'

Art and Illusion was concerned with a major historical phenomenon, the development of naturalistic Western art. Gombrich knew that a painting can never be a perfect copy of the real world. In stressing this fact, he also asserted that the problems of representation are by no means solved by photography and that, on the other hand, to welcome a completely abstract art too uncritically would be to lose contact with the great works of the past. But if a painting is not a perfect copy of the real world, what is it? During his attempts to answer this question Gombrich was forced to consider, not only what the painter does to a surface, but how a viewer of that surface perceives it. At this point in Gombrich's work it became necessary to attempt to find some common ground between the study of art and the science of vision.

Those of Gombrich's ideas which have been used to shape the following discussion can be crudely summarised as follows.

Any attempt to capture the appearance of the three-dimensional world on a two-dimensional surface is doomed to failure. There are two reasons for this. First, the projection of three dimensions on to two must result in a loss of information. The outline projection traced on Leonardo's window by the early users of central linear perspective is not uniquely determined by the layout of the surface beyond the window – there is an infinity of layouts which could give rise to the same outline.

Even then, if the 2D–3D limit could be overcome in some miraculous way, serious problems would remain. Chief among these is the fact that even a brief visual experience is too rich for the artist to capture, as it involves the fleeting but important effects of moving the head and eyes, the presence of stereoscopic cues to the relative depth of things (over short distances) and the awareness of the viewer's own body. For example, our noses are always present in the retinal image and are available to introspection; should the artist include them? Hardly, as in normal perceiving we usually fail to notice this intrusion. But already we are acknowledging at least two ways of seeing the world; which should the artist try to represent?

When the eye is offered groups of marks on a surface, two things happen. First, the marks tend to group and organise themselves in certain ways, revealing the influence of what seem to be basic perceptual processes. Second, the configurations which the marks have created can be seen as standing for other things, as representations. At this point it is necessary to consider the social and cultural context surrounding the viewer, for what is acceptable as a representation of something varies over time and across different cultures: Egyptian paintings differ from Victorian portraits; the swastika is unlikely ever again to recover its status as an innocent simple shape.

In art, however, it is not the case that anything can stand for anything else. The artist is a discoverer of possible equivalences, but these equivalences are limited by conventions which have been learned during a lifetime and which can be changed only during moments of real originality. There may be a range of different equivalences available to the artist at any one time, but this range has its limits. An original painting is, therefore, in one sense an experiment. The painter is trying to see what marks can best represent the objects or events to be depicted. This is the reason why art changes; more and more possible equivalences between objects and pictures are discovered and accepted by convention.

When marks on a surface come to look like something other than themselves, there is a sense in which this can be thought of as an illusion. It follows that there are important links between the psychology of illusion and the techniques of depiction. One of the most important tools available to the artist when creating an illusion of reality is, of course, the technique of perspective.

Art is not the only aspect of a culture in which depiction is important. The study of the language of vision can be enriched by considering techniques of depiction in, for example, instruction manuals, diagrams, posters and signs. (This particular aspect of Gombrich's work will not be dealt with here.)

I shall now give short accounts of some of the facts and theories in the scientific literature which was available to Gombrich when he was developing the ideas outlined above. Each account will then be followed by a brief description of some of the relevant discoveries or theories to have emerged in more recent years.

Perception as a constructive process

Between the 1940s and the 1960s there was one dominant paradigm in psychology: empiricism. Since the influential writings of Helmholtz (1821–94), most theorists have accepted the idea that sensory inputs are insufficient as data for complete and valid perception of the world. For example, if the visual image of an object shrinks with distance, but the object stays phenomenally the same, then the direct impact of the object on the perceiver, via its retinal image, cannot be sufficient for the (true) perception of the object's constant size. Clearly, some sort of compensation for distance must be occurring, and this necessarily involves more central processes.[1] On this view, perception is in large part a cognitive, constructive process; we can never be in direct contact with the real world.

The major texts which Gombrich cites in his early books, for example those by Osgood[2] and Woodworth and Schlosberg,[3] give numerous examples to support the empiricist (or constructivist) position. And these books were important sources for a generation of young researchers. As a result, the research literature in the next decade abounds in examples of perception being tricked in ways which reveal the involvement of knowledge, experience and familiarity – the types of central psychological processes held to be responsible for fleshing out impoverished sensory data. Publications of the time describe oddly-shaped rooms which appear normal when viewed through peep-holes, pictures and figures which are difficult if not impossible to decipher without verbal hints, delays in recognising briefly exposed words when these are threatening or taboo, and of course, many illusions. Showing the malleable and vulnerable aspects of perception under laboratory conditions increased the belief that this was how perception must be all the time. Perhaps the pinnacle of empiricism was reached when the distinguished psychologist, R. L. Gregory (with whom Gombrich has collaborated) announced that 'Perceptions are hypotheses.'[4]

The empiricist model of perception becomes even more complicated if the ideas of Brunswik are included.[5] Brunswik, whose influence is acknowledged in the introduction to *Art and Illusion*, held that the cues against which perceptual hypotheses are tested are themselves imperfect – cues which on one occasion may form reliable evidence concerning an aspect of the world may not do so on a second occasion. For Brunswik the perceiver, faced with this unreliability, was forced to act as 'an intuitive statistician', a role which demands flexibility and the ability to be able to switch between different sources of information.

One may guess that, for Gombrich, a major idea within empiricism was that, to a significant degree, perceiving is an activity which must be learned. Clearly, if seeing the world is something we learn to do as infants, we may be able to learn new ways of seeing parts of the world – representations for example – later in life. Add to this the apparent influences of knowledge, belief and experience on seeing, and one has a basis from which to develop explanations of the changes in artistic style across cultures and over time.

The question, of course, is whether perception is indeed a learned, constructive process. Is empiricism true? Contemporary research suggests that the picture may not be as simple as was once thought.

More recent work

Empiricism continues to dominate contemporary work in perception. There are, however, certain reasons for doubting whether the beliefs outlined above are true in their entirety.

A major challenge to the constructivist position can be seen in the later work of the American theorist, J. J. Gibson,[6] which was subsequently continued by his followers.[7] Gibson came to believe that perception of the real world is a direct process, requiring little in the way of supplementation through knowledge. His argument for this was that in the real world (in contrast to the artificial conditions of the laboratory) the eye receives more than the few simple rays depicted in traditional optical diagrams. In fact, the eye is bathed in a sea of *information*. Because it travels in straight lines, and because it is altered systematically by the medium it flows through and the surfaces from which it is reflected, light can carry information about where it has been; it can tell the visual system about the world it has illuminated. Vision, in Gibson's opinion, is mainly a direct, unlearned response to the higher-order information in this rich stimulation. Some of these higher-order properties, in the form of *invariants*, tell us about the surfaces and objects before us in the world. And whenever information is somehow inadequate or impoverished, observers take action; they move their heads and eyes, they walk around things. Observers do not have to learn to extract the relevant information from an optical array; just as the structure of the vertebrate visual system has been shaped by evolution, so too have its responses.

Gibson's most surprising assertion concerns the most abstract level of invariance, the *affordance*. Gibson came to believe that perceptual systems respond directly to those aspects of things which are relevant to behaviour: an apple is perceived as 'affording' eating, a stone 'affords' throwing, certain horizontal surfaces 'afford' sitting or walking. But are not these aspects of objects part of their *meanings*? Not surprisingly, this bold claim has been challenged by many modern theorists.[8]

As a personal friend of Gibson's, Gombrich was familiar with his views (see for example his sympathetic review of a book about Gibson's life and work).[9] Gombrich disagreed with Gibson's extension of his ideas to pictures, but was nevertheless in general agreement with several of Gibson's other key ideas.

It is possible to assert, more than a decade since Gibson's last writings, that some of the most recent work stemming from his Theory of Direct Perception is proving very fruitful. For example, the ways in which afford-ances can be perceived are being uncovered in an exciting manner. It now seems quite likely that we scale the perceived world in terms of our own body dimensions. As a rather esoteric example, consider someone approaching a horizontal aperture, such as a doorway. When the width of the doorway approaches the width of the person's shoulders, he or she will unconsciously rotate the shoulders prior to coming to the threshold. What is the basis of this decision? Is it possible to predict those door widths at which a particular individual will change from direct walking to walking plus an anticipatory rotation of the shoulders? The answer is that this correlates highly with the observer's *eye-height*.[10] It now appears that eye-height may be widely used as a scaling variable in various real-life situations; it could, for example, be the basis of accurate estimates of the size and distance of objects in the field of view.[11] Now if this last suggestion is true, then one of the classic problems in visual perception (and one that has exercised Gombrich), that of size constancy, is on the way to being solved. It is no longer necessary to puzzle about how the reduction in size of a retinal image with distance is 'com-pensated for'. If we can directly scale the world in terms of a stable body measure we can directly achieve correct perceptions of the real properties of the objects we see.

Should these successes continue, then it may be possible to show that much of our perception of the real world does not depend on learning; that not all percepts have to be constructed. But this raises a dilemma: Gibson himself made a clear distinction between perception of the natural environ-ment, which he held to be largely direct, and perception of the built or cultural environment, the meanings of which must be learned. Is this artificial world of signs and symbols perceived differently, by special processes? If so, and if the Theory of Direct Perception extends its successes, then theories of visual perception may be forced to split between those which can account for perception of the natural world and others which explain how we see, for example, paintings. This might set a limit on the usefulness of the science of perception for the explanation of the nature of art.

It must be re-emphasised that the work of Gibson and his followers on what has been called 'Direct Perception' is controversial. And when Gibson attempted to extend his theory to the perception of pictures, the result was not particularly convincing.[12] As stated earlier, it did not convince Gombrich.

However, there are other reasons for thinking that certain claims made within the empiricist tradition might need to be modified. Two provocative sets of findings will now be outlined: the results of some modern research into how infants see, and studies of blind people.

The American psychologist, William James (1842–1910), described the subjective world of the new-born infant as 'one great blooming, buzzing confusion'. This is also an important implication of the empiricist interpretation of perception – we must learn to overcome the confusion and build a stable perception of the world. However, modern work is increasingly supporting a contrasting view, namely that at birth a human infant is surprisingly competent. Briefly, this work has shown that a new-born infant prefers its mother's voice to that of a stranger;[13] the infant shows shape constancy, the ability to recognise an object as the same despite a change in its optical projection caused by its rotation about an axis;[14] presented with a head shape displaying normal features or one with scrambled features, the infant will track the former with its eyes more than the latter, and it will show this preference within five minutes of being born.[15]

A visual system which is sensitive to the differences between a scrambled and a normal face immediately after birth is likely to be heavily preprogrammed. It is therefore appropriate to ask about the extent to which a system with such a major genetic component is capable of modification by subsequent experience. Is it possible that when a viewer grows used to an novel form or style of depiction what is happening is not a change in perception *per se*, but rather some adjustment of a related cognitive system? Of course, as far as behaviour is concerned, it will always be hard to tell the difference. The problem rather is in predicting whether future explanations of basic processes of visual perception will assist the understanding of a more complicated question: how is art perceived? When we learn that a particular watercolour was painted by Adolf Hitler, our responses to it certainly change; but are these changes perceptual or emotional, or some complex blend of the two?

If we must learn to see, then the blind should lack visual concepts. One study is of particular relevance here. Kennedy has studied the pictorial abilities of a highly motivated self-help group of blind people in Toronto, some of whom have been blind from birth.[16] With great ingenuity, Kennedy found a way to make it easier for these blind people to draw. One problem in drawing is to know where next to take the line, but this is very difficult if one doesn't know where on the surface one is to start with. Kennedy overcame this problem by using a special plastic material which responds to a ball-point by blistering slightly.

Kennedy presented his blind collaborators with simple raised-line drawings of objects such as a fork, a hand and a man. Some of these could be identified by some of the blind immediately. Other drawings were misidentified in interesting ways; the fork mistaken for the hand, for example. One intriguing finding emerged when a blind person correctly identified an outline drawing of a man with his arms crossed – in other words, the convention of the occluding edge was immediately accepted.

When Kennedy watched his collaborators as they drew, and discussed the problems with them, he learned other interesting things. For example, two of the blind people suggested that when drawing railroad tracks, narrowing could be used to indicate distance; another person suggested that a line could be made thinner as the object depicted receded into the distance.

As a result of his studies of picture making and recognition by the blind, Kennedy makes the following remarkable claims:

1   The blind can recognise the problem of depicting three dimensions in two, and also that something special is required when representing, say, transparent objects.

2   The blind readily accept the idea of outlines as representations of solid things.

3   They understand the concepts of vantage point and line of sight.

4   They can appreciate the perspective distortion of circles into ellipses.

5   They can appreciate the necessity for occluding certain edges during depiction.

On the basis of these and other results Kennedy asserts that the blind have *an unlearned pictorial sense*: 'There seems to be some deeply rooted human capacity to understand outline depiction of features of solid objects, a capacity that applies the same rules to vision as to touch'[17] and: 'Picturing seems to be a form of communication meaningful to both vision and touch, without tuition.'[18]

As yet, there does not appear to be any independent support for these claims. But should Kennedy's findings be replicated with other blind people, then one can assert that this will be a wonderful puzzle for art theorists to worry over.

The organisation of marks on a surface

Some of the first scientific discoveries in vision concerned the automatic behaviour of peripheral mechanisms in vision, the workings of which extract contours from intensity gradients on the retina, enhance contrasts between bright and dark areas in the visual field (a phenomenon which Gombrich has discussed in relation to painting), and sharpen the resolution of the eye by means of inhibitory and excitatory processes in the visual pathway.

At a more psychological level, the early gestalt psychologists examined the spontaneous tendency in vision to split the world into figure and ground, and the rules by which groups of stimuli became grouped into wholes or *Gestalten* − Wertheimer's Laws of Grouping.[19]

More recent work

This interest in the early responses of the eye to stimuli continues today in the area of research known generally as artificial intelligence, and its more specific applications in the computational theory of vision. As this research proceeds more processes of a fundamental nature are becoming understood. For example, it is now known that the visual system behaves as a series of *spatial frequency channels*. The spatial frequency of a black-and-white grating (a tool with widespread applications in vision research) is the number of cycles of black and white stripes per degree of visual angle. The reader of this page is currently using a high spatial frequency channel to discriminate the printed letters. If the reader now screws up his or her eyes, the letters will blur, high spatial frequency information will be lost, and instead the page will appear as blocks of dark grey (the paragraphs etc.) − this is the low spatial frequency information.

The result of stepping back from an impressionist or pointillist painting is a loss of some of the high spatial frequency information − the inability to detect the detailed paint-strokes. Instead, the higher organisation of the painting and what it *represents* becomes dramatically apparent: 'We are back in the atmosphere and the period when the art-lover discovered the joy of stepping back from the canvas to enjoy the sensation of visible brush-strokes disappearing behind the emergent illusion.'[20] We now have a much more precise understanding of the visual processes at work during such enjoyable experiences. A similar account can be given of spatial averaging with distance, in which blobs of different hues on a canvas blend according to the laws of additive colour mixture.

One of the questions in this type of modern research is this: given that the first stage in seeing is the retinal image, how is this two-dimensional distribution of light processed to provide reliable information concerning objects and surfaces in the real, three-dimensional world? Generally, it is not retinal images that are scrutinised by researchers and their computers, but convenient substitutes such as photographs and simple displays. To give a flavour of the degree of care and rigour which is being given to such enquiries, I shall give a brief outline of a single experiment into the organis-ation of Glass patterns.

Figure 3.1 shows what happens when a random array of dots is rotated and superimposed on itself. This is a Glass pattern.[21] Such patterns can be formed by expansion and hyperbolic distortion as well as by rotation of the original. Glass patterns have proved valuable tools for investigating basic 'low-level' visual processes.

On first thought it might be supposed that the organisation seen in a Glass pattern is due simply to the fact that in a subset of dots the increased closeness to neighbours creates the pattern that we see. This, clearly, is how one would attempt to create such a pattern if one were drawing with dots. However, very precise studies of these patterns have shown that they cannot be explained solely on the basis of the proximities between certain dots. An ingenious experiment was performed as follows: each original 'source' dot in a random pattern was subsequently flanked by two other dots equidistant from it. One of these dots was placed in a position which could produce the Glass pattern associated with a rotation of the original source pattern, the other was placed in a position which could yield the Glass pattern formed by an expansion. Then each source dot was made equal in brightness to only one of its neighbours. The result was that of the two possible Glass pattern organisations, that formed by the interaction between the source dots and those dots which were equal in brightness was the one to emerge. The gestalt psychologist Wertheimer discovered the Laws of Proximity and Similarity many years ago when examining the spontaneous groupings which occur during the organis-ation of simple stimuli; this more modern research has shown that these two laws can interact in complex ways. It is now a distinct possibility that other gestalt laws will repay such meticulous re-examination, and that the results of future studies will be to provide a much deeper understanding of the ways in which marks on surfaces can become organised into configurations.

I have selected Glass patterns and spatial frequency analysis as examples of new ways of understanding visual processes mainly because they are relatively

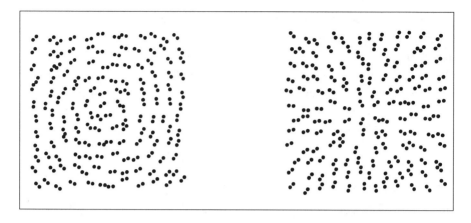

Figure 3.1 Two Glass patterns. The one on the left is formed from an original random display together with a rotation of itself; the one on the right is formed by combining an original pattern with an expanded version of the original.

easy to describe. Readers of a modern classic in the area of artificial intelligence, David Marr's *Vision*,[22] will find a very much fuller set of examples, such as the recovery of shape from shading, the abstraction of three-dimensional information from silhouettes, and the ways in which differences in illumination can be compensated for when perceiving variegated surfaces.

In developing his model of vision, Marr realised that many of his basic algorithms were of necessity viewer-centred; that is, they operate within a co-ordinate system centred upon the retina. But human vision is ultimately object-centred: the appearance of something does not change if one rotates one's head. Part of Marr's later work involved thinking about how vision moves from a viewer-centred to an object-centred framework.

Attempts have been made to relate the distinction between viewer- and object-centred parts of the computational theory of vision to differences in artistic styles and conventions. The most interesting discussion of this point to date, in my opinion, is the short article by Willats.[23] Willats asks whether Marr's distinction between viewer-centred and object-centred 'descriptions' of the world which the visual system is thought to create might be applicable to the general problem of depiction. On this hypothesis, central linear perspective is essentially a viewer-centred description, while other perspective systems, such as orthogonal projections, are object-centred. Similarly, not all of the lines in a photograph or an impressionist painting arise from, or represent, edges in the world; they must be interpreted, and hence can be described as viewer-centred. On the other hand, the lines of an architectural plan or an engineering drawing very definitely stand for parts of objects and can even be used to derive accurate measures of actual dimensions; they are object-centred. Willats himself admits, however, that this distinction is too simple; that most pictures fall somewhere between the extremes of totally viewer-centred versus object-centred accounts of the world. In this, I am sure that he is right. Nevertheless, the care and precision with which some modern workers are examining the extraction of information from the visual image is one of the most exciting developments in contemporary vision research. Gombrich is clearly aware of this new approach.[24] It is an intriguing question to ask how his thoughts might have been influenced had work of this quality been in progress when he was starting to write on art and perception. I shall end this section by simply asserting that all who are interested in linking the visual arts and science should be alert to the potential of this work.

Visual imagery

In my opinion, Gombrich is not always consistent in his use of the terms 'image' and 'imagery'. There is, however, a real and interesting set of problems here. When an artist paints something from memory, what is the nature of that memory? The main problem arises because most people experience some visual imagery, and it is natural to assume that this imagery is an essential aspect of memory. In addition, imagery is felt by many to be an aesthetically enriching component of consciousness. (When I published a journalistic account of experimental studies in this area many years ago, most of the many letters I received came from practising artists.)

The problem of imagery is easy to state, but has proved impossible to solve. The fact that a scene can be recognised (or painted) hours or days later is proof that it is somehow represented in the head. But many people would claim more than this; they would say that they have a *picture* of the remembered scene, that in a sense it can be seen 'in the mind's eye'. What is the status of such mental pictures?

Modern research

After a long period of neglect, imagery has once again become a very active area of research. Consider this experiment by Shepard and Metzler.[25] Observers were required to press one of two keys to indicate whether two shapes projected suddenly before them were identical or whether one was a mirror-image of the other: F versus Ⅎ, for example. When the shapes were oriented the same way, reaction times were as expected for a basically simple, two-choice reaction-time task. But when one of the shapes was rotated relative to the other, reaction times increased. In fact, the times increased as a direct function of the extent to which the shapes were rotated away from each other. It was as if the observers could not decide whether the shapes were or were not identical until they had rotated their representations of them.

There have been many similar studies, all of which suggest that an image 'in one's head' is not dissimilar from a direct visual percept − that the first is an analogue of the second − and such findings are of interest in that they suggest that mental imagery can be brought under experimental control.

Sadly, however, things may not be as simple as this. Ask a British person to say which is further north, Edinburgh or London, and the reply will be rapid and correct. But now ask which of the places is further *west*; the answer will be a long time coming. But if we have an analogue of the map of Britain in our heads, why should one of these questions be so much harder than the other? Why, too, do most people assert that they can easily form an image of a familiar object such as a bicycle, but when challenged to draw one from memory, find that they cannot produce even a working diagram? And why is it that when we think we have an image of, say, a room we were in recently, we are sometimes unable to describe a major detail, such as the colour of the carpet? How odd, too, that in such cases our mental picture, although demonstrably incomplete, never resembles a damaged photograph.

Such thoughts, and a number of experimental findings, have led some to attack the idea that a visual image is an analogue representation.[26] Rather it is suggested that what is stored in the head is a set of *propositions* which are not available to introspection. The 'pictures' we see happen to be available to introspection, and so we mistake them for the essentials of what is stored. On this view, the visual images we experience are epiphenomenal, interesting in themselves but irrelevant as guides to what aspects of the world are actually represented in our heads. The debate over the analogue versus the propositional nature of imagery will probably continue for a long time yet.

Psychology and perspective

Few early books on perception included any mention of the rules of perspective and their applications. Of the major textbooks of the 1950s, Woodworth and Schlosberg[27] has less than three full paragraphs on perspective, Osgood[28] contains no mention of it, and Stevens[29] spends less than a page on the subject. Most psychologists in the 1950s would have known that there is more than one perspective system and that there is something odd about art from the East, but not until Pirenne's work does one find anything much more sophisticated in the psychological literature.[30]

In the years since Gombrich's works first became widely known among experimental psychologists, there has been a growing appreciation of the importance of perspective as a source of empirical and theoretical problems. The main problems of perspective are dealt with elsewhere in this book. Following Pirenne's well-known treatment of optics, photography and perspective, the single most important work by a psychologist to appear in recent years is Hagen's *Varieties of Realism*.[31]

One of Hagen's most important contributions has been to demonstrate to those interested in perception and depiction the variety of ways in which it is possible to map a three-dimensional world on to a two-dimensional surface. Her book is a clear exposition of mappings and mapping functions, metric and similarity transformations, parallel projection, central projection on to parallel and intersecting planes, single versus multiple station points, affine and projective invariants.

From this solid base in the mathematics of transformations Hagen is able to do two things. First, she can make sense of much that initially strikes one as odd in children's drawings, art from the Far East and so-called primitive art. She shows that in all this, despite its immediate strangeness, there are principles of representation at work – systems of geometric projection that differ markedly from the familiar central projections of Western representational art. (Hagen also reminds us of the important fact that *most people in most cultures cannot use any depiction system competently*.)

Hagen's analysis of the world's paintings from 2000 BC to the present, using a systematic classification of the various representational styles which have existed, is likely to prove controversial. Her basic classificatory system comprises twelve compositional variables, such as the arrangement of the objects to be depicted, the picture planes and the projection lines used. For example, from 700–600 BC, much Egyptian art employed metric geometry, multiple station points, stratified object space and a uniform orientation of figures. Japanese art of the seventh and eighth centuries used affine geometry and a single station point. Cubism and art from the Pacific coast of North America used affine geometry and multiple station points. Hagen's conclusion is this:

> Even if we disregard all the criteria but that of improvement, it is probably not the case that the changes that take place in depiction style, in a culture or in an individual, reveal development toward any particular goal.[32]

Hagen adds that her analysis reveals no obvious developmental pattern across time or culture in terms of adoption of station point assumptions. Further: 'There is no evidence that cultures have ever moved systematically from Metric to Affine to Projective systems. Highly developed cultures have adopted each of these styles.'[33]

Hagen appears to have taken the analysis of what is involved in depicting the world on flat surfaces further than any other psychologist (and, incidentally, further than Gombrich). Although her conclusions are likely to be controversial, it is clear that Hagen's work has an implication which Gombrich would certainly agree with, namely that in order to understand *why* a particular style of depiction is adopted by any culture at any one time, it is necessary to discover what the depictions were trying to achieve: 'May not the conceptual, diagrammatic character of Egyptian images which has so often been described have as much to do with the function of these images as with the hypothetical 'mentality' of the Egyptian?'[34]

Concluding remarks

In this chapter I have reviewed some of the findings from experimental psychology which appear to have stimulated Gombrich during his theorising and have tried to show the directions in which some research areas appear to be shifting. It has not been possible to do this with any certainty; who knows what remarkable discoveries and theories may emerge from the science of vision in the next decades? Nevertheless, I hope to have shown that there is much in contemporary psychology which is deserving of the attention of art theorists.

So far, this chapter has been more concerned with perception and Gombrich than with Gombrich and perception. The reason for this is that there is a genuine problem when it comes to assessing Gombrich's influence on researchers in the general field of perception. The problem arises from the fact that while Gombrich has written so much that is insightful and stimulating about seeing, he does not, understandably, offer a theory of perception. Some of my very able students and I have spent hours discussing Gombrich's views and wondering how we could shape them into testable hypotheses, without a great deal of success to date. As an example, Gombrich has striking things to say about the role of schemata in the production and perception of art. His interest in schemata has been shared by several distinguished psychologists.[35] Some of these argue that the model of perception suggested by Gibson (described earlier in this chapter) cannot be made to work unless perceptions are organised by viewers' existing schemata. But as a concept, the schema has not had an entirely successful history. Introduced initially by the neurologist, Henry Head, it was of immediate appeal to psychologists such as Bartlett (1887–1969). But the schema remains somewhat amorphous, despite recent attempts to redefine it in some of the terminology of artificial intelligence, such as the 'frame'.

At the same time it is clear from interactions with other workers in vision that Gombrich is highly regarded, his work is well known, and many of his striking examples of novel visual effects have not been surpassed. His influence on perceptual research and theory may be considerable, but in my opinion it has mostly been indirect. He has presented us with a fascinating range of problems and has shown the enormous range of phenomena which can be subsumed under the general heading of 'seeing'.

I can, however, finish on a more positive note. I have suggested that Gombrich may not have had a measurable, direct influence on contemporary visual science. But is he read? Do his works continue to attract attention? The answer to both questions is a definite Yes. My search through recent European and American research literature resulted in well over a hundred recent references to Gombrich's writings. This is impressive. Even more impressive is the range of disciplines within which Gombrich has exerted his influence. Omitting all 'mainstream' perception publications, Gombrich has been mentioned recently in the following journals: *The American Journal of Archaeology*; *Annals of the Association of American Geographers*; *Behavioural and Brain Sciences*; *Biology and Philosophy*; *Cognition*; *Cognitive Neuropsychology*; *Developmental Psychology*; *Environment and Behaviour*; *Ethics*; *Geography*; *The Journal of Social and Biological Structure*; *Sociologie du Travail*.

I know of no other contemporary writer who could claim such a wonderfully diverse readership. Gombrich continues to arouse the sustained curiosity of all who read him.

Notes

1. Gombrich has some striking demonstrations of the role of *size constancy* in his 1975 review lecture 'Mirror and map: theories of pictorial representation', *Philosophical Proceedings of the Royal Society of London*, Series B, 270 (1975), pp. 119–49, reprinted in *Image and Eye*.

2. C. E. Osgood, *Method and Theory in Experimental Psychology*, New York 1953.

3. R. S. Woodworth and H. Schlosberg, *Experimental Psychology* (third edition), London 1955.

4. R. L. Gregory, 'Perceptions as hypotheses' (chapter 9 in S. C. Brown (ed.), *Philosophy of Psychology*, London 1974).

5. E. Brunswik, *Perception and the Representative Design of Psychological Experiments*, Berkeley 1956.

6. J. J. Gibson, *The Senses Considered as Perceptual Systems*, Boston 1966, and J. J. Gibson, *The Ecological Approach to Visual Perception*, Boston 1979.

7. See, for example, C. F. Michaels and C. Carello, *Direct Perception*, Englewood Cliffs 1981.

8. See, for example, the debate in S. Ullman, 'Against direct perception', *The Behavioural and Brain Sciences*, 3 (1980), whole issue.

9. E. H. Gombrich, 'Distinguished dissident', Review of E. S. Reed, *James J. Gibson and the Psychology of Perception* in *New York Review of Books*, 19 January 1989, pp. 13–15.

10. W. H. Warren and S. Wang, 'Visual guidance of walking through apertures: body-scaled information for affordances', *Journal of Experimental Psychology: Human Perception and Performance*, 13 (1987), pp. 371–83.

11. L. S. Mark, 'Eye-height-scaled information about affordances: a study of sitting and stair-climbing', *Journal of Experimental Psychology: Human Perception and Performance*, 13 (1987), pp. 361–70.

12. J. J. Gibson, 'On the concept of "formless invariants in visual perception"', *Leonardo*, 6 (1973), pp. 43–5.

13. A. J. DeCasper and W. P. Fifer, 'Of human bonding: newborns prefer their mother's voices', *Science*, 208 (1980), pp. 1174–6.

14. A. Slater and V. Morison, 'Shape constancy and slant perception at birth', *Perception*, 14 (1985), pp. 337–44.

15. C. C. Goren, M. Sarty and P. Y. K. Wu, 'Visual following and pattern discrimination of face-like stimuli by newborn infants', *Pediatrics*, 59 (1975), pp. 544–9 and S. Dziurawiec and H. D. Ellis, 'Neonates' attention to face-like stimuli: Goren, Sarty and Wu (1975) revisited', paper presented at the Annual Conference of the Developmental Section of the British Psychological Society, University of Exeter, September 1986.

16. J. M. Kennedy, 'Haptic pictures', *Papers in Language Use and Language Function*, 13 (1980), pp. 1–97, Scarborough College, University of Toronto.

17. *Ibid.*, p. 54.

18. *Ibid.*, p. 55.

19. M. Wertheimer, 'Experimental studies on the seeing of motion' (1912), reprinted in T. Shipley, *Classics in Psychology*, New York 1961.

20. *Art and Illusion*, p. 186.

21. L. Glass, 'Moiré effect from random dots', *Nature*, 223 (1969), pp. 578–80 and K. A. Stevens, 'Computation of locally parallel structure', *Biological Cybernetics*, 29 (1978), pp. 19–28.

22. D. Marr, *Vision*, San Francisco 1982.

23. J. Willats, 'The draughtsman's contract: how an artist creates an image' (chapter 16 in H. Barlow, C. Blakemore and M. Weston-Smith, *Images and Understanding*, Cambridge 1990).

24. See Gombrich, 'Distinguished dissident'.

25. R. N. Shepard and J. Metzler, 'Mental rotation of three-dimensional objects', *Science*, 171 (1971), pp. 701–3.

26. See, for example, Z. W. Pylyshyn, 'The rate of mental rotation of images: a test of holistic and analogue hypotheses', *Memory and Cognition*, 7 (1979), pp. 19–28.

27. *Experimental Psychology*.

28. *Method and Theory*.

29. S. S. Stevens (ed.), *Handbook of Experimental Psychology*, New York 1951.

30. M. H. Pirenne, *Optics, Painting and Photography*, Cambridge 1970.

31. M. A. Hagen, *Varieties of Realism*, Cambridge 1986. This, incidentally, bears a tribute to the late J. J. Gibson referred to above.

32. *Ibid.*, p. 267.

33. *Ibid.*, p. 269.

34. *Art and Illusion*, p. 103.

35. J. E. Hochberg, 'In the mind's eye', in R. N. Haber (ed.), *Contemporary Theory and Research in Visual Perception*, New York 1968 and U. Neisser, *Cognition and Reality*, San Francisco 1976.

4

Perspectives on perspective: Gombrich and his critics

David Topper

THIS chapter is confined to the specific issue of the interrelationship among linear perspective, perception and realism – avoiding, therefore, some of the more general matters of representation (such as metaphorical seeing). It is further restricted to the contemporary debate, approximately since the first edition (1960) of *Art and Illusion* (hereafter *A & I*), so that matters pertaining to the genesis and development of linear perspective will not be considered.[1] Finally, the term 'perspective' will be used for 'linear perspective,' unless the context dictates otherwise.

Rancour against Realism

> I have no doubt that [our] perception can be trained to see very different aspects of the world . . . But one should not carry this line of thought too far. I do not think that it is correct to say that people in the twelfth century saw the world differently. They did not . . . [Also] some people have been much too extreme in talking about the modification of perception through art. One of them . . . really did believe that the artist creates the world for us.[2]

A & I has been a mine of information and inspiration for readers from an extraordinarily wide range of disciplines. It is also a source of controversy regarding the issue of realism in art in general and the ontological status of perspective in particular. In a central section of the book Gombrich argues that the projective technique of perspective is a means for making realistic pictures; it is not, as some have proposed, a mere convention.

For some readers, this argument in *A & I* – coming after over two hundred pages of discussion on the roles of schemata, stereotypes, formulae, codes, projection,and so forth – appears to be an about-face, undermining what seems to be the book's thesis regarding a vocabulary or 'language' of art.

Indeed, the book was based upon Gombrich's Mellon Lectures of 1956, which were entitled 'The visible world and the language of art'. Also, in this book of almost four hundred pages, there are only about thirty pages devoted to perspective.[3] Is the perspective discussion in *A & I* therefore, out of joint with the rest of the book?

This problem was pointed out in an early review of the book by Nelson Goodman, who later became one of Gombrich's key protagonists. 'Though vision is relative to imposed schemata' according to Gombrich, Goodman wrote, 'Gombrich nevertheless holds that there are objective standards of representation.'[4] On the matter of perspective Goodman said that he found Gombrich's 'treatment of this subject . . . often puzzling'[5] and initiated his own critique, which was developed later in his 1968 book *Languages of Art*.[6]

More recently the same apparent disjunction was posited by Murray Krieger in his 1984 article 'The ambiguities of representation and illusion: an E. H. Gombrich retrospective',[7] which led to a subsequent exchange between Krieger and Gombrich. Krieger found inspiration in *A & I* for his own work in literary criticism: he interpreted Gombrich as undermining the traditional concept of 'imitation' and consequently showing 'how art represented "reality"'.[8] Thus the section in *A & I* on perspective, which posits 'the supremacy of the naturalistic tradition of perspective, with a consequent denial of conventionalism', Krieger saw as 'contradicting what most of us have taken as the main thrust of that book'.[9] According to Krieger, after writing *A & I* Gombrich distanced himself from those who found a conventionalist argument in the book. Krieger went so far as to accuse Gombrich of having 'retreated from the consequences of his own earlier claims . . .'.[10]

Gombrich, however, did not concede the apparent disjointedness in *A & I*. In his rejoinder to Krieger he spoke of 'the aesthetic misreading' of his book.[11] In the theory of schema-and-correction or making-and-matching, which represents probably the main thesis of *A & I*, it is implicit that there is a standard for depiction – for otherwise how would an artist know how to correct or match? Hence Gombrich wrote, 'I never felt compelled to abandon my central thesis.'[12] He went on to point out that his opposition to the theory that art creates reality is based upon his well-known critique of *Zeitgeist* historiography which posits that 'the history of styles' is a reflection of 'the history of the way in which the world was "seen"'.[13] Thus, to postulate 'two Gombrichs' – as Krieger did in his rebuttal of Gombrich's rejoinder – is really to misread the consistent viewpoint in *A & I* and later essays. In essence, Gombrich's position is this: the realisation of various conventions in depiction (because of different functions for images) does not subvert the possibility of realism (as may be conveyed by a perspective construction), for there *are* standards of depiction that overcome the conventions.

None the less Krieger may be right about his 'two Gombrichs' thesis; 'right' in the sense that subsequent readers have diverged in their interpretations of *A & I*. In his rebuttal Krieger distinguished between what he called Gombrich 'the sceptical humanist' and Gombrich 'the positive scientist'.[14] It seems obvious to me that the backdrop to this distinction is what may be called Krieger's anti-Western, neo-Romantic critique of science. He said that he prefers art 'to create the forms of its "reality" from within aesthetic norms, instead of to depend upon a reality imposed upon it by the authoritarian claims of a monolithic positivism masquerading as all the science there is'.[15] His animosity towards science was even more blatant when he said that 'the guiding science is *our* science, in tune with and growing out of *our* climate of pressures'; as a result, we are 'confusing nature with our institutional version of nature'.[16] This is surely a variation of the contemporary argument that all knowledge is relative to an individual's 'culture' – and this includes sciences as well as arts and customs.[17]

Similarly, W. J. T. Mitchell, in his 1986 book *Iconology*, reprimanded Gombrich for basing his ideas about art on the post-Newtonian scientific ideology with its underlying capitalistic, progressive and aggressive world-views.[18] As I stressed in my review of Mitchell's book, such arguments overlook the important issue of the truth or falsehood of Gombrich's thesis.[19] But, of course, within the framework of contemporary relativism there is no truthful standard outside of the individual or the collective viewpoints.

The most widely cited modern work propounding the conventionality hypothesis is Erwin Panofsky's now classic essay *Perspective as Symbolic Form*.[20] Put forward over seventy years ago, Panofsky's thesis was that ancient artists and theorists utilised a system of curvilinear perspective, where points are projected on to a curved surface rather than a flat plane (thus anticipating Leonardo's diagram of the Column Paradox, see Figure 4.3, discussed below). Panofsky pointed to Greek refinements (such as entasis) as embodying this principle. He did not go as far as asserting that curvilinear perspective is the way we really see the world, although he did speak of such curvature as 'the factual retinal image'; his approach was quasi-relativistic in positing that different 'artistic periods and regions' may adopt different systems of perspective, and in so doing reflect different 'symbolic forms'.[21]

More recent so-called 'post-modern' relativism is a continuation of an argument found, for example, in several essays written in the 1970s by Marx Wartofsky (who, I believe, was a student of Goodman). Wartofsky wrote of 'modes of perception' that change over time within and across cultures. He called this a theory of 'historical epistemology'[22] – the very sort of idea, with its *Zeitgeist* overtones, that Gombrich abhors. Our visual world, according to Wartofsky, 'is a cognitive construction, and is embodied in our represent-ations, as theories and models in science, and as pictures in art'.[23] I suspect Gombrich might see this as a *reductio ad absurdum* of his agreement with the dictum that there is 'no innocent eye', for Gombrich sees no contradiction in his beliefs in both an active theory of perception and standards of depiction. Features of the world – for example, that light travels in straight lines – provide boundary conditions, limitations, means of correcting or matching things in our perception of the world. But even this seemingly uncontroversial position would be attacked by Wartofsky, who, amazingly enough, does not believe in geometrical optics – one of the most solid subfields in all of science. Within the framework of 'historical epistemology' Wartofsky claimed that geometrical optics, which uses the rules of Euclidean geometry, is a convention of Western science, because of the relativity of Euclidean space. Furthermore, since the rules of perspective are based on Euclidean geometry, perspective too is a mere convention.[24]

In answer to Wartofsky – and, indeed, all cultural relativists – I can think of no better reply than the following quotation from Samuel Y. Edgerton jun.'s latest book. He argues that, despite the cultural context of the develop-ment of perspective, the fact remains that

> here was the first artistic method anywhere which had the capacity to map point by point and *to scale* the edges, surfaces, and relative distances apart of physical objects just as they are optically perceived from a fixed viewpoint . . . Indeed, any man or woman of any race or creed who wears spectacles must appreciate that the very laws of optometry that sharpen vision as one reads the newspaper are the same [laws of geometrical optics!] as those that were applied to perspective picture making in the Renaissance.[25]

Some day, I hope, the reasonableness (in both senses of this word) of Edgerton's position will drown out the screams of the cultural relativists, no matter how well-meaning they may be.[26] As with matters of human rights, for example, the issue here is not tolerance. It is truth.

Specifics on perspective

I sometimes think that there is no problem in the history of human thought in such a deep intellectual mess as the problem of perspective.[27]

On ambiguities, invariants and illusions

Perhaps another reason for the difficulty in grasping Gombrich's real view on perspective is that the first major discussion is found in Chapter 7 of *A & I*, entitled 'Ambiguities of the third dimension'. Here Gombrich stresses the 'inherent ambiguity of all images',[28] namely that the apparent visual size of a depicted object at which a picture could be produced, for example, by a larger object at a distance or a smaller one up-close, or a myriad of other possibilities. He points to the well-known Ames Room Illusion to confirm this fact of vision. Nevertheless, this ambiguity of images does not contradict the validity of perspective construction; in fact, the Ames Room Illusion confirms it − for one sees chairs and table in these 'rooms', not strangely skewed and disjointed objects. We do not see the ambiguity, Gombrich asserts; thus 'the theory of perspective is in fact perfectly valid, though the perspective image demands our collaboration' in recognising some things.[29] And this 'collaboration' does not controvert the objectivity of perspective.

In the preface to the second edition (1961) of *A & I* − in noting some misunderstandings among some readers − he stated unequivocally that 'the undeniable subjectivity of vision does not preclude objective standards of representational accuracy'.[30] Indeed, he has always acknowledged the ultimate subjectivity of 'how' we see the world based on memories, guesses, associations and so forth. 'To insist on the subjective element in our visual experience does not mean to deny its objective veridical component', he later wrote: 'It must be the aim of any improved theory to give subjectivism its due without making concessions to relativism.'[31]

The fact 'that we cannot look round a corner'[32] became one of the foundations of Gombrich's subsequent defence of perspective. He came to call this 'the eyewitness principle' − a negative rule, in that the artist must not include in a picture anything that could not be seen from a particular point at a particular time.[33] This principle is consistent with the laws of perspective, and makes irrelevant various apparent objections based upon the facts that we see with two eyes, that our eyes move in their sockets, that the retina is curved, that the retinal image is upside-down, that our eyes are continually moving in perception, that only the foveal area of perception is clear and so forth. In giving 'subjectivism its due' while holding to the eyewitness principle, Gombrich attempted to meet the major objections challenging the validity of perspective.

To begin to meet some of the objections concerning the realism of pictures that employ the rules of perspective, we need first to grasp the concept of an 'invariant'. This term was introduced by the psychologist James J. Gibson, who Gombrich increasingly drew upon for ideas about perception. Gibson used the term for the perception of constancies in the world, such as seeing a table-top as a rectangular form, or a plate as a circle *from any angle*. An alternative way of seeing such objects is to attend to their aspects, appearances or projections – that is, seeing the table-top as a trapezoid or the plate as an ellipse.[34]

Needless to say, such a 'projection' is related to the projective technique of perspective. Put simply, a picture in linear perspective is a depiction of an object in the world, as if the surface of the picture were a window upon which projections of the object to the eye are traced; the surface or picture plane is the intersection of the cone of vision. Using this technique results in a one-to-one correspondence (an isomorphism) between the object in the world and that in the picture – of course, only from this *geometrical* point of view.[35]

By the rule of geometry, therefore, pictures employing perspective (like most photographs) delineate the projection of the objects depicted. But – and this is crucial to the entire argument of this chapter – invariants are perceived in the *virtual* space of such pictures. It is true that a depicted table appears as a trapezoid and a plate as an ellipse on the surface of the picture; analogously their projections would be the same two-dimensional forms if we looked at the same objects through a window. But just as we seldom attend to the surface of a window that we peer through, so we seldom attend to the surface of a picture. Instead, we look *into* the virtual space of a picture. And, in so doing, we see the invariants in that virtual space.

This may be verified in a number of ways. A simple method is to move an object in a picture from the background to the foreground. *A & I* contains such a montage photograph of Constable's *Wivenhoe Park* (1816), a painting Gombrich introduces at the start of the book and uses as a kind of leitmotif throughout. The montage consists of 'moving' a distant house and a distant section of a fence to the foreground of the picture, with the result that the house and fence section look extremely small.[36] Such constructions reveal that we perceive constancies (or invariants) in the space of the picture; that is, we see the 'distant' house or fence as larger than their projection (or phenomenal size), just as we do with objects in a real space.

I believe this montage technique was extraordinarily important in the development of Gombrich's belief in the realism of perspective.[37] The one time I personally met him, and we were chatting outside a lecture-hall on these very problems, I well remember his directing me to a poster on a wall containing a landscape scene; he measured a 'distant' object with his fingers and then 'moved' this measurement to the foreground, saying something like, 'Look, see how much smaller it really is!' Of course he was right; there is a visual jolt, because we *are* seeing the 'distant' object larger than its phenomenal size – thus proving that we *do* see constancies or invariants in pictures.

For a more systematic test of this, William Simpson and I ran a series of experiments using a device invented by Richard Gregory, called a 'Pandora's Box', which permits the measurement of depth perception in images.[38] Gregory and others made use of the box to measure depth in contrived line drawings and some visual illusions, but we used images from the history of art, specifically pictures (mosaics and oil paintings) with varying degrees of depth in their virtual space. We found a progression of depth perception from a flat bulletin-board-type picture through a shallow medieval picture employing inverse perspective to a deep post-Renaissance painting in linear perspective. The experiments revealed two things: that depth (and hence invariants) are perceived in pictures, and that this depth perception is not confined only to pictures employing linear perspective (although it does render the deepest space).

The binary nature of pictures

The conclusion thus reached is that invariant perception in the virtual space of a picture is consonant with the isomorphism of the projective technique of perspective. But realising this does not mean that no disjunctions arise between the picture and the world. They do; indeed, these disjunctions are a major source of the apparent conventionality of perspective. One important disjunction is the ontological distinction between the spaces and projections: that is, on the one hand, the space in the world is real with the projection being a (geometrical) construction; in a picture, on the other hand, the (projected) surface is real (it is, in fact, a framed or bounded object in the world) with the space being, as noted, virtual. The fact that a picture therefore entails both a (real) surface and a (virtual) space constitutes its binary nature.[39]

Now, this does not a priori negate the isomorphism regarding perspective; it does, however, complicate the matter. For example, because of this binary factor, the rules of constancy apply to two-dimensional objects depicted in a picture that are parallel to the picture plane. A specific case should clarify this; consider the depiction of telegraph poles. An argument often used to support the apparent conventionality of perspective is that artists depict poles which are parallel to the picture plane as parallel to the surface, whereas they should be depicted converging (say to a vertical point overhead, like railroad tracks towards the horizon) – as poles (granted, very large poles!) would do in the real world. That artists usually do not depict telegraph poles converging shows that the rules of perspective are broken so that a picture looks correct. Hence perspective construction is a mere convention – or so the argument goes.[40]

But the argument is specious. Railroad tracks are drawn converging because they are orthogonal to the picture plane and by the rules of projection do so converge. Telegraph poles, however, are parallel to the picture plane. And a very important fact of geometry is that parallel lines project on to the intersection as parallel lines. Thus telegraph poles, being parallel to the surface, project as parallels. In fact, all two-dimensional forms parallel to the picture plane preserve their invariant shape; circles project as circles (not as ovals, as is sometimes erroneously assumed), squares as squares (not trapezoids), and so forth. (Only their size changes; the reduction being a function of the relative distances among the object, intersection or picture plane, and eye of the viewer.) But once the forms (lines, circles or squares) are *on* the surface of the picture, they then are forms in the world, and hence may be seen as converging lines, ellipses or trapezoids if viewed at various angles. (I have carefully used the phrase 'may be seen' because of the well-known and important phenomenon of visual compensation;[41] that is, since the picture is a surface in the world, then its form will also usually be seen as an invariant – thus viewers in movie theatres, for example, see the screen as a rectangle, even when viewing it from an angle.) So the artist is correct in drawing railroad tracks *converging* to the horizon and telegraph poles *parallel* on the surface. In fact, it would be doubly wrong to draw poles converging, for it would compound the convergence; the visual convergence would be 'added' to the depicted convergence. This highlights what is often called the 'El Greco Fallacy', derived from the erroneous assumption that El Greco drew elongated figures because he saw them that way (because of some peculiar perceptual pathology). But further reflection makes clear that even if he saw circles as ovals, he would still have drawn them as what we would see as circles, because drawing ovals would further exaggerate the distortion.

Other disjunctions between the picture and the world are sometimes manifested in three 'places' of a picture: in the extreme foreground, in the far background, and on the margins.

On some proximate and distant objects

In his widely read *Languages of Art*, Goodman emphasised two ways in which perspective pictures do not render a 'faithful representation'[42] of the world: there are distortions that arise with the enlargement of proximate objects and the diminutions of some objects in the far distance. As Goodman concretely put it, 'the photograph of a man with his feet thrust forward looks distorted, and Pike's Peak dwindles dismally in a snapshot'. Examples of this sort show why 'perspective provides no absolute or independent standard of fidelity'.[43]

In his 1972 article, 'The "What" and the "How"', Gombrich answered Goodman. He began with the reminder that our usual perception of the world in terms of invariants means that we rarely notice the appearances of things (that is, their projections), although we can attend to them — by say closing one eye and holding a pencil to measure the phenomenal size of things. In a sense, this is what the camera or picture does for us; it presents us with appearances that are accessible (but not usually attended to) in our perception of the world. But does this not contradict the argument presented here for the perception of invariants in pictures? For if invariants are seen, then why do the thrusting feet look too large and Pike's Peak too small?

The answer requires an appeal to the binary nature of pictures; that a picture both entails a depicted space and is a real surface. Recall that a depicted elliptical plate is generally seen as a round plate in the virtual space of the picture; but the viewer may also attend to its (flat) elliptical form. Of course, these are not mutually exclusive, as may be verified by the simple introspective act of peering at a depicted plate, or even a real one. I think Thouless's famous experiment supports this assertion.[44] In this experiment (published in 1931) viewers compared various angular views of round objects with a range of oval shapes. Thouless found that although the viewers could (qualitatively) see the objects as ovals, they (quantitatively) saw them as rounder than their actual projection; he called this a 'phenomenal re-gression to the real object', although we may wish to speak of it as a

'propensity towards the invariant'. This combination of invariant and projective perception Gibson once called (in a letter to me) a 'sort of in-between
perceiving'.[45] In his book he spoke of it as a 'concurrent specification of
two reciprocal things'.[46]

All of this is true – and important. Yet, in fact, certain features of a picture
are more amenable to the delineation of the projections (rather than the
invariants) than others – such as proximate objects. They appear rather large
in pictures, partially because they occlude a significant area relative to the
picture's surface. Recall the important fact that in the real world there usually
are no frames or bounds, so the phenomenal size of proximate objects is not
always realised. Thus Gombrich writes:

> in real-life situations we rarely have occasion to attend to such occlusions.
> If a small object cuts out a large part of our field of vision, we simply
> shift our head and are rid of the obstruction. It is only where our movement
> is impeded, as when we sit in a theatre and are bothered by the size of
> the hat of the lady in front that we notice the laws of perspective that
> make it obscure half the stage.[47]

I believe this argument meets Goodman's objection regarding the possible
looming of proximate objects.[48]

On the diminution of Pike's Peak, the problem is a bit more complex.
Since we know that distant mountains appear in pictures larger than their
phenomenal size (recall the montage), why then do some mountains in
pictures seem to diminish in size compared to their majestic on-site immens-
ity? Or put another way, why doesn't the invariant perception 'work' for a
picture of Pike's Peak? An answer is this: the diminution of Pike's Peak is
a subset of the more general phenomenon that most (non-proximate) objects
in a picture appear smaller than they would in the world. This is a fact; for
example, it is a common error among amateur photographers that they do
not get close enough to their subjects when taking pictures, so that they
often find that the subjects appear too small in the resulting photograph. To
repeat; with its frame and surface, a picture delineates the projection of things
(more so than the real world) – despite the concurrent perception of invariants
in the virtual space of the picture. The dwindling of Pike's Peak is, therefore,
an extension *into the background* of this diminution factor in picture perception
– which, in this case, overrides the otherwise invariant perception of the
distant objects.

Since all of this is compatible with the eyewitness principle, Gombrich

need concede nothing regarding the objectivity of perspective – at least
nothing yet.

On marginal distortions and curvilinear perspective

Marginal distortions appear in photographs of objects that are relatively close
to the picture plane, and they become increasingly distorted (elongated, in
fact) as they further approach the edges of the picture. Since such a photograph
entails perspective projection, then apparently this exposes an instance where
perspective is conventional, for artists seldom draw marginal distortions. Can
the isomorphism argument meet this challenge?

A marginal distortion is an example of the phenomenon of anamorphism,
where an object is elongated by the rules of perspective; for example, a
circle *expands* into an ellipse, in contrast to perspective foreshortening (see
Figure 4.1). Such forms, called anamorphs, may appear as distorted blurs
across the surface of pictures, like the famous one at the bottom of Holbein's
The Ambassadors (1533). Shadows, for example, can be natural anamorphs.
The viewer can see the original (non-distorted) form by viewing the
anamorph near its projection point, closing one eye, suppressing the surface
and so forth. This is not always easy: some viewers never see it, probably
because the compensation factor is so well-entrenched in our perceptual
experience. With diligence, however, the 're-formed' form usually pops into

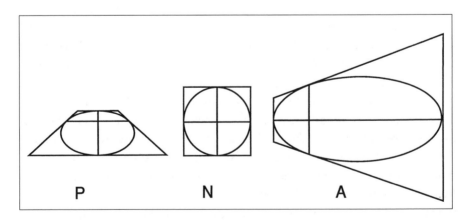

Figure 4.1 Comparison of perspective foreshortening (P) and anamorphic
elongation (A) of a circle (N) normal (orthogonal) to the line of sight. (Note
that this is only a schematic diagram; the ovals are not true ellipses.) In both
perspective foreshortening and anamorphic elongation the same geometrical rules
of projection apply (see note 49).

Figure 4.2 Anamorphic bicycle on a street. Bottom: the anamorph as seen orthogonal to the street. Top: the 'reformed' anamorph is best captured by a camera (since it 'obeys' the projective rules) – although, of course, viewers may do so on the spot, as by viewing the bottom photograph from an extreme angle.

view – hence the term 'anamorphism', from the Greek for 'form again'. We may think of anamorphs as two-dimensional Ames Rooms; and, like Ames Rooms, they obey the rules of perspective and require our collaboration. A straightforward example appears in Figure 4.2 of an anamorphic bicycle painted on a street.[49]

The most recent argument for the conventionality of perspective based upon marginal distortions is put forward by Norman Turner, who correctly points out that the famous Column Paradox (Figure 4.3) is really a subset of the marginal distortion dilemma for artists:[50] if a row of columns that are parallel to the picture plane is projected on to the flat intersection L, the columns will appear increasingly elongated as they 'recede' from the centre; that is, they become anamorphs. On the other hand, columns projected on to the curved surface C, decrease in width as they 'recede'. Hence, since the widths of a row of real receding columns do not appear to elongate,

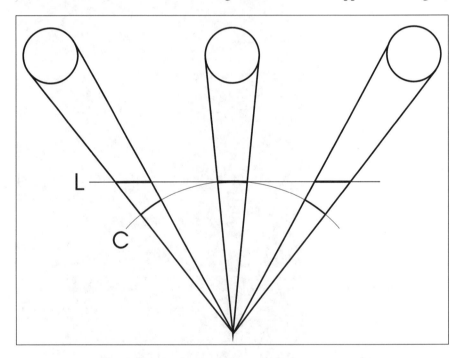

Figure 4.3 The column paradox. By rules of linear perspective a row of columns projects on to the intersection L. This results in marginal distortions, since the projected widths increase as the columns 'recede' from the centre. There are no marginal distortions, however, when the columns are projected on to the curved intersection C, for the projected widths decrease as the columns 'recede'. This projection results in curvilinear perspective. This paradox was probably first put forward by Leonardo.

some theorists have argued that so-called curvilinear perspective (rather than linear perspective) should be the correct technique used by artists wishing to attain realism; in this system all lines parallel to the pictorial surface are projected on to a spherical intersection.

In addition, the case for curvilinear perspective is sometimes coupled with the tenet that this is how we really see the world. Probably the strongest proponent of this is Robert Hansen.[51] Hansen asserted that straight lines in our *total* panoramic field of vision must curve. Consider, for example, railroad tracks seen from an aerial view; they surely would converge to two opposite points on the horizon and therefore must curve across our field of vision (a fish-eye camera can capture such a panoramic view). In his critique of curvilinear perspective, Gombrich – who called himself 'an unrepentant straightliner'[52] – proposed that a panorama is really a composite of a finite number of individual views across the field of vision, each of which obeys the rules of linear perspective.[53] So when the viewer spans across these views and they merge together, straight lines may 'really' be curved, but this is not obvious in normal perception. Indeed, Hansen admitted: 'I must say that straight lines appeared manifestly straight to me until I examined my vision closely'.[54] I believe Hansen is guilty of the El Greco Fallacy; if straight lines are really perceived as curved, should not the artist still draw them straight, since the act of perception will curve them?[55]

If curvilinear perspective therefore is rejected as a valid means of realistic depiction, we are back to the projection on to plane L in Figure 4.3 and the Column Paradox. Gombrich tried to resolve this paradox by arguing that, as circular objects, columns are a 'special case of ambiguity'[56] because they present both their 'fronts' and 'sides' at the same time. Replacing them by square columns should resolve the paradox.[57] Turner actually takes up Gombrich's ploy (see Figure 4.4) and shows that none the less the elongation remains for the projection on to the plane, since the diagonals of such squares increase as they recede from the centre. Turner is indeed correct.[58]

One way out of this, Turner notes, is for the viewer to learn how to re-form marginal anamorphs (what he calls 'anamorphic looking',[59] namely, seeing projections). But he goes on assert that this really will not do, since it requires an extraordinary way of viewing pictures (as compared to how we ordinarily see the world). Again, I agree with him – so far. To reinforce his case, he uses the example of Raphael's painting *The School of Athens* (1510–11). Here Raphael used linear perspective for the architectural space of this wide mural, but the spheres held by figures in the far right of the picture (which

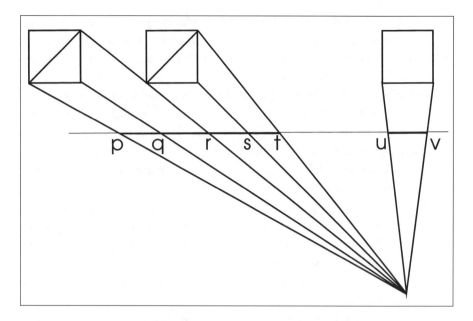

Figure 4.4 Marginal distortions. Although, by the laws of projections, pq equals rs equals uv, by the same laws, qr is greater than st. Hence the diagonals of the columns (square or circular ones) increase as they 'recede' from the centre.

should manifest marginal distortion) he depicted as round spheres (not as elongated anamorphs). By depicting the spheres as if seen from the front (indeed, the same may be said for all the human figures in the picture!), Raphael created a realistic picture by 'disregarding the laws of perspective'.[60]

Turner's facts are surely correct. But are we thus forced to accept his conclusion, that these facts are lethal to Gombrich's position, and that Gombrich's 'literalist idea of perspective is imperiled'?[61] I think not. First, Turner has failed to realise two important aspects of picture perception which I have stressed throughout this chapter: invariant perception in pictures and their binary nature. Second, and of utmost importance, is the following fact: marginal distortions are extremely difficult (I think impossible, see below) to see in the world. It is true that when depicted as anamorphs on surfaces, we obviously see the distortions. But in real space, even with the intervention of a projective plane (such as a window), marginal distortions are impervious to our perception.

I highly recommend that the reader verify this surprising observation by (say) drawing a marginal object on a window with a felt pen; the realisation of the extreme distortion is quite astonishing. Unlike foreshortened objects in the main field of vision – which, as we know, are relatively easy to attend to – the elongation of marginal objects, so to speak, *resists perception*. (I can think of no better way of saying this.) In other words, the invariants cannot be suppressed. I do not know why this is so; perhaps because in most of our everyday experience we do not attend to the margins of our visual world but simply turn our heads to see such objects.[62]

Since marginal distortions are almost impossible to see in the world, it is not surprising that Raphael did not depict them. In spanning a real space similar to that depicted in Raphael's large fresco, marginal distortions would resist perception. Since a picture is a frozen instance of this world on a surface, and we can and do scan this surface (with eye and head movement), then we expect to see objects in a picture keep their invariant shape across this surface – as objects do in the real world. So why should Raphael depict something that is almost impossible to see out of the corners of our eyes? He has merely accepted our invariant perception of marginal objects.

The conclusion thus reached is that an artist should not draw marginal distortions, since they are not a part of our experience of the visual world. A picture, accordingly, is realistic – but at a price; it does violate the rules of perspective at the margins. And here the word 'margins' may be taken both literally and figuratively.[63]

Ultimately, moreover, we must concede that a one-to-one isomorphism between the world and a perspective picture of it no longer holds. Hence Gombrich, in his reply to Turner, speaks of some 'flaws' arising when the three-dimensional world is projected on a flat surface. He also notes, as I have, that Turner 'ignored' an important experiential fact of picture perception: that distant objects in a picture look to be at a distance.[64]

In the end, Gombrich reverts to an analogy with music, specifically the adjustments that are made to a true system of tuning so that instruments may be played in different keys. Harmony is not sacrificed in spite of the departures from mathematical exactness entailed in the 'well-tempered' method. 'I believe', Gombrich concludes, 'the same to be true of the slight fudges sometimes demanded of the painter in eliminating lateral [or marginal] distortions. We can all thrill to Raphael's *School of Athens* without regretting that he painted the globe as a sphere and not like an egg.'[65]

Summary

A notable case for equating realism and linear perspective – a view consistently found in Gombrich's writings – may be made by the following eighteenth-century account by a Chinese painter and writer on the impact of Western art in China: 'The Westerners are skilled in geometry . . . When they paint houses on a wall people are tempted to walk into them . . . .But these painters have no brush-manner whatsoever; although they possess skill, they are simply artisans.'[66] Note that according to this narrative the Chinese saw little aesthetic value in the art of the West, and yet they were awed by the illusionist skills – even though they saw them more as tricks than as 'art'. But the tricks apparently amazed many of them. Another report of the initial viewing of a European picture states: 'The mandarins were amazed. They could not imagine how one could, on a single sheet, represent the halls, galleries, gateways, roads and alleyways so convincingly that at first glance the eye was deceived.'[67] Of course, we must always be cautious using such anecdotes. Nevertheless, the ubiquitous nature of the Western system of perspective – now adopted world-wide in computer graphics, for example – cannot seriously be accounted for by merely appealing to Western inculcation any more than the fact that all children learn Euclidean geometry is explained by Western imperialism.[68]

This is not to say, however, that there are no difficulties in equating perspective with a realistic depiction of the world. In particular, three features of pictures have been singled out as problematic: the looming of proximate objects, the dwindling of some distant objects, and the extreme distortions of marginal objects (the last, as manifested, for example, in the Column Paradox).

These problems may be met through a realisation of the special nature of pictures – as objects both *of* and *in* the world. We may see invariants in pictures as we see them in the world. And as with world perception, so with pictorial perception – often invariant and perspective perception are concurrent. Yet pictures themselves are objects in the world; they are surfaces within bounds and this makes the projections of depicted objects more amenable, more so than real objects – primarily in the main field of vision (especially some proximate and distant objects), although not at the margins. It is this interplay between the space and the surface of a picture that provides a basis for the resolution of problems raised by those theorists challenging the equation of linear perspective and realism – an equation that Gombrich has affirmed, with and since the publication of *A & I*.

Notes

1. For a masterly account of linear perspective, see M. Kemp, *The Science of Art: Optical Themes in Western Art from Brunelleschi to Seurat*, New Haven 1990. I have used the second edition of *Art and Illusion* (*A & I*).

2. *Eribon*, pp. 110–11.

3. For the discussion on perspective see *A & I*, especially pp. 242–62, 299–307, 329 and 393. Since writing *A & I*, Gombrich's major articles on linear perspective are: 'The evidence of images', 'Mirror and map', and 'Standards of truth', reprinted in *Image and Eye*, and 'The "What" and the "How": perspective representation and the phenomenal world' in *Logic and Art: Essays in Honor of Nelson Goodman*, Richard Rudner and Israel Scheffler (eds), Indianapolis and New York 1972, pp. 129–49.

4. N. Goodman, Review of *Art and Illusion*, *Journal of Philosophy*, 57 (1960), p. 597.

5. *Ibid.*, p. 598.

6. N. Goodman, *Languages of Art: An Approach to a Theory of Symbols*, Indianapolis and New York 1968.

7. 'The ambiguities of representation and illusion: an E. H. Gombrich retrospective', *Critical Inquiry*, 11 (1984), pp. 181–94.

8. *Ibid.*, p. 181.

9. *Ibid.*, p. 188.

10. *Ibid.*, p. 192; see also p. 182.

11. E. H. Gombrich, 'Representation and misrepresentation', *Critical Inquiry*, 11 (1984), p. 197.

12. *Ibid.*

13. *Ibid.*, p. 199.

14. M. Krieger, 'Optics and aesthetic perception: a rebuttal', *Critical Inquiry*, 11 (1985), p. 502.

15. *Ibid.*, p. 507.

16. *Ibid.*

17. In a particularly virulent footnote in the original essay Krieger said that Gombrich's position on realism is a 'reflection of Gombrich's development from an *émigré* savant into the privileged knight of English art historians' ('The Ambiguities', p. 194, n. 18). Such personal attacks are not uncommon among so-called post-modern deconstructionist writers, who strive to uncover the 'hidden agendas' of authors. But perhaps they would do well to review the *ad hominem* fallacy.

18. W. J. T. Mitchell, *Iconology: Images, Text, Ideology*, Chicago 1986.

19. D. Topper, Review of W. J. T. Mitchell's *Iconology*, *Leonardo*, 22 (1989), pp. 449–50.

20. E. Panofsky, *Perspective as Symbolic Form*, trans. C. S. Wood, New York 1991.

21. Panofsky, *Perspective*, pp. 33 & 41. Panofsky borrowed the term 'symbolic form' from Ernst Cassirer. The term carried with it an allusion to *Zeitgeist* historiography; Panofsky did not hold this viewpoint to be anathema, as Gombrich

has often noted (see, for example, *The Sense of Order*, p. 199 and my short essay on this, 'On a ghost of historiography past', *Leonardo*, 21 (1988), pp. 76–8). Panofsky's essay has frequently been used by those adopting some variation of the relativist position; for example, J. White, *The Birth and Rebirth of Pictorial Space*, New York 1967.

22. M. Wartofsky, *Models: Representation and the Scientific Understanding*, Dordrecht 1979, p. 189.

23. *Ibid.*, p. 195.

24. *Ibid.*, pp. 211–27; see my review in *Leonardo*, 14 (1981), p. 335.

It should not be necessary to mention – but I suspect, in this case, it is – that the curved space and bending of light entailed in Einstein's General Theory of Relativity is entirely irrelevant to all of this. Also, on the 'modes of perception' theory, the following story by Gombrich reveals the aberrant end to which Wartofsky was willing to carry his apparent logic:

> In a symposium I attended at Swarthmore College, Professor Marx W. Wartofsky made a drawing of a dog on the blackboard and wrote underneath the word 'dog'. He might also have written 'chien' or 'Hund'. He did it to assert that the words were neither more or less like the real animal than the drawing (*Image and Eye*, p. 284).

25. S. Y. Edgerton jun., *The Heritage of Giotto's Geometry: Art and Science on the Eve of the Scientific Revolution*, Ithaca 1991, p. 5.

26. It is also worth quoting the following statement by Edgerton, which succinctly summarises the relativist's position:

> In the current debate about critical theory and methodology there is increasing insistence that linear perspective and chiaroscuro be understood only as artificial symbols within a linguistic-like sign system expressing the peculiar values of Western civilization. Radical supporters of this latest relativism . . . argue that during the Renaissance, upper-class patrons championed linear perspective because it affirmed their exclusive political power. Single-viewpoint perspective, after all, encourages the 'male gaze', thus [giving rise to] voyeurism and the denigration of women, police-state surveillance, and imperialist 'marginalizing of the other' (*Ibid.*, p. 4).

27. J. J. Gibson, letter published in *Leonardo*, 6 (1973), p. 284.

28. *Ibid.*, p. 249.

29. *Ibid.*, p. 248.

30. *A & I*, p. xi.

31. *Image and Eye*, pp. 179 and 183.

32. *A & I*, p. 250.

33. *Image and Eye*, p. 253.

34. Gibson is most certainly correct in asserting that in everyday perception we see constancies or invariants in the world. But how or why we see them remains a matter of controversy. Gibson took the radical view, which many psychologists challenge, that invariants are directly perceived, contrary to the more widely-held position that invariants are built up from various aspects of the world by

mental and/or visual processing. This dispute, fortunately, is not of concern here; for it is a fact that our common perception of everyday things involves seeing invariants, and that to see projections usually requires an attentive act – except for some special situations, for example, when standing on railroad tracks and noticing their convergence at the horizon. I should also point out that some followers of Gibson would dispute my conflation of 'constancies' and 'invariants'; they have a more specific meaning of an invariant, one involving the so-called cross-ratio – a topic that would take us too far adrift. See, for example, the exchanges between K. Niall and J. E. Cutting in the *Journal of Mathematical Psychology*, 31 (1987), pp. 429–40. Gibson's ideas may be found in their most developed form in his latest book (*The Ecological Approach to Visual Perception*, Hillsdale 1979). See also my article on Gibson's changing ideas about picture perception, 'Art in the realist ontology of J. J. Gibson', *Synthèse*, 54 (1983), pp. 71–83. It is worth mentioning that Gibson and Gombrich were involved in a debate over the prehistoric origins of art and perspective perception. I avoid this debate here, for it is peripheral to the main topic; also I have discussed it in some detail in the same article (*Ibid.*, pp. 75–8). Recently Gombrich recalled this debate in the interview with Didier Eribon (*Eribon*, pp. 111–12).

35. See B. A. R. Carter, 'Perspective' in *The Oxford Companion to Art*, edited by Harold Osborne, Oxford 1970, pp. 840–61, and M. Kemp, *The Science of Art*, *passim*.

36. *A & I*, p. 304.

37. In at least two other places Gombrich also reproduced a similar photomontage from Ralph M. Evans's book, *An Introduction to Color* (1948) in which a distant lamp-post and fence-post are 'moved' to the front with the same resulting illusion that they look smaller in the foreground (Gombrich, 'The evidence of images' in *Interpretation: Theory and Practice*, edited by Charles Singleton, Baltimore 1969, p. 64, and *Image and Eye*, p. 19). Of course, the same experiment may be performed by looking through a window at the real world; it is always surprising how small the projections of distant objects 'really' are. Gombrich also created an 'opposite' montage for a seat number plate in a lecture-hall, in this case 'moving' the plate from the front row to the back wall so that the plate appears large in the back of the hall (*Image and Eye*, p. 199.)

38. See R. L. Gregory, *Concepts and Mechanisms of Perception*, New York 1974, pp. 482–91, and D. Topper and W. Simpson, 'Depth perception in linear and inverse perspective Pictures', *Perception*, 10 (1981), pp. 305–12.

39. See Gibson, *The Ecological Approach*, pp. 280–3; also Carol D. Brownson's (unfortunately) unpublished manuscript, 'Some failures of arguments for the conventionality of linear perspective rules'.

40. See Alan Tormey, 'Seeing things: pictures, paradox, and perspective' in John Fisher (ed.), *Perceiving Artworks*, Philadelphia 1980, pp. 59–75, esp. pp 67–9; David Carrier, 'Perspective as convention: on the views of Nelson Goodman and Ernst Gombrich', *Leonardo*, 13 (1980), pp. 283–7, esp. p. 284; and Topper,

'On the fidelity of pictures: a critique of Goodman's disjunction of perspective and realism', *Philosophia*, 14 (1984), pp. 187–97, esp. pp. 188–90.

41. See M. Kubovy, *The Psychology of Perspective and Renaissance Art*, Cambridge 1986, pp. 57–62.

42. Goodman, *Languages*, p. 15.

43. *Ibid.*, pp. 15 and 19.

44. Robert H. Thouless, 'Phenomenal regression to the real object', *Journal of Psychology*, 21 (1931), pp. 339–59, & 22 (1931), pp. 1–30. In a footnote (p. 340, n.1) Thouless makes a common error regarding perspective foreshortening. Since a rectangle projects as a trapezoid (a figure with only one axis of symmetry), it is sometimes erroneously inferred that a circle also projects as an oval with only one axis of symmetry. As he writes: 'The perspective shape is not, of course, exactly an ellipse, but a figure resembling an ellipse with one of the short semi-axes larger than the other.' But this is false, for a circle does project as a perfect ellipse (with two axes of symmetry) – however illogical this may seem (see Figure 4.1).

45. Letter of 6 March 1978; also quoted in D. Topper, 'Art in the realist ontology of J. J. Gibson', p. 79.

46. Gibson, *The Ecological Approach*, p.76.

47. Gombrich, 'The "What" and the "How"', p. 139; cf. *Image and Eye*, pp. 200–1.

48. Nevertheless, an important point made by John Ward in a letter to me (23 February 1986) should be added. Photographs with looming close objects usually have very close projections points. For example, the illustration of the man holding the ball close to the camera in *A & I* (p. 300) is a photograph with a projection point of only about two inches (for the small reproduction in the book). A normal viewing distance is therefore beyond the range of any compensation, and hence the picture looks distorted because it really is! See also Ward, 'The perception of pictorial space in perspective pictures', *Leonardo*, 9 (1976), pp. 279–88. Furthermore this reveals a connection between close-up objects and marginal distortions (discussed below). Thus the 'looming feet' may be less a puzzle of perspective and more an accident of photography.

49. Let me clarify the relationship between the foreshortening of objects in a picture and anamorphic elongation, since both obey the rules of perspective (such that circles become ellipses). Consider a circle which is parallel to the picture plane and in the centre of vision. This, as we know, projects as a circle on to the plane, its projected diameter (call it D) being a function of the relative distances among the circle, the plane and the eye. Now rotate the circle around a vertical axis; its projection will then be an ellipse, such that its major (vertical) axis is D and its minor (horizontal) axis, less than D, is a function of the angle of rotation. Keep rotating the circle until it is orthogonal to the plane; the projection will approach a very narrow ellipse (indeed, a straight line). Next, move the circle laterally towards the margin of the frame of the plane (keeping it the same distance from the plane, keeping the eye fixed, etc.). The foreshortened ellipse will then change such that its minor axis increases while preserving the major axis (D). As it moves, therefore, a point will be reached where the minor

and major axes are equal, and hence the projected shape will be a circle. After that, by continuing to move the circle towards the margin, the shape will become an anamorph, an ellipse where now the minor (vertical) axis is D and the major (horizontal) axis, greater than D, continues to increase. Thus there is a geometrical continuum between (foreshortened) perspective forms and (elongated) anamorphic forms. I have perhaps laboured all of this, but have done so because I have never seen these important relationships clarified this way – anywhere. Yet note that I am concerned here only with projections on to two-dimensional surfaces; there are other systems of anamorphism. See J. Baltrušaitis, *Anamorphic Art*, New York 1977, and F. Leeman, M. Schuyt and J. Elffers, *Anamorphoses: Games of Perception and Illusion in Art*, New York 1976. An expanded version of the latter was also published in 1976 as *Hidden Images: Games of Perception, Anamorphic Art, and Illusion*.

50. N. Turner, 'Some questions about E. H. Gombrich on perspective', *Journal of Aesthetics and Art Criticism*, 50 (1992), pp. 139–50.

51. R. Hansen, 'This curving world: hyperbolic linear perspective', *Journal of Aesthetics and Art Criticism*, 32 (1973), pp. 147–61.

52. 'The "What" and the "How"', p. 135.

53. *A & I*, p. 256; 'The "What" and the "How"', p. 138; *Image and Eye*, pp. 211–12. I believe Gombrich's argument is supported by the panoramic pictures produced by a camera with a swivelling lens. For an example see *The Camera* (a Time-Life series book), New York 1970, pp. 150–1.

54. Hansen, 'This curving world', p. 150.

55. See R. Klein, 'Studies on perspective in the Renaissance', in R. Klein, *Form and Meaning: Essays on the Renaissance and Modern Art*, New York 1979, pp. 129–40, esp. pp. 136–40.

56. *A & I*, p. 256.

57. *A & I*, p. 255; see also *Image and Eye*, p. 210.

58. Turner ('Some questions') is correct, but he could be more precise. For recall that two-dimensional forms that are parallel to the picture plane project as invariants; therefore, the fronts of the square columns do not elongate. But the sides, being orthogonal to the picture plane, become anamorphs (as explained in note 49 above), and thus they are the source of the marginal distortion of the diagonals of the columns (see Figure 4.4).

59. Turner, 'Some questions', p. 141.

60. *Ibid*, p. 142. See also G. ten Doesschate, *Perspective: Fundamentals, Controversials, History*, Nieuwkoop 1964, pp. 42–3; M. H. Pirenne, *Optics, Painting and Photography*, Cambridge 1970, pp. 120–23; and Kubovy, *The Psychology of Perspective*, pp. 112–16.

61. Turner, 'Some questions', p. 141.

62. That the camera, however, picks up marginal distortions further reinforces the argument put forward by theoreticians of perception, such as Gibson, that the human perceptual system does not operate like a camera (despite the fruitful analogue between the eye and a camera from a physiological viewpoint).

63. See M. Kemp, 'Seeing and signs: E. H. Gombrich in retrospect. An essay review of *The Image and the Eye*', *Art History*, 7 (1984), pp. 228–43, esp. pp. 230–33.

64. 'Additional thoughts on perspective', *Journal of Aesthetics and Art Criticism*, 51 (1993), p. 69.

65. *Ibid.*

66. Quoted in M. Sullivan, 'The Chinese response to Western art', *Art International*, 24 (1980), pp. 28–9.

67. *Ibid.*, p.12.

68. Cf. Tormey, 'Seeing Things', pp. 70–1 on an eighteenth-century Japanese encounter with Western perspective.

5

Art and Illusion:
A philosophical defence

Edmond Wright

ONE of Gombrich's own diagrams, a development of the Rubin's Vase Illusion, can be taken as an emblem of the argument to be presented here. The argument is a defence of the claim in *Art and Illusion* that perception in the everyday situation bears a close parallel to the specialised use of it in the observation of pictures, to the degree that the very term 'illusion' is applicable to both.

The word 'illusion' fluttered many a philosophical dovecote in the sixties and seventies; even some current writers are still performing anxious convolutions. This is not surprising, since in both the philosophy and the psychology of perception there was in those decades a marked distaste for any theory that saw percepts as basically ambiguous, especially if, in addition, the theory gave more than a secondary place to the sensory. Even Gombrich, who stood out against James J. Gibson's dismissing of the visual field, was nevertheless sufficiently impressed by the mounting objections to the old empiricist Sense-Datum Theory to agree that the notion of 'raw sense data' was utterly discredited.[1] He was strongly motivated by a desire to acknowledge what he calls 'the Beholder's Share' in perception, the searching activity of the brain in its normal perceptual commerce with the world. Indeed he calls his view a 'Searchlight Theory', seeing perception as a dynamic process involving the organism's 'probing and testing' of its experience.

But to probe and test implies handling tentative hypotheses. Such a theory, therefore, eschews certainty in perception, a feature that did not find favour with Wittgensteinians and Ordinary Language philosophers of the time, and there are others more recently who have endeavoured to cast a sceptical cloud over his achievement. These philosophers would undercut their praise for the scholarly breadth and abundant originality of the work by attributing to it a misconception of actual everyday seeing. In their view anyone whose theory mixes up seeing with seeing-as is left without any firm premises for his or her overall argument. Yet there is now a new theory of perception, which regards these old objections as begging serious questions. In particular, they neglect what is implied by such probing and testing if it is done by human beings who can communicate with each other about their hypotheses. This new theory also addresses the question of sensory fields, showing that there is a principled way in which they may be regarded as a necessary element in perception without in any way being a foundation for truth or even 'information' (as the Gibsonians will have it).

The diagram that initiates this argument was produced by Gombrich to show the effect of existing memory expectations upon features of the distribution of a visual field. He took the familiar Rubin Vase (Figure 5.1), which we can subject to a switch of gestalts between two profiles or a vase. He added clues which strengthened our expectations; first a pair of ears, which encouraged the Profile interpretation (Figure 5.2) or a few flowers at the top, which strengthened the Vase interpretation (Figure 5.3). His signifi- cant move was to include both sets of contextual clues (Figure 5.4). He points out that if you mask either set of clues 'the reading becomes assured'.[2] The interesting aspect of this demonstration is that the rival gestalts play over what is a contestable visual ground which cannot be described in the terms that are used of the gestalts *per se*. It is not the case that the distribution of lines has only two ways of being described. Consider Hamlet's mocking play with gestalts on a cloud:

HAMLET: Do you see yonder cloud that's almost in the shape of a camel?

POLONIUS: By th' mass, and 'tis like a camel indeed.

HAMLET: Methinks it is like a weasel.

POLONIUS: It is backt like a weasel.

HAMLET: Or like a whale?

POLONIUS: Very like a whale.

There is no guarantee that the various gestalts produced by this playing with the sight of some random distribution of water-vapour shared the same outlines: the 'camel' might have taken up one portion of a chance outline, the 'weasel' another, and the 'whale' yet another. It cannot be assumed that precisely the same portion of this continuum of water-vapour – for a con- tinuum is what it is – was captured by the gestalts that a fanciful imagination threw upon it. What is forgotten – and the temptation to forget it easily insinuates itself into our immediate understanding – is that there is a mode

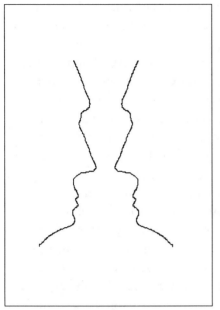

Figure 5.1 The Rubin Vase.

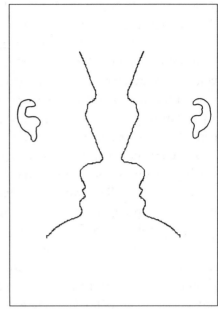

Figure 5.2 The Profile interpretation.

Figure 5.3 The Vase interpretation.

Figure 5.4 Complex combination.

of description of the field that is highly accurate but which makes no use at all of the terms employed to define the gestalts themselves. This distinction was first pointed out by J. B. Maund in a crucial article on the representative theory of perception.[3] He takes the example of a 'Movitype' display, one in which the appearance of moving pictures and words are presented by means of a matrix of tiny lights. These are commonly used nowadays in outdoor city advertisements. Take a typical sequence of images presented by such a matrix, such as the one I saw recently at Munich railway station: moving rows of German words were suddenly replaced by the appearance of a picture which grew out of some gathering collections of sparkles into the likeness of a Seven-Up can. The whole sequence was repetitive, so that when the sparkles came round again, helped by my Gombrichian 'expectations', I 'saw' the can assembling itself out of the sparkles rather earlier than before. It is obvious that any attempt to describe what was happening upon that matrix by means of the gestalts is quite inadequate if what is required is a precise account of the state of the matrix. After all, just when did 'the Seven-Up can' appear? 'The Beholder's Share' was fully in operation, because the first time round the collection of sparkles remained uninformative for quite a way into the 'assembling' sequence, but on the second occasion I was able to project a secure recognition much earlier. Yet the actual sequence on the matrix was precisely the same each time. In principle one can give a point-state description of the field without reference to what the field is showing as image to an eye with 'expectations'. Indeed, an electronics engineer could provide an exact computer printout of the point-states of the matrix, without any mention of German words or a Seven-Up can.

It is plain that there are two ways of describing a visual field; (A), an 'object-determinate' account, in which human beings may discuss what gestalts can most adaptively be applied to a given distribution; and (B), a 'field-determinate' account, which makes no mention whatsoever of any such selections from the field but gives a point-state description of the distributions in the visual field of an observer.

The same may be said, *mutatis mutandis*, of the television screen, for we as viewers can give descriptions in objective terms about what we see on the screen – say, a picture of Mount Everest – while the engineer could provide an accurate account of the state of the phosphor cells on the back of the cathode-ray-tube screen that made no mention of Mount Everest.

The computer scientist can even put us into what is described as an 'innocent eye' situation. He or she can feed on to the screen some randomised input that produces a succession of variations of shape and colour similar to hypnagogic visions. Note as a premise that what appears on the screen is not a representation of any kind; there is nothing objectified about it (as in the case with much of the hypnagogic sequences). One might play a kind of 'faces-in-the-fire' game with it, perhaps seeing 'Mount Everest' for an instant, or the profile of your maternal uncle; but of course, neither of these is in the program, and one does not have to play the 'faces' game. Indeed, the busy activity which Gombrich rightly says characterises much of our normal perception can shut down in such situations – should the viewer of the screen be fatigued (the observer of the hypnagogic sequences certainly is) – then it is remarkably easy to fall into the condition of a temporary experiencer (we shall not say 'observer') of a *non*-objectified visual field. There is nothing surprising in this, for it is an empirical fact that there are persons quite unable to objectify, to pick out gestalts at all; both brain-damaged persons ('agnosics') and certain autistic children can sense a visual field without being able to perform the activity of which Gombrich speaks. As one expert on the autistic has put it, 'They are able to hear and see, but they cannot listen and look.'[4]

As I have already argued elsewhere,[5] after-images give us a good example of non-objectified regions of the undeniably internal visual field subsequently yielding useful epistemic gestalts to an active perceiver. The apparently random after-image blot that has been 'interfering' with your perception can on inspection afford the fact that your partner has indeed brought you up a cup of coffee on the silver tray and left it on the window-sill in the sunlight: here unquestionably we have a simple case in which what is initially 'raw sense data' is transformed into a useful percept. Such transformations can be logically performed with all sense-data, yet there are many current denials of this empirical fact in the philosophical literature.[6]

One question has been begged so far in this argument. I have been assuming that the visual field is describable in point-state, non-epistemic terms. This is indeed the present conclusion of some neurophysiologists,[7] that the visual field appears in the form of a cortical display upon a 'raster', a matrix built up out of minute elements in a comparable manner to that of a TV screen or a Movitype panel. The points themselves are not discriminable, of course, but the analogue evenness of the field may be a product of a process that blends them into a continuous display.[8] Gombrich is thus correct to say that we cannot 'disentangle our nerve-endings'.[9] Furthermore, when the fact that its state bears no object-information within it is linked to the fact that it is not a copy of an externally coloured world, then it is clear that *neither* old Sense-Datum theory (with its canvassing of the notion of object- and property-similarity between the internal field and the external world), *nor* the old objections to Sense-Datum theory have any purchase upon the new position.

It was pointed out long ago by an insightful supporter of internal cortical displays, Roy Wood Sellars, that there is no pictorial resemblance between the internal display and the external distribution of light-rays arriving at the eyes.[10] What there is, is a *structural–formal* similarity. This is not a difficult notion: there exists a structural-formal similarity between the groove on an old gramophone record of Beethoven's Ninth and the laser-track on a modern CD of the same piece; between the intensities picked up by a metal-detector and the variations in the whine heard in the ear; between, to use Barry Maund's helpful analogy, the contours on a map and the topography they indicate. There is a mapping of intensities, no more; certainly no visual resemblance, the reason being that light-rays are not coloured. It is therefore self-contradictory to talk of there being a 'retinal image' at all. The display is in the cortex. There is also a radical conclusion which bears no relation to what the old objectors to Sense-Datum theory used to accuse it of, namely, a belief that there was some kind of pictorial similarity between what arrived at the retina and what was experienced within the brain. On the contrary, there is no such pictorial similarity, only an indirectly traceable structural–formal isomorphism. The new theory cannot, therefore, be called a 'sense-datum' theory, since it holds that there are no 'data' whatsoever upon the display, merely a causally induced array upon a raster that may or may not be subjected to gestalt-selection at the instigation of pain–pleasure/desire–fear. As I have expressed it elsewhere: 'A cortical field is an intermediary but not a facsimile: for the visual field its colours are not copies of colours.'[11]

Another key factor that can be deduced from this characterisation of the visual field is that its sensations are strictly not seen but *sensed*. Gombrich is correct to say that 'Nobody has ever seen a visual sensation',[12] the reason being that they are sensed, not seen. Colours and the phenomenal 3-D space being cortical constructs, they are not seen by the eyes, which are organs for picking up uncoloured light-rays; moreover, there are no light-rays in the cortex. One can have internal sensory experience without the 'Cartesian Theatre' of which Daniel Dennett makes such fun.[13] To change the modality, Dennett is claiming that the inner-sense theorist believes that, in the case of sound, there is air in the brain through which sound waves from some kind of loudspeaker could pass to another set of ears. Neither can there be a vicious regress of perceptions, an objection with which the old anti-representationalists (from Hermann Lotze to Gilbert Ryle) were fond of berating the Sense-Datum theorists.[14] Ryle mocked those who insisted that seeing was a matter of internal sensations by claiming that it reduced having sensations to not having them.[15] But this rejoinder was weak,[16] since it was clear that Ryle was unable to conceive of sensation without observation, that is, of the field as non-epistemic.

Gombrich has always been suspicious of James J. Gibson's claim that visual experience was an epiphenomenal 'luxury',[17] saying that he could not 'swallow Gibson's theory whole'.[18] Gibson even argued in the same article that 'visual perceptions are not necessary for visual perception'. Although we now know from the 'blindsight' experiments that minimal adaptive assistance can be derived from low-level registration of input, nevertheless to deny that sensation is not necessary for active perception amounts to a *reductio ad absurdum* of Gibson's own case.[19] However, it is easy to see why this assertion is being made, because Gibson, more than any other psychologist of perception, has drawn attention to automatic processes that alter the input in significant ways. He insists that the intake is not passive, because there are automatic alterations to it that render the result apt for successful perceptual and motor interaction with the environment. However, he has made a simple logical error concerning this pre-phenomenal processing of the input.

Let us take as a representative example the production of sharper 'edges' for outlines of regions within the field. The result is to produce the equivalent of turning up the contrast knob on the TV screen. But it is certainly not the case that producing such a change in the distribution on the screen is an automatic enhancer of information. Consider two persons looking at the bark of a tree: one is an expert entomologist, rather short-sighted; the other is one of his students, with excellent eyesight. In spite of these differences in sharpness of focus, the disadvantaged entomologist can nevertheless make out a camouflaged moth on the tree and accurately name its species, whereas the moth remains outside the perception of his sharp-eyed student. Another example: there is a large picture in the Albright-Knox art gallery in Buffalo, New York, which consists of a face seen through a sheet of glass textured with minute bubbles.[20] Close to the painting it is impossible to see the face; one must actively blur one's vision by retreating to an adequate distance before the face becomes visible. It is plain that *acuity* is not the same as *acuteness*. Discriminability at the level of the field bears no logical relation to accuracy of perceptual identification. Although on many occasions acuity is adaptively helpful, there are others in which it is not. No *epistemic* enhancement is provided by an 'edge'-improver: it is entirely a contingent matter. So the most that can be said is that such a Gibsonian process renders the field often more apt for current gestalt-selection, but does not provide any information whatsoever.

So what is actually happening at the point-states on the matrix? When the neurophysiologist of the future produces his list of the point-states of some visual field, no 'edges' will be mentioned in the list; all that could be observed would be *a narrowing of the regions at which transitions of intensity took place*. Although in some cases this might facilitate the application of a memory gestalt, there is no logical guarantee of it. The narrowing of a transition region provides no automatic deliverance of 'information'. Gibson was therefore using an insidious metaphor in applying the word 'information' to the improved discriminability of the visual field. The new theory of perception insists that the field is entirely non-epistemic and non-intentional; it is even an error to use the metaphor 'innocent' of it. Its structural–formal similarities to external distributions of light-rays are no more than elaborately processed effects of those causes. What they are taken to mean is another matter altogether.

For all Gombrich's saying that 'the innocent eye is a myth', that it 'is logically impossible',[21] he has acknowledged that the blind who regain sight are exposed to a 'smarting chaos' (confirmed by Sachs),[22] and that looking upside-down between one's legs at a landscape disengages normal perceptual habits.[23] At this level of sensory registration one cannot apply the terms that we normally do when perceiving, such as 'illusory' and 'veridical'.

Examine the mistake about illusions made by J. L. Austin and others.[24] Austin took it for granted that the bent stick in a transparent fluid is a logically safe example of what he called an illusion. But if the field can be probed by the searchlight of the active perceiving module, as Gombrich believes, then an interesting outcome emerges. Just as having the flowers on the Rubin picture changes the gestalt of the irregular lines in the middle, so viewing the bent stick with a different Gombrichian 'expectation' in mind can change it from being an illusion to being a clear instance of the discovery of real knowledge. What of the scientist who is expert in judging the refractive index of a fluid? Let him or her be provided with a series of pictures of sticks apparently bent in this manner. The scientist does not speak of illusion at all, the reason being that he or she now can pronounce with confidence upon the pictures in the following way: 'The first is in water; the second is in petrol; the third in benzene; the fourth, in amyl acetate;. . .' etc., etc. Has anyone since the beginning of time ever doubted the sight of the sun in the sky? – yet it would be an illusion by Austin's criterion, for the air is a fluid with a measurable refractive index, so the sun is never really where we think it to be. Yet no one has ever thought to call it a 'mirage'. Thus the field is open to endless interpretations in the service of organic life. Nothing on the non-epistemic field comes already marked with either illusion or reality, hence, with either information or distortions of information. Gombrich shows himself intrigued by the picture that Lawrence Gowing painted which records precisely the double-image effects produced by his focusing his eyes beyond a table:[25] again, this picture need not be viewed as an illusion, but as a precise indicator of (1) just where Gowing was focusing; and (2) the actual state at the non-epistemic level of the overlapping visual fields of the two eyes.

For philosophers such as George Pitcher, opposed to the distinguishing of sensation and perception, the double-image is not evidence of two internal fields because one is 'only seeing the same thing twice'.[26] What he forgets is that the two fields are distinct at every point because of the difference in perspective angle between the two eyes (the very difference of course that enables the brain to produce the 3-D phenomenal effect). Thus one cannot describe their differences in terms of some object that the subject presumes him- or herself to be seeing. In Gowing's picture there are two distinct 'tables', each seen from a slightly different angle. To agree with Pitcher would involve the inability to distinguish field-determinateness from object-determinateness. Furthermore, a simple experiment can make the difference startling: expose one eye to bright sunlight for several minutes, keeping the other covered – now go and squint at a red candle. What will be seen is a green candle overlapping a red one, proof that the two fields are different internal experiences, with sensation utterly distinct from percept.

Calling the visual field in the cortex (and the other sensory fields) non-epistemic implies that it is no more than an effect which is at the end of a complex causal chain frequently traceable to distributions at the retinas. Thus it is no more than a *natural sign* in H. P. Grice's sense;[27] because of its causal connections it can be used as an indicator. Just as we may see a cloud on the horizon and conclude that 'it means rain', so too we see distributions on the internal cortical field and have learned to associate them with consequences material to life. If it is no more than such a natural sign, then it bears no information whatsoever. Who would think of calling a cloud on the horizon a bearer of information? Yet Gibson was making what is logically the very same error. Gombrich, on the other hand, holds to the notion that 'pictures cannot assert',[28] to which must be added, neither do the sensory fields, this being the general reason why pictures cannot.

One has to move to a further conclusion, that, strictly speaking, the sensation fields of all the senses are not mental, except in the limited sense that they are in a brain. Perhaps Gombrich is moving towards this view when he says 'the optical world . . . is really part of the physical world'.[29] The term 'non-epistemic' must imply that there is no thought and no emotion at that basic level. Nothing intentional is selected from it until the gestalt-module, driven by the instigations of the algedonic system in the cerebellum, enforces a unifying of certain regions and their embedding in memory tagged with desire or fear. These gestalts are the result of what the psychologist Ernst von Glasersfeld calls 'attentional pulses';[30] this is where the *perceptual* activity repeatedly stressed by Gombrich is at work, not in the *sensory* registration itself. Only then, within this intentional activity, can we speak of the mental.

In his development of the Rubin Vase drawing, Gombrich acknowledges the 'Beholder's Share' as being responsible for the rival interpretations: the flowers are taken as a contextual clue to the presence of a vase, the ears to the presence of two profiles. It is an active engagement of the subject's memory that produces the two gestalts. Gibson, on the other hand, went to the extent of saying that in such cases 'the light itself was equivocal'.[31] Surely it would be hard to find in the annals of modern science a belief in the existence of rival thought-processes in some beams of light, quite apart from any human engagement: 'A physical event *in se* cannot have the property of equivocity'.[32]

Gombrich's searchlight is powered initially by pain and pleasure. These are what record gestalts in the memory and mark them with desire and fear. According to the new theory of perception, this gestalt module plays over the non-epistemic field and selects from it units that may prove to be reliable indicators of the repetition of rewarding or avoiding motor action. This is also a feature of Piaget's sensory-motor constructivism.[33] Learning in the rough-and-tumble of experience continually refines the selections being made, though they can never be anything other than viable. Piaget calls them 'mobile object schemata',[34] terms that match Gombrich's 'schema and correction'.[35] As Glasersfeld,[36] following Piaget, insists, what is achieved is no more than an adaptive fit with its perceptual construct, which cannot in any way be a replica of part of the environment. This meshes with the argument as it has so far proceeded, since the non-epistemic field is entirely open as far as the selection of gestalts is concerned.

It can now be seen that another criticism that has been levelled at Gombrich has no purchase upon his theory. Richard Wollheim argues that the whole notion of schema and correction is vitiated by the fact that there is nothing to stand in the place of what is being corrected. It cannot be the previous perception, because the very same challenge can be repeated again. The unfortunate philosophical result was claimed to be that trap of traps, a vicious regress. The same attack is repeated by Paul Richter,[37] and interestingly also turns up in attacks upon the Piagetian constructivists. Richard Kitchener claims that there can be no Piagetian transformation of one percept into another precisely because either there is nothing there before the transformation, or whatever it was must have been there from the beginning and so cannot be constructed.[38] Is it not less pretentious to take an evolutionary view of perception and see each organism endeavouring, by means of its pain–pleasure/desire–fear gestalt-system, to arrive at viable interpretations of the distributions of its sensory fields? There is then no danger of taking anything given as a 'timeless invariant'. What is valuable is the ability to change one's schema when its viability proves itself inadequate.

If, to quote Gombrich, 'to perceive is to categorise',[39] it is no surprise that each of us categorises slightly differently, and this is to be expected given the implications of evolutionary theory. As communicators, humans can therefore extend their corrections to the schemata of others and accept corrections in turn. To use Gombrich's improvement of the Rubin Vase picture as illustration: what we have to do is to bring, say, the *flowers* to the notice of someone who has been solely impressed by the *ears*, trying to show to others intentional relevances in the context that may bring about a gestalt-switch.

To achieve the necessary coincidence of our differing gestalts we have to hypothesise *pro tempore* that we have both identified the same portion of what exists. To use Gombrich's own example, that of R. V. Jones, the interpreter of air photographs during the war: he was able to identify what to others looked like a vague group of highlights and smudges as a V2 rocket with its shadow. When he said, 'Do you see *this*?', both he and they had to assume that 'this' was the same for all of them. It was impossible that they were each singling out *precisely* the same region of the photograph. Gombrich uses the case of a hunter who throws his spear at a rock, mistaking it for an animal:[40] notice that there is no requirement that all the hunter saw as 'the animal' was all he saw of 'the rock' — so where did his gestalt of the animal begin and end in his visual field? where did his percept of the rock? There is no guarantee that they were the same — only our habit of counting up to one makes us think so. As the Indian philosopher Dignaga said: 'Even "this" can be a case of mistaken identity.'[41]

Wittgenstein was mistaken when he claimed that there has to be agreement in judgements as well as in definitions.[42] Rather it is a question of acting as if those judgements were identical, to allow the correction to the schema to go through. Public agreements can hide all kinds of unknown differences at sensory and perceptual levels. The 'uncertainty in all seeing' has to be playfully ignored so that the separate perspectives can roughly coincide.[43] The separate 'seeing-as's' are to be treated as 'seeing that's'. At this meta-level, then, there is no distinction between so-called 'veridical seeing' and 'seeing-aspects'.[44] Such counsel can now be seen as no more than an exhortation to join in the game of there being a 'standard' entity common to everyone. *Strictly speaking, there are no such things as 'objects' or 'referents' at all*,[45] but only regions of the real continuum of varying extensions in space and time upon which persons with differing perspectives get a tenuous hold by pretending that they are surrounded by 'standard' versions of those 'objects'. Denotation cannot therefore be the principle of representation in pictures[46] since there are no objects to denote, being but elements in a necessary game of assumptions. As Gombrich has it, 'the layman is a partner with the artist in a game of equivalences',[47] which is no surprise if all intersubjective co-operation in perception is also such a game. Gombrich's insistence on the beholder's powers of projection, his reminder that emotion governs attention,[48] and his careful analysis of such situations as the V2 rocket photographs, show that he is conscious of the troubles that can arise from too complacent an acceptance of the received opinion of 'what' is denoted. The intelligence officer R. V. Jones, he says, was able to recognise the V2 rockets in photographs of Poland as he had done earlier in those of Peenemunde, but this later interpretation was rejected as amateur in an official memorandum. As Gombrich says:

> It is a story which should be widely disseminated wherever professionals claim a monopoly of wisdom. For the truth is, of course, that one can learn from the theory of interpretation that interpretation cannot be wholly learned or taught.[49]

This contradicts Wittgenstein's unwise reliance on the received opinion, taught only by those in the form of life who know they know better than their pupils. Interpretation is learned not from a teacher but from the active encounter with the ambiguities of vision, the 'illusions' that are everywhere.

Notes

1. E. H. Gombrich, 'The evidence of images', in Charles H. Singleton (ed.), *Interpretation, Theory and Practice*, Baltimore 1969, p. 62.
2. E. H. Gombrich, *Illusion*, p. 239.
3. J. B. Maund, 'The representative theory of perception', *Canadian Journal of Philosophy*, 5 (1975), pp. 41–55, later developed in, 'Representation, pictures and resemblance', in Edmond Wright (ed.), *New Representationalisms; Essays in the Philosophy of Perception*, Aldershot 1993, pp. 45–69.
4. B. Hermelin, 'Coding and the sense modalities', in Lorna Wing (ed.), *Early Childhood Autism: Clinical, Educational and Social Aspects*, Oxford 1976, p. 137.
5. E. Wright, 'Inspecting Images', *Philosophy*, 58 (1983), pp. 51–72.
6. G. Harman, 'The intrinsic quality of experience', paper read at the 1987 Chapel Hill Colloquium, provides a typical example.
7. For a survey, see J. R. Smythies, 'The impact of contemporary neuroscience and introspection psychology on the philosophy of perception', in E. Wright (ed.), *New Representationalisms: Essays in the Philosophy of Perception*, Aldershot 1993, pp. 205–31.
8. A. Clark, 'Qualia and the psychophysiological explanation of color perception', *Synthèse*, 65 (1985), pp. 377–405; see also A. Clark, *Sensory Qualities*, Oxford 1993, for a defence of internal sensory experience.
9. E. H. Gombrich, 'The evidence of images', in Charles H. Singleton (ed.), *Interpretation, Theory and Practice*, Baltimore 1969, p. 43.
10. R. W. Sellars, 'The epistemology of evolutionary naturalism', *Mind*, 28/112 (1919), p. 414; see also R. Chisholm, 'Sellars' critical realism', *Philosophy and Phenomenological Research*, 15/1 (1954), p. 41.
11. E. Wright, 'More qualia trouble for functionalism: the Smythies TV-Hood analogy', *Synthèse*, 97 (1993), pp. 365–82; see p. 375.
12. E. H. Gombrich, *Art and Illusion*, p. 252.
13. D. Dennett, *Consciousness Explained*, London 1991, pp. 101–38.
14. From H. Lotze, *Metaphysics*, Oxford 1884, pp. 92–93, to Gilbert Ryle, *The Concept of Mind*, Harmondsworth 1966, p. 173.
15. Ryle, *The Concept of Mind*, p. 215.
16. A. J. Ayer, *The Problem of Knowledge*, Harmondsworth 1957, pp. 105–8.
17. J. J. Gibson, 'The information available in pictures', *Leonardo*, 4 (1971), p. 31.
18. E. H. Gombrich, 'The evidence of images', p. 43.
19. L. Weisenkranz, *Blindsight: A Case Study and Implications*, Oxford 1986.

20. *Janet* by Chuck Close, 1992, oil on canvas, 100 in x 84 in.

21. Gombrich, *Art and Illusion*, pp. 251 and 264.

22. O. Sachs, *A Leg to stand On*, London 1986.

23. *Ibid.*, p. 67.

24. Austin is relied on, for example, by Richard Wollheim in his attack on Gombrich: R. Wollheim, 'Art and illusion', *British Journal of Aesthetics*, 3 (1963), pp. 15–37.

25. *Image and Eye*, p. 179.

26. G. Pitcher, *A Theory of Perception*, Princeton, New Jersey, 1971, p. 41.

27. H. P. Grice, 'Meaning', in P. F. Strawson (ed.), *Philosophical Logic*, Oxford 1967, pp. 39–48.

28. *Image and Eye*, p. 175.

29. *Ibid.*, p. 176.

30. E. von Glaserfeld, 'An attentional model for the conceptual construction of units and numbers', *Journal for Research in Mathematics Education*, 12 (1981), p. 87.

31. J. J. Gibson, *The Senses Considered as Perceptual Systems*, London 1968, p. 247.

32. R. J. Richards, 'James Gibson's Passive Theory of Perception: a rejection of the doctrine of specific nerve energies', *Philosophy and Phenomenological Research*, 37 (1976–77), p. 227.

33. J. Piaget, *The Child's Construction of Reality*, trans. Margaret Cook, London 1955.

34. *Ibid.*, p. 93.

35. *Art and Illusion*, p. 231.

36. E. von Glaserfeld, 'An introduction to radical constructivism', in Paul Watzlawick (ed.), *The Invented Reality: How Do We Know What We Believe We Know? Contributions to Constructivism*, New York 1984, p. 25.

37. P. Richter, 'On Professor Gombrich's model of schema and correction', *British Journal of Aesthetics*, 16 (1976), pp. 338–46.

38. R. F. Kitchener, *Piaget's Theory of Knowledge: Genetic Epistemology and Scientific Reason*, New Haven 1986, p. 114.

39. 'Image and code' in *Image and Eye*, p. 21.

40. Gombrich, 'The evidence of images', p. 48.

41. B. K. Matilal, *Perception: An Essay on Classical Indian Theories of Knowledge*, Oxford 1986, p. 332.

42. *Philosophical Investigations*, New York 1953, 242.

43. Gombrich, 'The evidence of images', p. 47.

44. See T. Wilkerson, 'Representation, illusion and aspects', *British Journal of Aesthetics*, 18 (1978), pp. 45–58.

45. R. L. Gregory, 'Hypothesis and illusion: explorations in perception and science', in Edmond Wright (ed.), *New Representationalisms*, Aldershot 1993, p. 259 and E. Wright, 'The Entity Fallacy in epistemology', *Philosophy*, 67 (1992), pp. 33–50.

46. N. Goodman, *Languages of Art: An Approach to the Theory of Symbols*, London 1968.

47. *Art and Illusion*, p. 276.

48. Gombrich, 'The evidence of images', p. 48.

49. *Ibid.*, p. 47.

6

A conceptual dimension of art history

B. R. Tilghman

E. H. Gombrich's investigations into the history of art have led him to discuss several topics that have absorbed the attention of philosophers, especially the notions of human action, intention and emotion. In the art of painting these notions intersect in very interesting ways, and it is through an understanding of them that we can gain insights into the problems faced by artists in their task of representing the human figure and into the problems faced by historians, critics and spectators in their practices of understanding and appreciating what artists have done.

I will focus attention primarily on two of Gombrich's papers, 'Ritualized expression and gesture in the arts' and 'Action and expression in Western art', but also mention two others, 'Moment and movement in art' and 'The evidence of images'.[1] In these essays the representation of human action and much that surrounds it is discussed. My aim in this chapter is not necessarily either to question or disagree with anything that Gombrich has done, but is rather to reveal a dimension of the topics he treats that is not generally noticed and that I hope will shed some light on the nature of the work that he has done in art history.

The concepts of action, intention and emotion are logically interconnected. We can see this by recalling the ways in which we describe actions, that is, what people do. A man, for example, sits down to write a lecture, stoops to pick up a tennis ball, or flirts with a woman.[2] The descriptions of the actions include the intentions with which they are done. This inclusion is necessary in order for us to understand what is being done. I see the man yonder and notice that his legs are bent and his arm is extended so, but I can't make out what he is doing. The tennis ball has to come into the picture in order to complete the description.

Emotions are not only reactions to circumstances, as when one becomes angry, afraid or falls in love; they can also provide reasons and motives for action, they can characterise how an action is done and they can characterise people themselves. One can strike a blow out of anger, bar the windows out of fear, send flowers out of love, one can stoop to retrieve the tennis ball angrily, fearfully or even lovingly, and an individual can be quarrelsome, timid or loving by temperament.

These logical connections between these concepts have consequences for the understanding of painting. The antique tradition of art inherited by the Renaissance defines it as 'the imitation of men in action' and it is the painterly representation of human action that concerns Gombrich. It follows, then, that painting must make clear the character, intentions and emotions of its figures if the action it represents is to be understood. Our understanding of what is going on in a painting must be parasitic upon our understanding of what is going on in our commerce with people in the course of our lives.

Gombrich makes a distinction among the kinds of gestures and expressions that are characteristic of human emotion. He describes these as 'symptoms' and 'symbols'.[3] A symptom is a natural expression of emotion, such as spontaneous laughter, a cry of pain or throwing up a hand to ward off a blow. A symbol, by contrast, is a conventional or even ritualised gesture. Putting the hand on the heart is such a ritualised convention of sincerity. The two are not thought of as mutually exclusive, but as ends of a spectrum. Clapping the hands is an example of a social convention for expressing approval of a performance, and may be done quite perfunctorily and simply 'out of politeness', but once this convention has taken hold it can also be a genuine and spontaneous reaction to a masterful performance. Many conventionalised gestures have been borrowed for use in painting and have become, in effect, conventions of painting. The Christian gesture of blessing with a hand with two fingers extended is one such.

The use of the terms 'symbol' and 'symptom' in the description of the relation between emotion and its various expressions points towards a view of that relation whose ancestry in art theory can be traced at least as far back as Xenophon's report of the conversation between Socrates and the painter Parrhasius.[4] Parrhasius does not understand how emotions can be represented in painting, because they are invisible. Socrates reminds him that emotions are displayed in a person's postures, gestures, facial expressions and the like; the artist can certainly paint these. Renaissance literature on painting from Alberti to Le Brun is full of remarks to the effect that the task of the painter is to represent the inner emotions and character of the figures in the painting by the outward appearances that the inner states are supposed to cause. Gombrich quotes Leonardo to the effect that the most important thing in painting is to show the movements that *originate* from mental states (my emphasis).[5]

This traditional distinction in artistic theory between the inner and the outer is reflected in Gombrich's description of natural and spontaneous emotional reactions as "symptoms". To speak of them as symptoms suggests that the emotion itself is an inner state of which the visible bodily manifestations are at best bits of evidence from which the true condition of a person must be inferred. To the philosopher this inner/outer, emotion/symptom distinction strongly suggests a commitment to the kind of philosophical dualism that makes a theoretical distinction between mind and body.

The philosophical thesis of mind/body dualism can be stated quite simply. Thoughts, feelings, intentions and everything that we are inclined to label 'mental' are non-physical entities known only by the one who experiences them. Only I can feel my pains, think my thoughts and know my intentions. Your mental states are not available to me and mine are not available to you. Our bodily postures and movements that are publicly observable are only contingently related to the inner mental states of which they are presumably symptoms or for which they are presumed to be evidence.

The immediate consequence of this dualism is scepticism with respect to other minds. If this theory is true, we can never know what another person is thinking or feeling, because it is theoretically impossible to establish any correlation between outward bodily behaviour and inward mental state.

Given that the traditional aim of art was to imitate people in action, that is, to show us what they are thinking, feeling and doing as well as what is happening to them, painting must accomplish this aim by representing, among other things, the gestures, postures and facial expressions of the figures. Gombrich's emphasis on this representation is, of course, exactly right. How else could human character and feeling be shown? For many, however, the ghost of dualism still hovers over our thinking about this, and we are nagged by the question, 'How can bodily postures and gestures − including the painted representations of them − reveal human character and feeling?'

At this point it will be useful to take another look at Socrates' response to Parrhasius when he said that human emotions are displayed in the face and in attitudes of the body. There is a temptation to construe this talk about facial expressions and bodily attitudes as references to one half of the mind/body dualism. Whatever philosophical theory of the mind that may have lain behind what Socrates said, we do not have to understand his words as implying any form of dualism, or any other theory, for that matter. Let me suggest that we construe them as what Wittgenstein calls grammatical remarks, that is, remarks that remind us how the words of our language are used.

Taken in this way, Socrates' words remind us that the attitudes of the body that concern us are not the behaviourist's 'colourless bodily movements,' to be described in the vocabulary of physics and physiology, but are, instead, the gestures, expressions and actions of people, to be described in the full vocabulary of human character and emotion. It is the face itself that is described as angry or sorrowful, the gesture itself that is described as fearful or emphatic and it is the whole bodily attitude that is aggressive or submissive. As Wittgenstein said, 'The human body is the best picture of the human soul.'[6] This is meant as a grammatical remark and is part of an explicit rejection of dualism. It is in the light of this remark of Wittgenstein's that it is possible to understand Socrates in the way that I have suggested. Socrates can be taken as telling us, in effect, that the human body is the best picture of the human soul. Mind/body dualism with its attendant scepticism and 'other minds' problem is intellectually incoherent. I will assert this dogmatically as an assumption of the discussion that follows and leave it to the reader to seek its justification in other places.[7]

Although some of the theorising on the practice of painting in the Parrhasius–Leonardo–Gombrich tradition can suggest philosophical dualism, the philosophical theory can play no role in the *practice* of painting, just as it can play no role in our dealings with people in the stream of life. There is no logical room for theoretical scepticism in the stream of life. It makes no sense to wonder whether we can ever know what another person is thinking or feeling. If art is the imitation of life and of people in action, then there is no logical room for theoretical scepticism in painting, either. It would be a conceptual mistake to suppose that painters must limit themselves to the representation of what is visible, that is, gestures, movements, facial expressions, and the like, because they cannot represent the real emotions and intentions which are believed to lie invisibly behind them. The representation of the body is not something painters must resort to *faute de mieux*.

There is, to be sure, a common-or-garden variety of scepticism that is logically independent of philosophical dualism and its theoretical scepticism about other minds. In particular cases we can be unsure of what a person is thinking, feeling or intending, because we are fully aware that people can conceal their thoughts and feelings and that they can lie to us about these things. In the stream of life it makes perfectly good sense, in certain situations at least, to doubt what a person says and to wonder what that person is really up to.

There is no logical room in art, however, for even this 'garden' variety of scepticism to get a foothold. It makes no sense to ask whether the kneeling figure of the Magdalene with her attendant skull and crucifix is truly repentant or only putting on an act, say, to ingratiate herself with the other Mary, or whether the girl in Zurbaràn's execrable *The Virgin as a Child* is only affecting a pious face to please the nuns. Why this kind of scepticism makes no sense with respect to art is easy to understand.

At one point Wittgenstein asks,

Why can't a dog simulate pain? Is he too honest? Could one teach a dog to simulate pain? Perhaps it is possible to teach him to howl on particular occasions as if he were in pain, even when he is not. But the surroundings which are necessary for this behaviour to be real simulation are missing.[8]

There are people who are too open and honest to lie. It may never occur to them to do it, or if they try, they can't do it convincingly. Their whole manner and expression betrays them. Wittgenstein, of course, wants us to realise that it makes no sense to speak of a dog lying. The conceptual surroundings for dissimulation are simply not there.

The figures in a painting cannot lie either; but it is not because they are too honest. The conceptual surroundings for intelligibly ascribing a lie include such things as the possibility of discovering ulterior motives, overhearing sinister conversations, facing the culprit with the truth and the like. All that would have to entail acquaintance with the figures in a life outside the painting, and this is where we bump against the limits of intelligibility. It makes no sense to question whether the figures in a painting are really feeling what they are painted as feeling.

While there is no place for scepticism about how it really is with a figure in a painting, pretence and dissimulation can, of course, be shown in a painting. Giotto did it in a masterly fashion in his Arena Chapel panel of the kiss of Judas, where Christ looks directly into Judas' face as if to say, 'I know exactly what you are doing.' Rembrandt also succeeded magnificently in a similar task in his painting of Peter's denial of Christ.[9]

Although the aim of painting is to represent human feeling and action, it faces certain problems in doing so, and Gombrich has called attention to some of these. There is too much about people that painting cannot represent. Art cannot, for example, represent speech, and so poor St Sebastian cannot tell us how much it hurts, but neither can it show the head nodding or shaking, a sudden blush or eye movement. It thus lacks 'most of the resources on which human beings and animals rely in their contacts and interactions',[10] that is, the resources that we need to understand how it is with another. Leonardo advised artists to make careful observations of the actual gestures that people make in everyday life. Gombrich notes, however, that such observation could not produce great works of art, because 'life in movement is just too rich and too manifold to allow of imitation without some selective principle'.[11] Consequently painting must rely on a somewhat restricted range of conventional and ritualised gestures already familiar to its audience in order to help make clear what the figures are about.

The resources, in all their richness and manifoldness, that we need to understand other people needs further comment. I would like to look at it this way. Leonardo's gestures of everyday life can, of course, be captured by the draughtsperson. Too often, unfortunately, these gestures appear to be, as many would say, without meaning. What the notion of meaning comes to here, I suspect, has something to do with description. A sketch, or snapshot, of a gesture (posture, face, etc.) taken *sur le champ* may not permit us *to describe* and hence understand the gesture as one of anger, resignation, emphasis or whatever. The problem that Gombrich has pointed out is partly a conceptual one concerning the application of appropriate descriptions.

There is not much logical room in painting for the understanding of even those nuances that can be represented by the lift of an eyebrow or the curl of the lips. Appreciating and understanding nuances as expressions of thought and feelings often depends upon the kind of close knowledge of an individual that includes an awareness of his or her characteristic and habitual ways of reacting to situations, as well as the observation of patterns of behaviour manifested over time. Art and life are importantly different in this respect. Since it makes no sense to speak of encountering the figure in the painting apart from the represented scene, there is nothing that can be called becoming more fully aware of its mannerisms, its characteristic ways of acting, its likes and dislikes, or anything of that sort.

The question for Gombrich in its most general form is to determine what the relation is between the gestures performed in real life and those represented in art. More specifically, however, the question is this: if we are to understand what is going on in a painting, or sculpture for that matter, the figures must make use of ritualised gestures. In life, ritual can take the place of genuine feeling. In art the representation of ritual can become an empty formula. The problem for the artist, therefore, is how to use the conventional gestures to express genuine feeling. This, I think, is a practical problem and not a theoretical one, at least not one with any philosophical overtones. It is a matter of the artist's sensitivity and skill. Some can do it and some cannot. Zurbaràn fails with his *The Virgin as a Child* and Rembrandt succeeds with his *David in Prayer*, to invoke two of Gombrich's examples.[12] There seems little else to be said.

Gombrich's answer to the general question about the relation between the gestures of life and the gestures of art is twofold. On the one hand, the artist, as already pointed out, must make use of ritualised gestures whose significance has been conventionally established. On the other hand, these gestures must be understood in an appropriate context in order to realise their full significance for the action being represented. It is in this contextual requirement that the principal conceptual dimension of Gombrich's work is found. An appropriate context is necessary for the intelligible application of descriptions of people's actions and reactions. Contexts enter into Gombrich's work in two different ways. These two ways can be illustrated by the example of his discussion of Rembrandt's *St Peter's Denial*.

He contrasts the Rembrandt with a mosaic of the same scene in S. Apollinare Nuovo.[13] In the earlier work the maid extends her hand in a conventional speaking gesture and Peter recoils and raises his hands in another conventional gesture. The gestures and postures are stylised and theatrical – 'theatrical' in the sense of being broad and exaggerated in the way that is necessary if they are to be recognised from the cheap seats where nuances simply cannot be seen. Gombrich says that the gesture of Rembrandt's Saint Peter raising his hand is much less unambiguous than in the mosaic. He says that

> taken in isolation the figure may simply be shown to speak or even make an inviting gesture asking one of the other figures to come forward. But the figure is not in isolation and thus Rembrandt compels us to picture the whole tragic scene in our mind.

The figure is not in isolation, and Rembrandt compels us to picture the whole tragic scene. It is in terms of this remark that we can understand the two ways in which context plays a role. The figure is not in isolation, in that it is shown in relation to and reacting to the other figures in the painting and it is not in isolation in that it is part of a representation of an episode in a larger history that both precedes and follows the moment.

Whatever an emotion is – and it is not necessary for us to decide that – it is not, as William James had it, an inner turmoil of physiological reactions and the sensations produced by them. There are, to be sure, physical and physiological reactions characteristic of emotions, but for these to count as *emotional* reactions they must be seen in appropriate contexts; the individual must be reacting *to* something. This is sometimes put by saying that emotions have objects. This is another grammatical remark. Fear, for example, is always fear *of* something and anger is always anger *at* something or someone. A person's reactions, facial expressions, gestures and so on can be recognised as manifestations of a particular emotion only when understood in relation to a possible object of emotion.[14]

It is his failure to provide any context and hence any object of emotion that explains why Le Brun's attempt to teach aspiring artists how to represent the emotions by the examples of his notorious drawings of what he imagines the proper facial expression for each to be cannot possibly work. Several of the faces seem quite interchangeable; 'fright' and 'anger' for two, and without some indication of what the expression is a reaction to, one can only shrug one's shoulders.

Such a context is certainly not lacking in Rembrandt's painting. Peter is clearly reacting to the woman and the two 'tough soldiers', as Gombrich describes them. There is, nevertheless, something lacking for understanding. What is it about these people that produces Peter's reaction? If we compare this painting with any number of versions of the *Pietà* we can see what is lacking. A *Pietà*, whatever else it may be, is a representation of a woman grieving over a dead man. Since the woman's expression is focused on the dead body it can usually be recognised unambiguously as grief; it is clear what produces her reaction. To understand that the expression is one of grief the spectator does not have to know any more than that grief is a characteristic human response to death; the knowledge that the dead man is Christ and that the woman, Mary, his mother, does not have to enter into it; the juxtaposition of the two is enough. The juxtaposition of Peter and the others, however, is not enough.

To understand what is going on in Rembrandt's painting we must know that this is Peter, that it is Christ in the background, looking over his shoulder at him, and that the others have just accused him of being one of the followers of Jesus. In other words, we must know something of the whole story of which the painting portrays only one incident. This is an example of the second of the two ways in which context enters into the understanding of emotion and action in painting.

I said earlier that our understanding of what is going on in a painting must be parasitic upon our understanding of what is going on in our commerce with people in the course of our lives. In the course of our lives we must often know, as it were, the 'whole story' in order to understand what people are doing and how they are reacting in various situations. As an illustration of this, let us consider the incident mentioned earlier, represented in Giotto's Arena Chapel fresco of the kiss of Judas. Christ is shown looking directly into the eyes of Judas as he delivers the betraying kiss. The eyes say, in effect, 'I know exactly what you are doing.' We understand what Judas is doing because we know the story. Had we been spectators of the actual event we would have had 'to know the story' too, in order to understand the kiss as dissimulation. That is, we would have had to know something about Jesus and Judas, the situation with the authorities, Judas' dealings with them, and so on. Giotto's accomplishment lies in the way he portrays the gaze of Christ, that makes clear to us, who understand, the depth of his discernment. As spectators of the original we could well have noticed something unusual in the way that Jesus looked at Judas, but recognised it as seeing through the disciple's motivation only after we had learned more about what was going on.

Gombrich has devoted considerable attention to the way that the 'whole story' enters into our understanding of paintings. He questions distinctions such as Lessing's between the arts of time and the arts of space, but sees a problem in how images of allegedly 'arrested' action, such as paintings or even photographs, can appear to proceed from what has gone before and to presage what will come after. He makes an appeal to what psychologists have supposed to be explanations of these alleged facts in order to justify the claim that there is no such thing as an identifiable *point* in time that a painting or photograph can be said to capture.[15] The psychological machinery that is claimed to be responsible for our perception can be exchanged for the grammatical point that pictures are usually seen and understood as illustrations of a *story*.

The fact that we understand paintings as illustrations of stories makes clear the nature of at least one aspect of the interpretation of paintings and explains why there is frequently a problem about interpretation. One task of interpretation is to determine what the story is that is being illustrated, and that involves identifying who the figures are, what they are doing, how they are reacting, and so on. This task is sometimes made easier by the fact that the painting is part of a history already familiar to us, as is the case with Rembrandt's painting of Peter's denial. It would be possible to read the painting in a different way; Peter is not denying Christ and proclaiming his own innocence, but instead is expressing horror at the false accusations that the people are bringing against Christ. This is consistent with the figure of Christ looking back: he is expressing thanks for this bit of support that he knows will be of no avail in the end. This is, of course, not the way to understand the painting, because it demands that we tell another story, and we already know what the real story is.

Sometimes, however, we don't know what the story is, and consequently we can't know what is going on in the painting. The logical interconnections noted earlier between concepts of action, intention and emotion come into play here. To understand what people are doing, what their intentions and emotional reactions are, often demands a wider acquaintance with the history of their projects and relations. Where that wider history is not known the art historian must try to construct a tale that will make sense of it all. Gombrich discusses a number of fascinating examples involving elaborate inferences and hypothetical constructions that art historians have employed to try to wrest sense out of various recalcitrant paintings.

In order to know what people are up to we must know something of their intentions and projects, and this involves knowing a story about them. The identification of a person, however, does not have the same conceptual ties to action and intention. We can identify people and the representations of them in art without knowing what they are doing.

This conceptual point, as well as the other conceptual point, that what is going on in a painting can be described in more than one way, depending upon the narrative that surrounds it, can be brought home by means of a joke that is really a conceptual joke. A humorous caption has been supplied for Albrecht Dürer's *The Knight, Death, and Devil* that reads 'Dragon? Ain't no Dragons 'round these parts'.[16] There is no problem about the identification of the figures. We know that here is an anonymous knight, Death and a devil, but there are controversies about just what is going on.[17] The joke line imposes a certain perspective on the engraving, although it is a crazy one.

In one reading suggested by this line, Death becomes a curious yokel. This interpretation, however, does not take account either of the hourglass or the figure of the devil. That could be easily remedied by assuming that we are in the presence of a Monty Python skit. The madman of the woods carries an hourglass instead of a pocket-watch, but can't keep count of how many times he has turned it. And as for the devil, you can find anything in Monty Python's woods. The Python people once complained of the commercial editing of their television shows, which interrupted the flow of the comedy. A remark was made to the effect that if you are going to milk humour out of a *non sequitur*, then there is going to have to be something for it not to follow from. Anything can be found in Python country; the devil figure is a visual *non sequitur*.

I have tried to show that our understanding of what people are doing in paintings is based on our understanding of what real people are doing. This is the foundation of much of Gombrich's work in the interpretation of painting. I have also tried to show that not all of the conceptual connections that link the notions of action, intention and emotion in life have application to art, and that it is this lack of application that is responsible for many of the problems about the interpretation of particular works of art.

Notes

1. The first three of these essays are collected in E. H. Gombrich, *Image and Eye*, 'The evidence of images' is in Charles S. Singleton (ed.), *Interpretation: Theory and Practice*, Baltimore, 1969. I am indebted to Richard Woodfield for calling my attention to this last essay.

2. I have deliberately borrowed three of John B. Watson's examples of behaviour that he believes are free from intrusions of the 'mental'. It is more than ironic that he must describe behaviour in terms of the intention with which it is carried out, especially after explicitly ruling out any appeal to 'purpose'. See *Behaviorism*, Chicago 1957, p. 16 (the book was originally published in 1924).

3. 'Ritualized gesture and expression in art', p. 64.

4. Xenophon, *Memorabilia*, 3. 10. 1–5. Gombrich refers to this passage in 'Action and expression in Western art', p. 85.

5. 'Ritualized gesture and expression in art', p. 68.

6. Ludwig Wittgenstein, *Philosophical Investigations*, trans. G. E. M. Anscombe, New York 1953, p. 178.

7. See, for example, David Cockburn, *Other Human Beings*, Houndsmill, Basingstoke 1990, and B. R. Tilghman, *Wittgenstein, Ethics and Aesthetics*, Houndsmill, Basingstoke 1991, chapter 5.

8. *Philosophical Investigations*, §250.

9. See Gombrich's account of Rembrandt's painting in 'Action and expression in Western art', pp. 98–9.

10. 'Action and expression in Western art', p. 78.

11. 'Ritualized gesture and expression in art', p. 70.

12. *Ibid.*, pp. 72–3

13. 'Action and expression in Western art', pp. 98–9.

14. The grammatical, or conceptual, aspect of emotion is argued for in A. I. Melden, 'The conceptual dimensions of emotion', in Theodore Mischel (ed.), *Human Action*, New York 1996, and B. R. Tilghman, 'Emotion and some psychologists', *Southern Journal of Philosophy*, 3 (1965), pp. 63–9.

15. These matters are discussed in 'Moment and movement in art'.

16. Bob Reisner and Hal Kapplow, *Captions Courageous*, New York 1958. Gombrich refers to this book in 'Action and expression in Western art', p. 86.

17. Gombrich discusses varying interpretations of Dürer's engraving in 'The evidence of images', pp. 98–102.

7

Form and its symbolic meaning

Chang Hong Liu and John M. Kennedy

GOMBRICH once mentioned a game using the sounds 'ping' and 'pong'.[1] He presented people with 'ping' and 'pong', along with word pairs such as 'elephant' and 'cat' or 'hot soup' and 'ice cream'. He asked people which of the pair was 'ping' and which was 'pong'. Most people paired a cat with a 'ping' and an elephant with a 'pong'. The hot soup was 'pong' and the ice cream was 'ping'. The striking finding in these games is the high consensus, despite the novelty of the judgements. We believe much can be learned about symbolism by proceeding further with Gombrich's game. Let us play a similar game, but to connect more closely with pictorial art, let us play the game this time with shapes. Imagine we show people a circle and a square and ask them to match the shapes with pairs of words, such as 'soft' and 'hard', 'mother' and 'father'. How would they pair them? We found that 100 per cent of 47 undergraduate subjects paired 'soft' with the circle and 'hard' with the square. Also, 94 per cent paired 'mother' with the circle and 'father' with the square.[2] Gombrich's game is clearly not restricted to 'ping' and 'pong'. We believe it is fundamental to the use of shapes as symbols in artistic representation. Here we explore form symbolism and its relation to other forms of representation.

Our plan in this chapter is as follows: we will examine the consensus shown by subjects playing Gombrich's game with circles and squares. We show the consensus is not an all-or-nothing affair – it has intermediate degrees. We also show it covers a wide range of referents, though not everything can be matched with a shape with significant consensus. We will mention forty pairs of terms tested in various ways. We will suggest that form symbolism is distinct from variables used by Charles Osgood in what he called the 'semantic differential'. Then we will ask whether intermediate levels of consensus are due to mixtures of people, each person having firm views, but different people having different views. We will tackle this issue with reaction-time measures. Finally, we will discuss the intellectual basis of symbolism, comparing it to analogy and metaphor.

Consensus on matching words with shapes

Liu and Kennedy report experiments in which subjects were asked to match twenty pairs of words to a circle and a square.[3] Table 1 illustrates the pairs used in these experiments and their results. The consensus ranges from high (100 per cent) to chance (51 per cent). High consensus pairs were soft–hard (100 per cent), gentle–harsh (97 per cent), happy–sad (94 per cent) and mother–father (94 per cent), all of which were matched with circle and square respectively. A chance level is shown by pairs such as deep-shallow (51 per cent) and playing-resting (56 per cent). The rest of the pairs fell in between these two extremes.

Table 1: *Consensus on matching words with shapes*

Circle	Square	Experiment 1	Circle	Square	Experiment 2
Soft	Hard	100	Gentle	Harsh	97
Happy	Sad	94	Beauty	Ugliness	90
Mother	Father	94	Liquid	Solid	84
Love	Hate	89	Floating	Sinking	74
Good	Evil	89	Whole	Part	74
Bright	Dark	87	Sweet	Bitter	71
Alive	Dead	87	Water	Soil	71
Light	Heavy	85	Art	Science	65
Summer	Winter	81	Coward	Brave	65
Warm	Cold	81	Go	Come	65
Fast	Slow	79	Defense	Attack	61
Weak	Strong	79	Inclusive	Exclusive	61
Spring	Fall	74	Interesting	Boring	61
Cat	Dog	74	Red	Blue	61
Quiet	Loud	62	Young	Old	61
Walking	Standing	62	Philosophy	Religion	58
Even	Odd	57	Low	High	58
Animal	Plant	53	Classic	Modern	58
Far	Near	53	Remembering	Forgetting	58
Deep	Shallow	51	Playing	Resting	55

Note: The values in the table represent the percentage of occasions that the first word of each pair was matched with the circle and the second word of the pair was matched with the square.

Several things are suggested by these results. First, high levels of consensus are most likely reached without following well known, standard conventions linking each pair of words with each pair of shapes. While the interpretation of a symbol's fit with a particular word is not arbitrary, it does not depend on established norms, as the word 'cat' does for its referent. Second, the wide gradient from high consensus to no consensus suggests the relation between a symbol and its referent is a continuum rather than a dichotomy. Third, there is significant consensus for many referents but not all. Fourth, the high-consensus pairs are not synonyms; e.g., mother–father is not synonymous with alive–dead or good–evil. Last, the results show shapes can symbolise complex ideas, such as love and hate.

Explanation by Semantic Differential ruled out

An important approach to connotative meaning was developed by Charles Osgood and his colleagues.[4] Their instrument was the 'Semantic Differential', or SD. The SD used three major factors or axes called 'Evaluation', 'Potency', and 'Activity'. In the SD, concepts are measured on a scale using antonyms, such as good–bad, kind–cruel, wise–foolish, humble-proud, etc. Each pair of adjectives anchors a seven point scale. Subjects are given a concept and these scales, and they are told to rate the concept on the scale. Osgood claims that the results represent much of the connotative aspects of meaning. Osgood, May and Miron, for example, apply the Potency factor to metaphors:

> Potency is connoted by qualities like *strong* and *deep* when Colors are being rated; when Forms are being rated, properties like *hard, angular,* and *sharp* carry the Potency connotation; and when abstract words like LOVE, WAR, ART and PEACE are being rated, we find that qualities like *real, distinct,* and *near* acquire Potency implications. We have here the stuff from which metaphors are made. When we say of an abstract notion like LOVE that is *near* and *real,* or of a color like RED that it is *strong* and *deep,* or of a form that it is *hard* and *sharp,* we are conferring the feeling of power equivalently.[5]

The SD theory has three major defects: first, in Osgood, May and Miron,[6] how and why people come to assign a particular value to a referent on the Potency factor is completely unexplained. The account may even be circular, as if the fact that a form is rated as powerful is explained by the fact that it has a high Potency rating. Hence the theory does not explain symbolism and metaphor, as opposed to documenting their existence. Second, so far as shape symbolism is concerned, it is not difficult to invent counter-examples to any general rule based on SD's factors. For example, it might be contended that 'circles' were generally 'good'. This would explain why a circle fits with SOFT or LIFE. But both positive meanings and negative meanings apply to the words that fit with 'circle'. Not only 'good' and 'happy' can be assigned to 'circle', but also 'weak' and 'dull'. Third, what SD measures is not word meaning, but chiefly the affect, or the 'emotive influence' of words.[7] Words like 'nurse' and 'sincerity' have near-identical scores on Semantic Differential scales, yet they have completely different denotative meanings. As Osgood, May and Miron themselves admit, the Semantic Differential does not by any means exhaust the connotative meaning of concepts.[8] Hence, if a sample is suitably chosen, alternative factors will emerge. As Tversky rightly points out:

> An adequate analysis of connotative meaning should account for man's ability to interpret metaphors without specific prior learning. Since the message conveyed by such expressions is often pointed and specific, they cannot be explained in terms of a few generalized dimensions of connotative meaning, such as evaluation or potency.[9]

The same argument can probably be given for shapes acting as symbols for particular referents.

Why consensus has levels

We suggest that levels of consensus reflect the aptness or strength of the symbolic relation between the shapes and their referents. A high consensus indicates a strong symbolic relation. But there is another possibility; the intermediate levels of consensus could be due to mixtures of people, each group of people with firm views, but each group having different views from the others. In this case, the symbol-referent strength of all the pairings in our experiments could be the same for each subject, but the consensus would be low. However, this view may be tested using reaction-time measures. If there is no difference in the strength of the symbolic relation at different levels of consensus, the reaction times for high-consensus and low-consensus pairs should be equal. To test this, we gave a new group of subjects the same shape and word-pair task as before, but asked the new group to make their match as fast as they could. Their reaction times to each pair were recorded. Our hypothesis was that if the symbolic relation in a low-consensus pair is unsure, decisions should be difficult, and the reaction time to judge the relation between the items should be especially long. Thus, on average, high-consensus words should result in shorter reaction times than low-consensus pairs.

The results show that reaction times were inversely correlated with levels of consensus ($r = -0.65$, $p < 0.001$). That is, the higher the consensus, the less the reaction time required. This confirms our hypothesis that levels of consensus reflect the aptness of the symbolic relation.

Probing the intellectual basis of form symbolism

Since the word-pairs and the shapes were novel, we suggest that the matching judgements are probably reached by a 'constructive process', rather than by a retrieval process relying solely on pre-set stored information. Retrieving stored information is a characteristic of many categorical tasks. For example, answering the question whether a robin is a bird depends on retrieval of a known or 'stored' fact – that a robin is indeed a bird. In the symbol-matching task, however, the answer is not pre-stored and then retrieved, but rather created on the spot, we suggest. The mechanisms of symbolism are a kind of problem-solving rather than an automatic spreading of activation between related concepts.[10] The problem to be solved is to decide whether a con-nection can be established between a symbol and a meaning, where the connection is often not already established and available in memory. But what is the nature or intellectual basis of this match, and the related con-structive process?

Understanding the intellectual basis of form symbolism is in part a question of finding out how form symbolism relates to other kinds of non-literal meanings such as metaphor and analogy, to which we now turn.

Symbols and metaphors have several important properties in common. A circle may be a good symbol for INFINITY for example. But of course, it is not necessarily infinite. Similarly, we may say 'Juliet is the sun', but she is not actually. As a result, both symbols and metaphors deal with things standing in for things they are not. Also, both are asymmetric. They cannot be reversed without their meaning changing. Juliet may be the sun, but the sun is not Juliet. 'Surgeons are butchers' is no compliment to surgeons, but 'butchers are surgeons' praises butchers. Similarly, a circle is a symbol of a mother, but a mother is not a symbol of a circle. Similarities like these seem to have led many authors either explicitly or implicitly to take symbolism to be a form of metaphor.[11] Gombrich uses the term 'visual metaphor' for colour symbolism: 'A simple example of what I shall call a visual metaphor is the use of the colour red in certain cultural contexts. Red, being the colour of flames and of blood, offers itself as a metaphor for anything that is strident or violent.'[12] If colours are visual metaphors, shapes might also be called 'visual metaphors' for referents such as love or softness. Hausman[13] explicitly states that what Langer[14] calls 'symbols' in the arts are equivalent to what he calls 'metaphors' in the arts. Indurkhya calls religious and artistic symbolism 'non-linguistic metaphors'.[15] These strong claims, which equate symbols with metaphors, may be called the 'metaphor identity view'. An important implication of the identity view is that metaphor forms the basis for symbols, and hence theory of metaphors can invariably apply to our understanding of symbols.

Here we will vex the 'metaphor identity' view with the results from some demonstrations. We put the question this way: When subjects agree that certain meanings fit well with a pair of shapes, does it follow that the shapes can be used in 'metaphors' with those meanings? In criticising the 'metaphor identity view', we will examine an alternative view, in which metaphors and symbols serve different functions. We argue that metaphors involve class-inclusion. For example, in 'surgeons are butchers', surgeons are said to belong to the class of butchers. In contrast, symbols involve representation or reference, like a sign or label. A symbol is used to stand for something; a religious or national symbol stands for the religion or the country. In this connection, a circle is a more appropriate symbol for a mother than a square. There is no implication that a circle is an example of 'mother', and 'mother' is not a member of the class of circles. Rather, the function of a symbol is to highlight or draw attention to some aspects of the referent.

Far from being metaphors, symbols may be closely related to analogies, although they also differ in many ways, as we will discuss below. Gentner and Jeziorski define an analogy in Aristotelian fashion as 'a mapping of knowledge from one domain (the base) into another (the target) such that a system of relations that holds among the base objects also holds among the target objects'.[16] A symbol such as a circle may be taken to be a member of a set of forms, such as the geometrical forms circle, square, triangle, etc. Similarly a symbol's referent may be taken to be a member of a set. A mother may be understood to be a member of the set mother, father, daughter, son, aunt, uncle, etc. One domain may be mapped on to the other. Perhaps any time a symbol is used, a mapping between a set of symbols and a set of referents is at work. Thus analogy and symbol may be related fairly closely.

To test whether metaphors, analogies and symbols could be treated in a same way, let us evaluate some statements in the form of metaphors, analogies and symbols. A typical metaphor format is 'A is B', as in the example 'the surgeon is a butcher'. The relation between a shape and a word can be translated into a statement following this format, using circles and squares as the vehicles, for example, 'softness is a circle'. The typical analogy format is 'A is to B as C is to D.' A and B can be assigned to a pair of words and C and D to the two shapes, a 'circle' and a 'square'. An example is 'softness is to hardness as a circle is to a square'. In constructing statements about shapes as symbols, we may use the form 'A is a symbol for B', where A is either a 'circle' or a 'square', and the B is a word. An example is 'a circle is a symbol for softness'. Other examples are shown in Table 2, columns 1, 2 and 3, respectively.

Table 2: *Forms used in metaphors, analogies and symbols*

Metaphors	Analogies	Symbols
A mother is a circle.	Mother is to father as a circle is to a square.	Circle is a symbol for mother.
Summer is a circle.	Summer is to winter as a circle is to a square.	Circle is a symbol for summer.
Softness is a circle.	Softness is to hardness as a circle is to a square.	Circle is a symbol for softness.

The question is, which uses of the shapes seem apt, which are forced and which lack any kind of appropriateness? If metaphors, analogies and symbols are comprehended in a similar way, all of these sentences should be equally apt. We suggest the metaphor statements appear particularly opaque. We can agree that a circle is an apt symbol for 'mother', and that a mother and a father are related as a circle is to a square, but 'a mother is a circle' is obscure. The same holds true for SOFTNESS or SUMMER. An apt symbol may very often not be an apt metaphor. On the other hand, an apt symbol may be related to an apt analogy in which the possible implicit comparison involved in the symbol is made explicit. If our impressions are correct, symbolism is probably distinct from metaphor, and closer to analogy.

What could account for differences in the ways in which forms can be involved in metaphoric, analogical and symbolic relations with their referents? What are the key factors here?

Fundamentally, metaphor is a kind of class-inclusion statement contending that 'an A is a B'. 'All surgeons belong in the class of butchers' is implied by 'surgeons are butchers'. Surgeons are examples of butchers.[17] Yet symbols are not examples of their referents. A mother is not an example of circle. This could explain why 'mother is a real circle' fails, surely. This is a principled reason for distinguishing symbols from metaphors, even if both symbol and metaphor share some features at times.

If a symbolic relation is not a class–inclusion relation, what is it, then? A symbolic relation is, in part, a referential relation, like a sign. A cat in the world is represented by the sign 'cat'. The sign 'cat' is in no way a subclass or a supercategory of a cat. Likewise, a symbol is not a subclass of its referent, or a superordinate category. The difference between the form symbols used here and a sign is that the referential relation between these symbols and their referents is not purely arbitrary, whereas the relation between a sign and its referent is. A symbol that is not a convention must share a key feature with its referent. That is, the symbol has a property that allows the symbol to mean that the referent is courageous or comforting or conflicted, for example. To put this abstractly, if X symbolises Y, X implies Y has properties, and X has related properties.

Now let us discuss the relationship between analogies and symbols. Since the symbol has properties and implies its referent has appropriate properties, it is likely that two related symbols can convey the relationship between two referents, i.e. function as an analogy. However, symbolism is not identical with analogy. A crucial distinction is that in typical analogies taking the form A:B :: C:D, there are often only arbitrary connections between A and C, and B and D. For example, in 'an electron is to a nucleus as the earth is to the sun', there is no apparent connection between 'electron' and 'the earth', and 'nucleus' and 'the sun', in the absence of the analogy. 'The earth is an electron' is obscure. Only when the two sets of relations in the sentence are considered do the comparisons between 'electron' and 'the earth', and 'nucleus' and 'the sun' become meaningful. In contrast, in 'a mother is to a father as a circle is to a square', we suggest we see connections between 'mother' and 'circle', and 'father' and 'square' without solely relying on relating the two sets in the sentence.

In addition, when analogy is used, the ideas in the target domain are often understood via the source domain. For example, the relation between an electron and a nucleus is often understood through the relation between the sun and the earth. When an analogy is explained explicitly and succinctly, it is usually satisfactory, e.g. the electron is taken to be a small body circling a larger one, via the solar-system analogy. The analogy functions 'as an explanation', allowing the observer to appreciate new properties of the target. In contrast, in the analogy and symbol examples in Table 2, we are unlikely to arrive at a way to understand MOTHER via a circle. Quite the reverse; we judge that MOTHER can be symbolised by a circle because we already know a set of relevant features of both MOTHER and circle. In analogy, properties of the vehicle are attributed to the referent when an analogy functions as an explanation. However, form symbolism does not seem to function as a tool for understanding one domain via the other in the same fashion. Rather, the symbol is used to bring attention to some of the properties we already know are present in the target. The symbol functions to emphasise or bring forward features and produce eloquent – or as Saussure put it, 'natural' – labels for ideas they stand for.[18]

There is yet another respect in which symbols are unlike analogies. Curiously, a symbol's use is often difficult to justify when it is explained openly. We have noted that people may explain a circle is soft, symbolically, because 'it is round and smooth'. But many round, smooth objects are not soft, as Kennedy points out (e.g. stones in a stream can be worn round and smooth).[19] In contrast, once an analogy's basis is made explicit, it is justified, e.g. both electrons and the earth orbit a central, powerful body.

Last, we would like to consider how to position other forms of representation in our general picture of these non-literal devices. We think that metaphor, analogy, and form symbolism may become more understandable if they are considered along with synaesthesia and expression.

The metaphor-identity theory of symbolism argued that metaphor and symbolism are equivalent. Likewise, other theories also view synaesthesia and expression as metaphors. Marks speaks of a 'metaphorical match' across sensory domains and of 'synaesthetic metaphor'.[20] Gardner gives as the reason why he uses the term 'metaphor' to describe synaesthetic mapping: 'the ability to utilise metaphors presupposes the capacity to perceive relations among disparate phenomena. For a loud noise to be compared to a bright colour, the common "expansive" property of both entities must be recognized.' Also, 'A task requiring perception of a common property between diverse elements and the ability to capture this relation in a verbal formula thus models central aspects of the production of a metaphor.'[21] Goodman grants expressive elements in paintings the status of metaphors and regards them as 'metaphorical exemplifications', since a painting cannot be literally happy or sad.[22] These authors often attend to the common features of metaphor, symbolism, analogy and synaesthesia, such as their non–literalness. Indeed, they may all be subsets of a general problem. But are they the same? We shall argue that they are not. In order to make the relations between them clear, we would like to draw attention to some unique features that may reside in one but not in others, and partial overlap between some of them.

Synaesthesia seems to play an important role in form symbolism. A circle is regarded as 'soft' and 'warm', and the square is regarded as 'hard' and 'cold', as the consensus showed. However, synaesthesia should not be confused with form symbolism or metaphor. In synaesthesia, there is generally a symmetrical relationship between the senses under comparison. For example, when a high tone is taken as analogous to a bright colour, usually its reverse is also true: a bright colour is analogous to a high tone. Hence, the two senses under comparison are symmetrical. In contrast, for both metaphor and symbolism, asymmetry is crucial: the meaning of 'lawyers are sharks' is lost in 'sharks are lawyers'. Similarly, a circle may symbolise mother but mother does not symbolise a circle. The same holds true for conventional symbols. Thus bread and wine may represent the flesh and blood of God, though the flesh and blood do not represent bread and wine. Goodman regards asymmetry as a general characteristic of representation, including depiction: 'A painting may represent the Duke of Wellington; the Duke doesn't represent the painting.'[23]

Synaesthesia can be used in symbolism. A circle could readily represent softness in which the synaesthetic mapping between the roundness of the circle and softness is used. But notice that in symbolism we treat the circle, not just its attribute, such as roundness, as the representation of softness. So we may say 'a circle represents softness', not just 'roundness represents softness'. The equivalence of roundness and softness involves synaesthesia. Representing softness with a circle involves symbolism that applies synaesthesia.

In some respects synaesthesia resembles form symbolism but not metaphor. Unlike metaphor, but like symbolism, a synaesthetic relation is not a class-inclusion relation. One sense may evoke the other, without being a subclass of the other. For example, the relation between a bright hue and a high pitch is not a class-inclusion relation. Hence, neither 'a bright colour is a high tone' nor 'a high tone is a bright colour' make much sense as metaphors. The two senses are not at different category levels. At best, the two sentences are elliptical versions of 'a high tone is related to bright colour'.

Physiognomy and expression are often used to refer to the same phenomena in discussions of synaesthesia. They have a narrow and a broad usage. In their narrow usage, both terms refer literally to facial (and sometimes also bodily) expressions. In their broad usage, however, both terms refer to expressive qualities in both animate and inanimate things.[24] The expressive qualities are often synaesthetic, e.g. 'he looks hard' or 'he has a hard face'. The broad usage of the terms physiognomy and expression is often not literal. A sunset could be deeply moving and appear 'joyous', but the scene itself is not joyous, since it does not have emotional states, and so the description is metaphoric, notes Goodman.[25]

Much as form symbolism may use synaesthesia, it may also use physiognomic perception. For example, some people may perceive a cheerful or a happy expression in a circle, and a stern one in a square. In turn, the expression may cause us to judge that happiness can be symbolised by the circle. It is noteworthy here that what is relevant is decided at times by a two-step relationship. A circle may act in a physiognomic manner, and the physiognomy may act as the basis for symbolism. The result is that there are intricate relationships between form symbolism and related areas. Synaesthesia and expression may be nested in form symbolism and at same time be distinct from it.

Table 3: *Kinds of relations between forms and referents*

	Symbolism	Analogy	Metaphor	Synaesthesia	Expression
Non-literalness	+	+	+	+	±
Asymmetry	+	+	+	−	+
Class–inclusion	−		+	−	
Relational mapping	+	+			
'Natural'	+	−	−	+	+
Labelling	+	−	−	−	−

Table 3 gives a summary of our discussion of the features that are shared by different devices. The horizontal heading is a list of devices discussed in this chapter. The vertical heading is a list of features. A '+' sign indicates the presence of a feature. A '−' sign indicates the absence of a feature. A '±' sign indicates that the feature may or may not be present, depending on the particular example of a device. As the table shows, 'non-literalness' is shared by all the devices except expression, where it depends on the medium being considered (e.g. a person or painting). 'Asymmetry' is shared by all the devices except synaesthesia. Some questions, such as whether analogy can be considered as class-inclusion, have not been debated in this chapter and are left blank.

In this chapter, we have mainly focused on relationships between some non-literal devices, following up Gombrich's provocative comments on pairing referents with 'ping' and 'pong'. Our demonstrations show that an apt symbolic relation could be a poor metaphorical relation. Hence metaphoric and symbolic comprehension are not equivalent. In contrast, symbol comprehension is more like analogy comprehension, though the two are distinct, since individual symbols may often operate quite well, but analogies require pairs of terms. The symbolic relation is asymmetric, in that the symbol represents the referent, and draws attention to features of the referent, but the referent does not represent the symbol. The symbol makes salient some of the many features of the referent with which it is paired.

Notes

1. *Art and Illusion*, p. 314.
2. C. H. Liu and J. M. Kennedy, 'Symbolic forms and cognition', *Psyke & Logos*, 14 (1993), pp. 441–56..
3. C. H. Liu and J. M. Kennedy, 'Symbolic forms can be mnemonics for recall', *Psychonomic Bulletin & Review*, 1 (1994), pp. 494–8.
4. C. E. Osgood, J. G. Suci and P. H. Tennenbaum, *The Measurement of Meaning*, Urbana 1957.
5. C. E. Osgood, W. H. May and M. S. Miron, *Cross-cultural universals of affective meaning*, Urbana, Illinois 1975, p. 399.
6. *Ibid.*
7. V. Weinreich, 'Travels through semantic space', *Word*, 14 (1959), pp. 346–66.
8. *Cross-cultural universals.*
9. A. Tversky, 'Features of similarity', *Psychological Review*, 84 (1977), p. 349.
10. D. Sperber, *Rethinking Symbolism*, Cambridge 1977 and D. Sperber, 'Is symbolic thought prerational?' in M. L. Foster and S. H. Brandes (eds), *Symbol as Sense: New Approaches to the Analysis of Meaning*, New York 1980.
11. E.g. E. H. Gombrich, in *Meditations*; 'The use of art for the study of symbols', in J. Hogg (ed.), *Psychology and the Visual Arts*, Harmondsworth 1969; 'Icones symbolicae', in *Symbolic Images*; C. R. Hausman, *Metaphor and Art: Interactionism and Reference in the Verbal and Nonverbal Arts*, Cambridge 1989; B. Indurhkya, *Metaphor and Cognition*, Cambridge, Mass. 1992; M. Johnson, *The body in the mind: The bodily basis of meaning, imagination and reason*, Chicago 1987.
12. 'Visual metaphors of value in art', in *Meditations*, p. 13.
13. Hausman, *Metaphor and Art.*
14. S. K. Langer, *Philosophy in a New Key: A Study in the Symbolism of Reason, Rite, and Art*, Cambridge, Mass. 1942.

15. Indurhkya, *Metaphor and Cognition*.

16. D. Gentner and M. Jeziorski, 'The shift from metaphor to analogy in Western science', in A. Ortony (ed.), *Metaphor and Thought*, Cambridge 1993, p. 449.

17. For class-inclusion theories on metaphor comprehension see S. Glucksberg and B. Keysar, 'Understanding metaphorical comparisons', *Psychological Review*, 97 (1990), pp. 3–18; J. M. Kennedy, 'Metaphor: its intellectual basis', *Metaphor and Symbolic Activity*, 5 (1990), pp. 115–23; *Drawing and the Blind: Pictures to Touch*, New Haven 1993; J. M. Kennedy, C. D. Green and J. Vervaeke, 'Metaphoric thought and devices in pictures', *Metaphor and Symbolic Activity*, 8 (1993), pp. 243–55.

18. F. de Saussure, *Course in general linguistics*, New York 1966.

19. *Drawing and the Blind*.

20. L. E. Marks, *The Unity of the Senses*, New York 1978 and 'Synesthetic perception and poetic metaphor', *Journal of Experimental Psychology*, 8 (1982), pp. 15–23.

21. H. Gardner, 'Metaphors and modalities: how children project polar adjectives onto diverse domains', *Child Development*, 45 (1974), p. 85. See also R. Wagner, E. Winner, D. Cicchetti and H. Gardner, 'Metaphorical mapping in human infants', *Child Development*, 52 (1981), pp. 728–31.

22. N. Goodman, *Languages of Art*, Indianapolis 1968.

23. *Ibid.*, p. 4.

24. E. H. Gombrich, 'On physiognomic perception', in *Meditations*; M. S. Lindauer, 'Physiognomy and art: approaches from above, below, and sideways', *Visual Arts Research*, 10 (1984), pp. 52–65; H. Werner, *Comparative Psychology of Mental Development*, Chicago 1948; H. Werner and E. Kaplan, *Symbol Formation: An Organismic-Developmental Approach to Language and the Expression of Thought*, New York 1963.

25. *Languages of Art*.

Response from E. H. Gombrich:

3 March 1995

Dear Professor Kennedy,
Dear Mr Chang Hong Liu,

I must ask you to forgive me for this long delay in thanking you for your interesting paper on 'Form and its symbolic meaning' which Richard Wood-field passed on to me. I read it with pleasure and amusement, but as you will see, you did not entirely convince me in the distinction you propose between symbol and metaphor. In fact I ventured to make a 'thought experiment' of my own to test your experiment about the responses to round or square forms.

My purpose was to demonstrate that these forms or their descriptions can operate very easily as metaphors in certain linguistic contexts. So here we go:

> When my father, hard and *square*
> Met me, with a frosty stare,
> What a comfort I then found
> In my mother, warm and *round*.

My little experiment consists in nothing but in permutations of the dramatis personae. You can easily substitute 'master' for 'father', and 'sweetheart' for 'mother', or any other male and female roles, but you cannot, I contend, switch the sexes or genders round. The verse would become odd indeed. Which goes to show, I have come to think, that the old insight is confirmed that women have 'curves' and men have not (or few). Our awareness of this basic biological distinction is surely deep-rooted, and hence our ready response to your questions, but in my view they could also extend to metaphors, as I have tried to show above.

I hope that I have not misunderstood you and that you find my observations not totally irrelevant. In any case, you see, they made me return to some of my pet subjects, and contributed to my amusement.

I hope you forgive this brief comment, I am well aware of the fact that more might be said, but I really am compelled to ration my time.

With all good wishes and thanks
Yours gratefully and respectfully

Ernst Gombrich

8

Four theories of artistic expression[*]

E. H. Gombrich

WHEN we speak of 'expression' in ordinary life, we mostly think of the visible or audible signs of emotion in man and also in animals, such as the symptoms of joy or of rage, the howl of pain, or, speaking of human beings, the melancholy sigh or the radiant smile. There is no strict dividing line between these outlets of emotion in life and in the various arts. A child may jump with joy or a group of adults may perform a joyful dance during a ritual, just as a sad occasion like a funeral may be accompanied by mournful wailing and gestures of grief. No wonder, therefore, that the relation between the expression of emotions in life and art has attracted the attention of philosophers and critics ever since the arts became the subject of reflection, which happened, in the Western world, in classical antiquity at the time of the ancient Greeks.

But as soon as we study and analyse the ideas of critics and philosophers about the role of expression in art, we discover that underneath a similarity of words, we often find a difference in meaning. It is to this difference that I should like to draw your attention; for it seems to me that in the history of Western aesthetics, we can distinguish three distinct theories which I should like to characterise briefly before I shall venture to present my own interpretation which will be the fourth; I hope you will forgive me if I shall formulate these theories in a somewhat schematic form, almost like a sequence of diagrams. I am well aware of the fact that the history of ideas is never so clear-cut and tidy; the various theories I have singled out are rarely formulated in isolation; on the contrary, they are often blended in various ways, but even these mixtures may be more easily understood if we first look at the abstract possibilities in isolation.

These abstract possibilities have long been the concern of students of language and other systems of communication; and looking at art from the

---

[*] 'Four theories of artistic expression' was originally published in the *Architectural Association Quarterly*, 12 (1980); it was based on a lecture given in Japan in April 1980.

aspect of communications, it is best to take the result of their analysis as a starting-point. There are three functions which can be distinguished in any such context. I have mentioned the first of them already: I mean the function of the symptom which can be interpreted as an indication of an inner state, almost like a pointer-reading on an instrument panel. We can say that frowning is such a symptom of anger, blushing a symptom of embarrassment. This function, as I also said, is common to men and animals; the dog wagging its tail to welcome its master displays such a symptom.

The second function is also common to animals and men; I am referring to the possibility of arousing emotions through visible or audible signs. Animals may utter a call which functions like a signal; the hen may thus call the chickens to their food or warn them of impending danger. Such signals may be rooted in symptoms, but they need not. They can arouse reactions by themselves, as do the warning colours displayed by certain animals.

Finally, signs can be used to represent or depict emotional states, as when a writer describes a scene and makes us understand the feelings of his hero. This possibility of pure description is a function which only human language and other human systems of communication have acquired; I shall speak of them as the symbolic function. Symptom, Signal and Symbol; these are three convenient terms which I propose to use to distinguish the three main theories of artistic expression which have succeeded each other in the history of European thought. But they did not occur in that order.

I believe in fact that what I have called the signal function is the one which plays the most significant part in the earliest discussions of art, and on reflection you may find this quite natural.

The discovery that human emotions can be influenced by external agents must go back very far in history. Any mother who has sung her baby to sleep discovered for herself the power of art over the inner states of the child. The lullaby which the mother sings is not, you will realise, a symptom of her own feelings, it is not she who wants to go to sleep, but she sends the child the signal that it should sleep and this signal tends to work; it something like a spell, a magic formula which compels a response. It cannot have remained hidden from early civilisation either, that this power over the emotions is not confined to words or tones. There are substances which influence feelings: drink, as we are told in innumerable poems throughout the world, can make us cheerful; it can also make us melancholy. Many religious rituals have also taken recourse to drugs together with incantations to induce the desired emotional states. I believe it is this kind of action on the emotions which was the first to be discovered and discussed in the philosophy of art; I should like to call it the magico-medical theory, to allude to the link with magic spells and with drugs. The greatest and most influential exponent of this theory in ancient Greece is Plato, whose dialogues, written in the fourth century BC, remained of such incalculable importance for the history of Western thought. The most explicit formulation of this theory occurs in Plato's discussion of music and its relation to the emotions. In ancient Greece, music played a great part in education, and in his dialogue *The Republic*, Plato is very anxious to select only that kind of music for his ideal state which should have the right effect on the emotions. It is well known that Plato condemned some instruments and some kind of music for the bad influence they had on the soul. He wanted all music which exhibited sensuality or which was found too relaxing banned from the curriculum and indeed from the state, and only to permit invigorating modes, something like military music. Of course, he was not the last teacher to express these misgivings, which you can hear echoed today when modern dance music is being discussed; nor would I say that he may not have been right that music can indeed act like a drug on the human mind. Music is not the only one of the arts to which the ancient world attributed such magic power over the emotions. The art which stood in the centre of interest in classical antiquity was the art of oratory, of eloquence; for anyone who wanted to succeed in politics or in the law had to master the skill of playing on the emotions of his audience. Many profound remarks about these effects are to be found in the Greek and Latin writers on rhetoric, and often the impact of great speeches is likened to that of music. But perhaps the most famous application of what I call the magico-medical theory of artistic expression is to be found in the *Poetics* of Aristotle, though it is not always interpreted in that way. I am referring to his description of the effects of the drama, which he describes as *katharsis*. The term is, in fact, a medical one, meaning purgation; but what is to be purged, according to Aristotle, are the passions. Watching a tragedy should change our state of emotion in a way reminiscent both of a religious ritual and a medical treatment. We emerge cleansed from this profound experience of fear and of pity. I have spoken of music, of oratory and of the drama in connection with the theory of artistic expression. What about the art which interests me most: paintings and sculpture?

Here, we know, the theory of art as imitation largely holds sway, but not entirely. For the Greeks and the Romans certainly considered the effects which images had. The most naive form which this interest takes is to be found in the anecdotes telling of the effects paintings had on animals: birds came to peck at the grapes Zeuxis painted, horses neighed when they saw a horse painted by Apelles. We need not take these anecdotes too seriously, but they still betray a link with the performance of magic, the compelling power of the artist. Just as the mythical singer, Orpheus, in Greek legend, attracted all the animals of the wilderness by the sound of his lyre, so the great painter could cast a spell on humans and non-humans alike. There is no civilisation or tradition, I believe, in which this belief is not manifest in the use of images for religious or superstitious purposes; in my recent book on decoration, I drew attention once more to this universal function of threatening masks, such as the Chinese t'ao-t'ieh, to turn away evil influences. It is from this ancient tradition that there developed the great tradition of the Temple Guardians fashioned by Chinese and Japanese sculptors to protect the sacred shrine. Their fierce and awe-inspiring appearance is intended to strike terror into the heart of unseen powers. It is a belief which shades over into the attitude of awe accorded to certain images because of the power they were said to have over the human heart. It was said of the statue of the Goddess of Love by the Greek sculptor, Praxiteles, that it aroused desire in everyone who saw it, just as the statue of Zeus by Phidias filled the beholder with religious awe.

The point I should like to stress in this first theory of the power of art over human emotions, is mainly that it is a theory of art, not of artists. Just as I said of the mother who sings her child to sleep that she need not feel sleepy, so, in this theory, it is not necessary for the artist who casts his spell on the audience to feel the same emotion himself. He can, if he does it may even help him to achieve more power, but what matters is the power of his creation, not his personal feeling.

I think I have said enough to illustrate this first of my four theories of artistic expression, which I called the magico-medical one, for its affinity with the effects of spells and of drugs. It is a theory which certainly has its parallels also in the great traditions of India, China and Japan. I am thinking, for instance, of the creation of moods by the flute-player in a Nō play, or by the great gardens of Kyoto.

I would not say that this theory was ever consciously abandoned. When we study the writings of critics and artists in the Italian Renaissance, we find that they often quote the admired ancient authors and wanted to follow them faithfully. And yet, in reading these later discussions of music, of painting or of poetry, in the sixteenth, seventeenth and early eighteenth centuries, you may find that the emphasis has changed. What is now the centre of interest is the capacity of all the arts to depict or portray the emotions; in other words, what I have listed as its symbolic function, though in this context of artistic expression it may be best described as the dramatic function. The artist is taught to study the expression of the emotions, in order to imitate it convincingly on the stage, in his painting or music. We find this emphasis very clearly in the writings of one of the greatest painters of the Italian Renaissance, in those of Leonardo da Vinci. In one of the passages of his Treatise on Painting, Leonardo remarks that the good painter has to depict two things, man and his mind.[1] The first, he says, is easy, the second is difficult, because the mind can only be represented by outward signs such as gestures and movements. He asks the beginning painter to study these movements constantly in real life, and to note them down in his sketchbooks. He goes so far as to suggest that the artist should pay special attention to the gestures of the deaf-mute, who have to communicate with movements alone; and if you remember his famous *Last Supper*, you can realise what he meant, for there we see the excitement and questioning of the disciples of Jesus and also His gesture of resignation.[2] Not that this emphasis on the need for the dramatic and accurate representation of the expressions of emotion made Leonardo forget their effect on the beholder. He hoped that the beholder of the painting will be caught up in the relevant emotion, or, to quote his actual words,

> If the narrative painting represents terror, fear, flight, sorrow, weeping and lamentation, or pleasure, joy, laughter or similar conditions, the minds of those who view it ought to make their limbs move so that they seem to find themselves in the same situation which the figures in the painting represent.[3]

Actually, Leonardo elsewhere slightly qualifies this demand. He says in his comparison of the arts that a picture of a laughing man may make you laugh, and, interestingly, a picture of a yawning man may also be contagious, and make you yawn; but sober scientist as he was, he did not think that any painting could make you weep, for, as he says, tears are too great a disturbance to be caused by a painting.[4] Be that as it may, the study of symptoms of emotion in the movements of the body and the muscles of the face became an important part of the artist's training, for it was only in this way that he could convincingly represent the stories from the Bible, the life of Christ or the loves of the ancient gods. And like the painter, the poet had to study the human heart, and depict in his works the reaction of the heroes to what was usually described as the 'passions of the mind', that is grief, anger, joy or despair.

Telling a story in an epic poem or in prose, he had to dwell on the effects of love and on the effects of courage or despair on the people in his story; and the more his description conformed to our own experience, the more his narrative would move us. The main place for this depiction of the passions, of course, was the theatre, the stage; there is no more famous discussion of its role than the passage in Shakespeare's *Hamlet* when the prince converses with actors whom he wants to perform a particular scene, and says, in words which were a commonplace at the time, that the purpose of playing is 'to hold the mirror up to nature' (Act 3, Scene 2). Once more, Shakespeare makes it abundantly clear that in learning to depict human passion, the actor need not, and perhaps cannot, express his own feeling. He makes Hamlet comment on the performance of an actor who has been playing a scene from a drama, where Aeneas tells the Queen of Carthage how the King of the Trojans was killed in front of his wife Hecuba. In telling this tale of horror, the actor himself turns pale and tears fill his eyes, and Hamlet reflects on this feat of the imagination:

> Is it not monstrous that this player here,
> But in a fiction, in a dream of passion,
> Could force his soul so to his own conceit
> That from her working all his visage wann'd;
> Tears in his eyes, distraction in's aspect,
> A broken voice, and his whole function suiting
> With forms to his conceit? and all for nothing:
> For Hecuba:
> What's Hecuba to him, or he to Hecuba,
> That he should weep for her?
>
> (*Hamlet*, Act 3, Scene 2)

Once more we are reminded that art is artifice, it is the skill of depicting the symptoms of grief. We do not blame an actor if he feels no grief for Hecuba, provided only that he can represent that grief.

And as with drama, so with music. The two, in fact, are closely allied in the development of artistic expression in Europe; for it was in the musical drama, in opera, that music was first given the explicit task of representing human passions.

Opera-goers sometimes express regret and bewilderment because so many librettos of the best operas are rather irrational and crude. But this criticism slightly misses the point. The writer of the libretto saw it as his main task to give the composer of the opera, and of course the singers, as many opportunities as possible to express the extremes of emotion, love, fear, hope, revenge, courage and despair; there must be scope for martial music and for a sad lament by the heroine; there must be a villain pouring out his fury, and a hero singing about his steadfastness. It matters little how these various situations are justified by the plot, if only they come about and make us admire the composer's mastery in depicting these contrasting feelings which the singers must learn to render. I dare say there is no great difference here between the scope of opera in the West and that of various forms of drama in the East. We go to see the human heart bared, and if the expression of the emotions convinces us, we gladly forgive the unconvincing plot.

I mentioned that, by and large, this dramatic conception of artistic expression held sway in art and criticism till the second half of the eighteenth century. At that time, another important shift occurred in the theory of artistic expression, which can be connected with the Romantic movement. Briefly, what this movement stressed was the need for sincerity, for genuine emotion. And so the emphasis was laid not on expression as a signal or as a symbol, but on expression as a symptom of emotions; for the first time, the critics wanted to know what the artist himself felt; they wanted him to bare his own heart.

One of the best books on the history of criticism deals with this momentous change; I am referring to the book by M. H. Abrams, *The Mirror and the Lamp*, subtitled *Romantic Theory and the Critical Tradition*, which was first published in 1953, but has not lost in importance. The 'mirror' of the title is precisely the mirror of which Hamlet speaks, when he calls it the purpose of the dramatist or actor to hold up a mirror to nature, to reflect or represent the various passions of man. His mission is to observe, record and depict, and the clearer the mirror, the better it will perform this task for him. The lamp is different: it does not reflect, it illuminates the world, and the brighter it burns, the more it reveals. In the new theory of the Romantic movement, the artist is like a lamp; he sends the rays of his feelings into the world where they are received by the public who will turn towards this source of light. His light is his art, whether poetry, painting or music; and when we now speak of artistic expression, we mostly mean the expression of the artist which is embodied in the work of art.

This Romantic theory has been so universally accepted in the Western world by countless artists and critics, that it takes a moment to realise how new and revolutionary it was. Let me repeat, therefore, that neither in the ancient world, nor in the Renaissance, was the artist himself the centre of interest. It was his work which was judged: in antiquity, for the power it exercised over the emotions; in the later theory, for the fidelity with which it portrayed the emotions. Now this was no longer enough. The emotion found in a poem was suspect, if not worthless, if it was not thought to be the artist's own emotion at the time when he wrote the poem. Clearly, this theory applied most easily to lyrical poetry in which the artist pours out his feeling of love or his admiration for the beauty of nature; indeed, the English poet Wordsworth wrote in 1800 that poetry is the 'spontaneous overflow of powerful feelings', and almost thirty years before, one of the characters in a play by Goethe had already said that what makes the poet is 'a full heart, over-full with one emotion'.[5] What distinguishes the poet or, quite generally, the artist from other human beings, therefore, is not his skill, his mastery, but the intensity of his feeling; and it is this intensity alone which really matters. A work of art produced without feeling, in cold blood, is really a fake; it is dishonest and immoral, for the public is deceived if a poet writes of a love he did not really feel in his heart.

Consequently, the circumstances under which a poem was composed suddenly began to matter to the critic and the public. In earlier times, this was much less the case. Nobody would have been upset to learn that an ode mourning the death of a person was written on commission, and paid for by the man's relations. To the Romantic theory, which we have inherited, this possibility was somehow disturbing. The poet or the artist should only express his own feelings spontaneously and unprompted by anybody or anything except the urge to express himself, to unburden his heart. Only then, the theory implies, would the feelings reach the reader or listener who will come to experience the identical emotions. The German poet, Friedrich von Schiller, explicitly propounded his view in a letter to Goethe: 'I call a poet anyone who is able to put his state of feeling into an object so that this object compels me to pass into the same state of feeling.'[6]

This is the theory of artistic expression as a communication of emotions: the transmission of feelings from man to man. As you know, the new doctrine of communication was applied not only to the expression of feelings in poetry, but to all the arts. The great English landscape painter, John Constable, put it succinctly when he said, 'Painting is for me just another word for feeling',[7] and Delacroix, the champion of the Romantic conception in painting, wrote that 'painting is nothing but a bridge set up between the mind of the artist and that of the beholder; cold accuracy', he continues, 'is not art'. For what matters is, as he had written earlier, that every painter should express his soul. 'If you cultivate your soul it will find a means to express itself.'[8] And in the next generation, Zola wrote, 'what I look for in a painting is a man, and not a painting'.[9]

I need hardly say that the art which lent itself best to this interpretation of expression is music. The moving words which Beethoven wrote on the score of his great *Missa Solemnis* testify to his artistic faith: 'Vom Herzen, moege es wieder zu Herzengehen' (From the heart, may it also go to the heart).

Theoretically, this identification of art with the expression of the artist's mind and soul should have made it hard to appreciate the art of the past: the many works and monuments made by anonymous masters and craftsmen, about whose personality we know nothing and can know nothing. But here another theory came to the rescue: the theory of collective mind, which took a variety of forms. The art of former epochs, the style of ancient Egypt, of Greece or of the Gothic Middle Ages, was conceived as the product of the national spirit of the Egyptians, the Greeks, or of the spirit or *Zeitgeist* of the Christian Middle Ages. These so-called 'Spirits', which manifested themselves in such diverse forms and styles, were almost regarded as super-artists, expressing their innermost self, and revealing the essence of the nature and the age. To look at an Indian temple or a Japanese shrine was to be in contact with the spirit of India or Japan.

I believe that my own subject, the history of art, owes its rise and popularity partly to the impulse of this optimistic doctrine of art as communication; but I have, nevertheless, felt compelled in many of my writings to analyse and criticise its logical justification, and some of its manifestations in the historiography of art. Briefly, I have come to the conclusion that it is far too simplistic to be of any help for the historian and critic. I have been equally critical of the theory of art as the communication of the artist's feelings; or, as modern parlance often has it, of art as self-expression. Of course, I am not the only writer on art who has doubted the usefulness of this idea, which gained such a wide acceptance in this century through the artistic movements of German Expressionism and American Abstract Expressionism. I think, indeed, that empirically the weakness of this idea is manifest. No doubt it will be true that any creation of a work of art will also be linked with the personality of its creator, but saying this, one does not say very much, for it is surely untrue that those who respond to the work will thereby come to know the maker. One of the most famous artists of the Renaissance, Benevenuto Cellini, has left us his autobiography, a splendid account of an irrepressible personality, violent, adventurous, untamed; but who could guess these personality traits from the elegant and refined works of his hand, the *Perseus* in Florence, the golden salt-cellar in Vienna? Or what do we really know of the personalities of Shakespeare or of Bach? Would we recognise them if we met them anywhere? nor can it be very useful to think of any great work as the outflow of a particular mood which came over the artist at a particular moment. It has often been pointed out by critics of this theory, that it would really demand that a composer who wrote a symphony would have to wait for a melancholy mood to write the adagio, and for a cheerful mood to write the scherzo. Art cannot be as simple as that.

What these objections reveal, in my opinion, is the need to come up with a better theory of artistic expression. In some respects, as I have indicated, we have had such better theories in the past. The dramatic theory of the Renaissance was reformulated by Suzanne Langer in her influential book *Philosophy in a New Key*,[10] but I do not think she added much that had not been said before. The theory of effects which I identified as the leading theory of classical antiquity has also moved again to the centre of interest; for the concerns which Plato felt about the dangerous effects of bad art have become topical again, with the debates about the effects of television on the minds of the young. But this, in a way, is a side-issue compared with the main question of the relation between the artist, his work, and his audience. He would be a bold person indeed who would dare to solve this complex question, and he would be a foolhardy man who would undertake to do so in the few minutes during which I still want to ask for your attention. To put it briefly, I believe that the fourth theory, which we need, should incorporate the three preceding ones, but modify them in the light of such criticism.

I said that the theory of art as an expression or manifestation of the artist's feelings which he communicates to his audience, comes close to identifying the expression of emotions with the symptoms of emotions, such as we know them in real life, as frowning in anger or jumping with joy. Such symptoms can certainly be catching or contagious, for emotions can be spread through a crowd, at a festival or an assembly. And yet, if we look

at the situation more carefully, we see that even here the common notion
of the process is somewhat over-simplified. As I have said elsewhere, it rests
on the idea that we have a feeling which is subsequently expressed or
squeezed out in the form of a sign or a symptom.[11] The direction is all
from inside outwards, centrifugally, as it were: first the feeling, then the
sign, then the response to the sign on the part of others; so that feelings
are carried by the symptoms, like a message on the waves of a radio
transmitter. But the psychologist has long known that this relationship
between feeling and symptom is not all so one-sided. To put it crudely,
the symptom can cause the appropriate emotions. This observation is known
in psychology as the James–Lange theory of emotion, a theory which stressed
the unity of mental and physical states in both animals and men. I remember
reading somewhere that when the cockatoo feels happy, it nods its head up
and down; allegedly, it is easy to change the mood of the bird from anger
to happiness, simply by grasping its head and moving it up and down. I do
not vouch for the accuracy of this observation, nor do I subscribe to a
complete identity of physical and mental events; but in a way, we are all
such cockatoos. My mother, who was a piano teacher, would advise her
pupils who had to play a cheerful passage to lean back and to smile, and
this deliberate action passed into the expressiveness of their performance. As
a matter of fact, orators and actors had discovered the James–Lange theory
long before the science of psychology was established. The orator or the
actor must always talk and act himself into the emotional state he needs for
his purpose. Remember Hamlet's surprise about the real tears shed by the
actor reciting the tragic tale of the Fall of Troy: 'What's Hecuba to him?'
But then, the actor did not weep because he mourned for the Queen of
Troy; he got into the emotion by reciting the speech the playwright had
composed for the purpose. It is not the grief that creates the impassioned
speech, but the impassioned speech that creates the grief, or at least all the
symptoms of grief, including tears.

I shall try to make a case for a theory which lays more stress on this
inverse relationship between feeling and expression. I have proposed elsewhere to call it, in contrast to the 'centrifugal' theory, the 'centripetal' theory
of expression. The expressive signs come first, and it is they which release
the emotional response in the actor, the orator and, and I should like to
believe, in any artist, whether painter, poet or musician. Using a term
borrowed from engineering, I should like to call this fourth or centripetal
theory of artistic expression a 'theory of feedback'; it is a theory which stresses

the constant interaction between the feeling and the form, the medium and the message.

Though my field is really the history of the visual arts, I should like, with your permission, to stay for a moment with the theory of artistic expression in poetry, for it is here that the shift of emphasis which I should like to advocate is most easily explained. The poet's medium is his language; he can only express ideas or emotions for which the language offers him words or forms. His art consists in bending his medium to his purpose by selecting the right word, tone or form which corresponds most closely to what he wishes to express. But, once more, it is an over-simplification to think of his feelings and sentiments coming first; feelings which he subsequently clothes in the words of his mother tongue. As with the symptoms of expression, only more so, it will be language which suggests and arouses his feelings in a constant movement of interaction. As the great English critic, I. A. Richards, increasingly stressed, after he had himself turned to the writing of poetry, it is the language which inspires the poet.[12]

Once more we can speak of the centripetal theory of expression: language offering the poet the means to shape his feelings or thoughts into artistic creation.

I owe an extreme, though somewhat eccentric, example of this share of language in expression, to the book by Sigmund Freud on 'wit' or on 'the joke'.[13] Freud is often thought of as a simple expressionist, who sees the artist as a man under overflowing pressures of emotions. But this is to misunderstand his best thought on art, which is to be found in the book I have mentioned. For, in discussing jokes, Freud concentrates on the play on words, the kind of pun which exploits the accidents of the language. The examples he analysed are, of course, taken from Freud's native German, and his translators have had a problem selecting equivalent jokes in English. One used by his translator is the jocular description of Christmas vacations as 'alcoholidays'. Not a very good joke, but enough to illustrate the dependence of the expression on the language. I dare say it is not only in England that some people look forward to the holidays as an opportunity of getting drunk; but their wish or hope would not have to be specially formulated; it is the accident of the English language, rather than the love of alcohol, which is responsible for the joke, such as it is.

Needless to say, language can offer more to the artist in words than such a flat joke. All poetry is derived from language. This is obvious if you consider the importance of rhymes and metres in certain poetic traditions; I also read in Arthur Waley's book on the Nō plays of Japan, that the lyric portions of these plays make frequent use of pivot words and puns, particularly puns on place-names, which are called *kakari-kotoba*. It is the accident of the language, combined with the ingenuity of the writer, which creates the lyric.

What matters to me in my present context is the role which the medium of the artist is thus seen to assume in the process of artistic expression. Now the arts of architecture, gardening, painting, sculpture, music or the dance, do not operate with such distinct symbols as does language, but even they could not function without a tradition which offers the artist certain choices and possibilities. In a paper I wrote some time ago on 'Expression and communication in art',[14] I argued that we should not ignore what we have learned from the theory of communication. Communication between any transmitter and receiver always presupposes a code, for as has been said, the signals do not carry meaning as trucks carry coal. The signal can only communicate a message to a recipient who has certain expectations; a prior knowledge of possibilities or probabilities from which the signal helps him to select one or the other. It may seem absurd to relate artistic expression to this arid theory of information worked out by communication engineers, and I am aware of the enormous distance that separates any of the arts from the simple codes discussed in this mathematical theory. Even so, the student of art can profit from this new discipline if he learns to see the role which prior expectation always plays in our responses. The fully expected is hardly registered, and the wholly unexpected will seem meaningless. It is the right proportion between the expected and the unexpected which constitutes the charm and magic of artistic expression. It would not be possible without an established medium which permits the artist to play upon the expectations of his audience, confirming, denying, teasing or surprising them. Where the theory of art as communication also goes wrong, in my view, is in the tacit assumption that even a great artist can plan all these effects in advance without the benefit of feedback. At every stage of the creative process, he must be his first audience and his first critic.[15] He will explore his medium and observe how any combination of shapes, colours or tones, affects himself. In this watchful play with the possibilities of his art, the painter will no less exploit happy accidents, than will the poet who explores the language. It was the great English landscape painter, Turner, who liked to admonish his students, 'Never lose an accident.'[16] I believe that the alertness to the accidental variations of the medium also played an important role in certain Far-Eastern schools of painting. It has done so again in the Abstract Expressionism of twentieth-century art, but there is an important difference here. Only within a firm tradition can the artist fully rely on the slightest nuance, being sure that his refined audience will catch every hint, and respond to every shade to which he himself responded. I believe that in this respect the arts of the Far East, of China and Japan, are often more subtle than those of the West.

In any case, I need hardly elaborate on the degree to which the literature and art of every culture articulates certain emotional states and feelings: the response to nature, the attitude towards love, the concepts of heroism or saintliness, which are embodied in the art and literature of every nation. I have alluded to the popular idea that all these can be regarded as manifestations of the national character or the collective spirit, but here, as elsewhere, I would plead for a theory of feedback. It is not only the national character which finds expression in a nation's art, it is also the nation's art which shapes the national character. The language, the medium, the tradition reacts back on those who inherit and use it. To separate and analyse this subtle interaction is impossible. Suffice it to realise that it always takes place.

I should like to stress that what I have ventured to call the fourth theory of artistic expression does not contradict the previous three I have sketched; it merely amplifies them, while taking from each one an important element. The first theory, that of the ancient world, which concentrates on the effects of art on the emotions, almost as if the means of the artist were comparable to incantations or even to drugs, seems to me the most important of them all. But I would urge that the first to feel this effect, and indeed to seek it out, is the artist himself who discovers and selects the kind of emotion he wishes to cultivate and express.

His attitude here need not necessarily contradict what I have called the second, or dramatic, theory of artistic expression. He studies the manifestations of feelings which he finds in the tradition he has inherited, as something objective and truthful; but he does not study them with a cold heart. On the contrary, I should like to suggest that there is much to learn from the Romantic theory of expression; for I believe that in his search and in his quest for discovery, the true artist will encounter feelings to which he is attuned, emotions he can authenticate in his own heart.

If I may use an illustration by way of summing up, taking a simple example from the language of music; consider a trumpet-call. The ancients would have stressed its capacity to arouse the emotion of courage and aggression; the Renaissance would have used it, say in an opera, to represent martial feelings; a Romantic composer might have inserted a trumpet-call into his symphony to express his emotion of triumph: all these interpretations seem to me legitimate. But we must never forget that the trumpet-call is part of the tradition of the culture, and that the composer who used it discovered its power by studying his own response. Having done so, he can find new applications, new variants and new feeling tones, and make us realise that this trumpet call is his and his alone. In this way, but only in this, can we interpret the idea of art as self-expression.

Notes

1. Leonardo da Vinci, *Treatise on Painting*, edited by A. P. McMahon, Princeton 1956, no. 248.
2. *Ibid.*, no. 250.
3. *Ibid.*, no. 267.
4. *Ibid.*, no. 33.
5. *Goetz von Berlichingen*, Act 1.
6. 27 March 1801.
7. Letter, 23 October 1821.
8. Diary entries, 25 January 1857, 14 May 1824.
9. *Mon Salon*, 4 May 1866.
10. S. Langer, *Philosophy in a New Key*, Cambridge, Mass. 1942.
11. 'Freud's Aesthetics', *Encounter* 1966 [republished in *Reflections* – editor's note].
12. Notably in his Presidential Address of 1978 to the English association, *Verse v. Prose* [and see now 'The necessity of tradition: an interpretation of the poetics of I. A. Richards' in *Tributes* – editor's note].
13. S. Freud, *Der Witz und seine Beziehung zum Unbewussten*, 1905.
14. E. H. Gombrich, *Meditations on a Hobby Horse*.
15. As my friend, Sir Karl Popper, likes to stress.
16. J. Ruskin, *Modern Painters* 1988, volume 5, p. 177.

9

'A lost art': optical refinements in classical Greek marble sculpture

Göran Sörbom

WHEN we now, at the end of the twentieth century, look at Greek sculpture from the classical period, do we 'see' the same things as the Greeks of that period saw? We have the same physical objects in front of us, although colours may have faded, some parts may have been damaged and some are lost. But our experience and understanding are certainly different from theirs, as are our ways of talking and writing about them. We encounter the sculptures mostly in museums, which is a cultural context very different from their original setting. As twentieth-century spectators, we are equipped with knowledge and cultural habits far beyond the horizon of the classical Greek audience. Just a few examples can hint at some of these formidable differences: we have a concept of pictorial space and we have cultural habits when looking at images which are strongly influenced by the ideas of the central perspective of the Renaissance; we treat classical Greek sculpture as works of art, a practice just a few hundred years old, and we look for and enjoy aesthetic form in the sculptures; we distinguish between representation and expression, whereas the ancient Greeks did not. These differences are basic, and it is difficult to see their consequences for our understanding of the classical Greeks' appreciation of their sculpture.[1]

In this chapter I will discuss a more simple and direct factor which is of immediate importance for our perception and understanding of classical Greek sculpture: the spatial relationship between sculpture and spectator. When we nowadays meet Greek sculture in museums and in pictures, in books and periodicals, etc., the normal position of the spectator or the camera is a straight frontal view, with the spectator or the camera on about the same level as the sculpture. Now this is not the way in which many of the Greek sculptures actually were seen when placed in their original positions. Many of them were placed high up as akroteria on temple roofs, on pediments, as reliefs in metope and triglyph friezes or as friezes inside or outside on cella walls, on columns or in other high positions. How many sculptures were seen high up or at least clearly above eye-level and how many were seen at about the same level as the spectator is difficult to say. But it is a fair guess, at least, that in classical times, and perhaps in antiquity in general, more important sculptures were in a high position than is usual in our modern world. What did the ancient Greeks think about the position of sculptures, and did these thoughts affect their ways of making sculptures?

Textual evidence

It was recognised in antiquity that seeing things far away or high up changed the perception (*aisthesis*) of them. This was also discussed in connection with paintings and sculptures. The earliest articulated example we know of is from Plato's *The Sophist* (235D–236A), in which Plato tries to define the nature of the sophist. In so doing picture making is discussed:

STRANGER: I see the likeness-making art as one part of imitation. This is met with, as a rule, whenever anyone produces the imitation by following the proportions of the original in length, breadth, and depth, and giving, besides, the appropriate colours to each part.

THEAETETUS: Yes, but do not all imitators try to do this?

STRANGER: Not those who produce some large work of sculpture or painting. For if they reproduced the true proportions of beautiful forms, the upper parts, you know, would seem smaller and the lower parts larger than they ought, because we see the former from a distance, the latter from near at hand.[2]

Because of their 'unfavourable' positions, their makers abandon the true and beautiful proportions of their pictures, Plato argues. Such pictures are not even similar to their beautiful originals, but only appear to be so. And the stranger also maintains that 'this is very common in painting and sculpture'.

The practice to which Plato refers is called 'optical correction' or 'optical refinement'. A similar practical knowledge was also exploited by architects. It is obvious that Greek architects and builders often worked with subtle changes of ideal proportions in order to gain strength, power, vitality and other, what we now call aesthetic qualities of the building.[3] Vitruvius also mentions that buildings must have their proportions changed in order to make them look beautiful.[4]

This practice was codified into a 'techne' named skenographia. Aristotle mentions that 'Sophokles added skenographia' to the theatrical practice.[5] Proclus describes skenographia in his Commentary on Euclid as a part of geometry and arithmetic: skenographia is the theory of 'how appearances should avoid giving the impression of being ill-shaped or ill-formed in pictures, based on the distances and the height of painted figures'.[6] 'Damianos' of Larissa (fourth-century) expresses a similar view:

> What is skenographia? The skenographic part of optics seeks to discover how one should paint images of buildings. For since things do not give the appearance of being what they in fact are, they look to see not how they will represent the actual underlying shapes, but rather, they render these shapes in whatever way they appear. [Architects are mentioned as using the same technique.] And it is also a procedure of this sort which brings about the appearance of commensurability in his creation for a maker of colossal statuary, so that the work has a satisfactory form for the vision and is not, in a futile fashion, worked out according to real commen-surability. For works set up at a great elevation do not appear to have the form which they in fact have.[7]

Finally, Tzetzes (twelfth-century) tells an anecdote about a competition between Phidias and Alkamenes. They were asked to make one sculpture each to be placed high up on a column. When the sculptures were completed, they were exhibited, presumably on the ground and not in their intended places, and people were invited to look at them. The audience found Alkamenes' sculpture far better than Phidias'. But when the sculptures were placed in their intended spot high up, it became clear that Phidias had used optical refinements in order to make the sculpture look beautiful when it was placed in its correct position.[8]

Monumental evidence

These texts demonstrate an awareness of the practice of painters, sculptors and architects of changing their works in order to improve their appearance when they were seen from so-called 'unfavourable positions'. When we go to the monuments themselves, it is, according to a common view, more difficult to see whether the few sculptures still in existence are modelled with the help of optical refinements or not. Eva C. Keuls expresses, I believe, a common outlook when she writes: 'To my knowledge, no monumental evidence for optical proportions in statuary survives.'[9]

No Greek monumental paintings have survived which could demonstrate the practice of optical refinements. The Roman and Pompeian wall-paintings are discussed more with regard to the possible use of perspective than as applications of optical refinements. The only group of surviving monuments that could tell us something about the use of optical refinements in pictorial representation is Greek monumental sculpture. Bente Killerich has commented upon the use of such optical refinements, and she maintains that they were used in the production of the Parthenon frieze; she compares them to the optical refinements of the building itself.[10] For one thing, she remarks, the frieze is not completely vertical; the upper parts lean out somewhat towards the spectator. The same thing has been observed to be true of the metopes of temple C in Selinus, upon which Killerich comments: 'Seen from below the reliefs have another effect than when seen at eye-level. When you look up to them, something of the compactness disappears, which they have when you look at them at eye-level.'[11] Other ways of making optical refinements are, she claims, the change of proportions, asymmetrical structure of faces and bodies, light and colour and consideration of whether the spectator is supposed to stand still or to move along or around the monument.[12] Further, Killerich claims, optical refinements have been used also in the creation of some *kouroi* and *korai*. Her conclusion is, however, that optical corrections do constitute an aspect of Greek sculpture, an almost completely unexplored territory in archaeology and art history. But she offers no demonstrations of how such optical refinements might work; she only refers to what she herself has seen and experienced.

In a review of the great exhibition *The Greek Miracle: Classical Sculpture from the Dawn of Democracy to the Fifth Century* (Washington and New York 1992–93) Garry Wills reports an experience similar to that of Killerich.[13] Having observed the fragments of the Parthenon frieze from the position of lying on the floor close to them, he comments:

> Seen from that angle, the cavalry frieze gave me a strikingly foreshortened view past the horses' rumps and their prominently veined bellies. The heads and bodies of the riders are only partly seen, projecting out over the horses' anatomy – bridles and other accoutrements would have flashed at one in the shadowy roof area. The angle recalls the shots, imitated from John Ford's *Stagecoach*, of horses thundering over a movie-camera.

Wills asked the curator why the frieze was hung at eye-level and not at its original height, and was given the answer that they were not allowed to hang them at their original height, and, besides, 'it is hard to see from that angle'. Wills comments: 'What the curator meant, of course, is that we would not be able to see the frieze the way we want and expect to see it – "liberated" from its cult site for inspection *sub specie aeternitatis*, as befits ideal works.'

Recording the monuments in a new way

My own first attempt to look at Greek monumental sculpture in the original way, from below, was made back in 1968, when I visited the British Museum and lay down on the floor just under the Parthenon frieze. The sculptures did change their look, and sometimes amazingly so. This experience convinced me that it must be important to try to record, in some way or other, what you see in this, the original perspective of Greek monumental sculpture. In an attempt to record and communicate something of what it is possible to see in classical Greek sculpture, when seen in its original position, I tried to simulate the original relation between monument and spectator with the help of the camera. The idea is simple enough. We know the exact position of several of the remaining Greek sculptures from the sixth and fifth centuries, and a number of them were set high up – for example, the metopes from temples C and E at Selinus, the pediments from the temple of Athena Aphaia at Aigina, the pediments and metopes from the temple of Zeus at Olympia and from the temple of Athena Parthenos on the Athenian Acropolis, the interior cella frieze of the temple of Apollo at Bassae, Paionios' Nike at Olympia and the Nike parapet, again on the Athenian Acropolis.

This material was sufficient and the works important enough to merit some experimental investigation. Starting from our knowledge of the high position of these sculptures it proved possible to simulate, to some extent at least, how these sculptures once looked in their original positions.[14]

In the usual way of exposing and photographing ancient sculpture the spectator is almost at eye-level with the monument. This horizontal relation is part of what I call the 'museum handbook' attitude to ancient painting and sculpture, the 'inspection *sub specie aeternitatis*' Wills mentions.[15] The ancient spectator was often in a much lower position than the usual one of the modern spectator. Whenever you deviate from the horizontal one-to-one correspondence between monument and spectator, a sort of right-angled

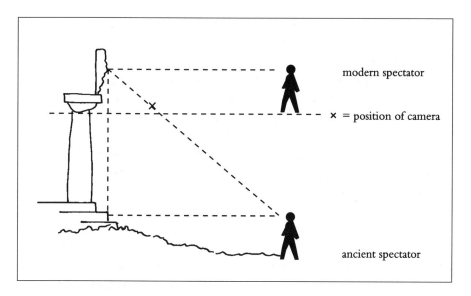

Figure 9.1 The ancient spectatorial triangle.

triangle appears, created by the height of the monument above eye-level in relation to the position of the spectator. In some cases it is possible to calculate the ancient spectatorial triangle with some precision, since the position of the sculptures, the height of the temple and the topography just around the temple are known.[16] The simulation consists in putting the camera somewhere (usually as far 'down' as the museum floor permits) along the hypotenuse of the ancient spectatorial triangle as demonstrated by Figure 9.1.

In the spring of 1992 I started to take photographs of fifth-century Greek sculpture according to this scheme of simulation. There are, of course, technical problems in so doing. For instance, what lenses and lighting should be used? When the sculptures are exhibited just slightly above the eye-level of the spectator, it is, of course, impossible to re-create the original distance between spectator and sculpture. The photographs will, however, in that position show us the sculptures in a way which is, in a sense, better than what was possible when the sculptures were seen in their original positions; we can actually see more detail in them than was possible in antiquity.[17] This does not, however, frustrate the possibilities of testing the hypothesis put forward in this chapter: that the Greek sculptors, in making monumental sculpture in stone to be put in high positions, actually changed the proportions of their works, as is maintained in a number of ancient texts, and that these changes do matter for our experience and understanding of the sculptures.

The result of my photographic work is a series of coupled photographs with one photograph representing the 'museum handbook' aspect of some piece of Greek monumental sculpture, in the way we usually see it in a museum or a handbook, and another photograph simulating the 'original' aspect of the same sculpture.[18] The remaining figures illustrating this chapter are of such a kind. There is not space enough here to make detailed comments and comparisons of all the figures; readers are invited to look and think for themselves. Here are just a few general comments on some particularly striking features that I believe come to light from a comparison between the two kinds of photograph.

The representation of life

Let us start the discussion from a given position: what did the Greeks themselves regard as the most important characteristics of their sculptures? Or, when the classical Greeks talked and wrote about sculpture, what sort of language and what sort of concepts did they use, i.e. under what description did the Greeks experience, understand and interpret classical sculpture?[19]

From the early classical period onwards an important issue in talking and writing about sculptures is their lifelikeness. In a fragment from a satyr play by Aeschylus, a sculpture is said to lack only a voice; otherwise it would be experienced as perfectly alive.[20] In his *Memorabilia*, Xenophon lets Socrates maintain that the most important quality of the sculptor Kleiton's works is not their beauty, but their ability to render the quality of life, their lifelikeness.[21] And all through antiquity the representation of life plays a dominant role in the discourses on sculpture. Here are some further examples: in a mime by Herodas a woman describes a sculpture by saying that 'you could expect the sculpture to speak, if you did not see that it is made of stone' and she continues that 'the time will come when man will also be able to put life into the stone'.[22] Another revealing example is from Petronius' *Satyricon*. Trimalcho brags about his fortunes: 'Myself I have a great passion for silver. I own about a hundred four-gallon cups engraved with Cassandra killing her sons, and the boys lying there dead – but you would think they were alive [et pueri mortui iacent sic ut vivere putes].'[23] Petronius ridicules not only Trimalcho's mistake in mythology (Cassandra did not kill her sons, Medea did) but also his misuse of the way we speak about pictures in praising them for their ability to render life. In *The Greek Anthology* we find other examples: 'The Bacchante is of Parian marble, but the sculptor gave life to the stone, and she springs up as if in Bacchic fury.'[24] and 'A cunning master wrought me, the Satyr, son of Bacchus, divinely inspiring the monolith with breath.'[25] Even Plotinus asks: '[A]re not the more lifelike [*tsotikotera*] statues the more beautiful ones, even if the others are better proportioned?' And he answers: 'Yes, because the living is more desirable; and this is because it has soul.'[26]

The predominance of interest in lifelikeness, which we find so abundant in ancient texts, has often, in the nineteenth and twentieth centuries, been (mis)understood as ancient Greek attempts towards realism and naturalism. The theory of imitation was seen as a simple-minded recommendation that paintings and sculptures be made as similar to individuals or things as possible.[27] Such simple realism does not fit what Greek art shows us, it was argued. The Greeks' verbal formulation and description of their experience and understanding could, then, be sorted out as uninteresting, particularly in light of the experience of bourgeois realism of the nineteenth century and the victory of formalism.

The much-sought-after lifelikeness can, however, also be understood as attempts to render the most important feature of human life, namely life itself, understood as the interplay between body and soul.

From the fifth century BC the Greeks developed a way of understanding body, soul and life as three necessarily coexisting things: life is defined as the conjunction of body and soul; a corpse is a body bereft of its soul; the soul of a living being cannot exist without a body. The soul is presented as the essence or the form of the living body: '[T]he soul is in a sense the principle of animal life.'[28] The triumph of classical Greek sculpture was, as I have argued elsewhere,[29] the development of means to represent this, according to Western thought, most essential aspect of human existence. The ability to represent the body–soul unit is the remarkable innovation of the classical period which changed the whole history of picture-making and picture-understanding.

Some comments

Now, if we look at and interpret the coupled pictures of figures 9.2 to 9.7 with the understanding that it was central to classical Greek picture-making to try to represent the essence of living organisms as body–soul units, it is quite obvious that when the monuments are seen from below, this ambition is more easily perceived than in the 'museum handbook' aspect. There is a greater sensual closeness and presence in the persons represented when they

Apollo, from the west pediment of the temple of Zeus at Olympia.
Figure 9.2 (*left*) 'Museum handbook' aspect.
Figure 9.3 (*right*) Simulation of aspect as seen from the ancient spectatorial position.

Heracles fights the Cretan bull. Metope (west, 4) from the temple of Zeus at Olympia.
Figure 9.4 (*left*) 'Museum handbook' aspect.
Figure 9.5 (*right*) Simulation of aspect as seen from the ancient spectatorial position.

Theseus and centaur from the west pediment of the temple of Zeus at Olympia.
Figure 9.6 (*left*) Museum handbook aspect.
Figure 9.7 (*right*) Simulation of aspect as seen from the ancient spectatorial position.

are seen from below. The spectator becomes aware of the presence of a living body and the persons represented seem to be aware of their existence in a body. The persons represented are not just physical things represented with fidelity in a three-dimensional space but bodies in every small detail full of the soul of a living individual; the bodily actions as represented in the sculpture are the works of the soul, as Xenophon expresses it.[30] Or, 'life seems to enter the marble', as Gombrich characterises the enormous innovation of the classical period, echoing the ancient critical language.[31]

Further, the figures become more independent of the background in the reliefs when seen from below; they become surrounded by a natural space and are not tied to a flat background.[32] Take, for instance, the metopes of the temple of Zeus at Olympia and those of the Parthenon in Athens. When we look at them from eye-level, the metopes are seen as square surfaces against which the persons act. But when seen from below, the square becomes an oblique form, loses something of its power as a visual object and recedes in favour of the actions represented.[33] Probably this is what Bente Killerich refers to when she writes: 'When you look up to them [i.e. the metopes of temple C at Selinus], something of their compactness disappears.'[34] This effect is also magnified by the fact that, seen from below, parts of the figures are outside the frame of the metope.

In several of the sculptures there is more than one figure, and the figures interact. When seen from below, the acting figures often seem to be in greater contact with each other than when viewed at eye-level in the traditional manner.

The consistency of the visual evidence in my photographic material, hinted at in the few figures in this chapter, leads to the conclusion that the strikingly different characteristics and qualities which appear when one observes much classical Greek sculpture from below are intended by the Greek sculptors. The strength and uniformity with which the greater lifelikeness, realism, space, adequacy of action and sensous presence appear in classical Greek sculpture when seen from below show that these qualities cannot be the result of chance or some characteristic of the camera; they are the result of conscious planning and skill. These characteristics are also the ones that are stressed in many ancient texts as the most important ones.

Literary sources tell us that the Greek sculptors knew how to adjust their sculptures with regard to the intended positions of their finished works. And they knew it both in theory and in practice. *Skenographia* was not only an art (*techne*) in the sense of a handbook telling how to do things and giving theoretical descriptions of and justifications for the practice; it was also a practical (tacit) knowledge handed down from generation to generation.

Naturally, some questions present themselves: when did this skill first appear and for how long was it a part of the sculptor's trade?[35] And maybe also: when was the knowledge applied? The dimensions of some Greek sculptures are quite small, and yet the photographs from below distinctly indicate adjustments for the spectator's low position. Questions of this kind are too large to be answered in this chapter. Much more empirical work has to be done to secure a foundation for such descriptions and conclusions.

There is also another possible loss of content when you look at some classical Greek monumental sculpture within the 'museum handbook' attitude. Something of the loftiness and magnificence of the world represented is lost. The horizontality of the 'museum handbook' attitude may imply a sort of equality between monument and spectator in the aesthetic act, an *ich–du* relationship in a nineteenth- and twentieth-century sense. The high position of many sculptures in antiquity may demonstrate the difference between the heroic world and our own. Aristotle writes in the second chapter of his *Poetics*:

> Since the objects of imitation are men in action, and these men must be either of a higher or lower type . . . it follows that we must represent

men either as better than in real life, or as worse, or as they are. It is the same in painting.[36]

Tragedy, for instance, represents human actions on a higher level than everyday life. The low position of the spectators of many Greek monumental sculptures may stress this difference. We literally look up to this higher world of gods and heroes. In the 'museum handbook' aspect the spectator is mostly on the same level as the god or hero. This equality of level works against Aristotle's conception of the difference between the existential level of gods and heroes on the one hand, and ordinary people on the other. When seen from below there is a loftiness, magnificence and a high tension in the bodies and actions of the gods and heroes which is diminished when we are on the same level as them.

My conclusion is that *skenographia* may be in itself a lost art, but that there is an abundance of traces of it in the form of the optical refinements we see in at least some monumental classical Greek marble sculptures. The examples chosen have such a central place in the history of sculpture that we cannot disregard what they show us as something peripheral. Rather they show us that the techniques and practices mentioned by ancient writers were an important part of sculpture-making in the classical period.

Notes

The author of this chapter would like to acknowledge the financial support given to him for the research involved in this project by The Bank of Sweden Tercentenary Foundation.

1. I am working on a monograph about such theoretical questions with a discussion of the so-called Greek revolution in art as a primary example. In some ways this project is a continuation of E. H. Gombrich's discussion of the Greek art revolution in *Art and Illusion*, chapter 4. In a review ('The art of the Greeks', reprinted in *Reflections*, pp. 11–17) Gombrich has hinted at the line of interpretation I have chosen to develop.
2. Translated by Harold North Fowler in the Loeb Classical Library edition of Plato's *Theaetetus and Sophist*, London 1961.
3. See William Henry Goodyear, *Greek Refinements: Studies in Temperamental Architecture*, New Haven 1912.
4. For instance, 3.4.5: 'The level of the stylobate must be increased along the middle by the *scamilli impares*; for if it is laid perfectly level, it will look to the eye as though it were hollow a little' (translated by Morris Hicky Morgan in

Vitruvius: The Ten Books on Architecture, New York 1960). Let us, following Goodyear (p. 19), distinguish between 'optical correction' and 'optical refinement'. The former is what Plato refers to: a change of proportions in such a way that the thing seen seems to have right proportions. The latter denotes a change of proportions in order to improve the aesthetic qualities of the thing seen (for example, the passage from Vitruvius quoted above). Optical correction and optical refinement are identical only if you presuppose that beauty resides in given proportions and that beauty is the goal of picture-making.

5. Poetics, 1449a18.
6. Quoted from J. J. Pollitt, *The Ancient View of Greek Art: Criticism, History, and Terminology*, New Haven 1974, p. 233.
7. *Ibid.*, pp. 233–4.
8. J. Overbeck, *Die antiken Schriftquellen zur Geschichte der bildenden Künste bei den Griechen*, Leipzig 1868, Nr. 772. See *Art and Illusion*, pp. 161–2.
9. *Plato and Greek Painting*, Leiden 1978, p. 111.
10. *Græsk skulptur fra dædalisk til hellenistisk*, Copenhagen 1991, p. 126: 'Such optical relations answer to the optical corrections which were made in the architecture of the Parthenon.'
11. *Ibid.*, p. 248.
12. *Ibid.*, p. 248. On p. 250 she writes: 'Asymmetry can also be counted as a form of optical correction.'
13. 'Athena's magic', *The New York Review of Books*, 17 December, 1992, pp. 47–51.
14. The material on which the following discussion is founded is the result of rather extensive photography by myself and my wife in the following museums: The National Gallery in Athens, The Acropolis Museum in Athens, The Museum of Olympia, The British Museum and The Glyptothek in Munich. In this context, I would like to offer my thanks to these museums for their kind cooperation in this experimental work. The photographs of the Olympia sculptures for this chapter were taken by Marie and Craig Mauzy.
15. This is a very complex attitude, built up through the centuries. It is an attitude which is constituted by our conceptions of art, by our habits of exhibiting works of art and by what we look for when we experience them, and by the archaeological and art-historical knowledge of the time, among other things. It is impossible to explore this notion in this context.
16. Richard Stillwell has made a careful study of the appearance of the Parthenon frieze to the ancient spectator in his article 'The Panathenaic frieze: optical relations', *Hesperia*, 38 (1969), pp. 231–41. He does not, however, touch upon the problems discussed in this chapter.
17. Mary Bergstein has, in her paper 'Lonely Aphrodites: on the documentary photography of sculpture', *Art Bulletin*, 74 (1992), pp. 475–98, clearly and vividly demonstrated many of the perils of the documentary photography of sculpture. She does not, however, consider the problems of simulating the original positions of sculptures in a high position. This problem is discussed by Robert Munman in the preface to 'Optical Corrections in the Sculpture of Donatello', *Transactions of the American Philosophical Society*, 75, part 2, Philadelphia 1985.

18. Robert Munman (see note 17) has made a detailed study of the sculptural work of Donatello with regard to the positions of the work and the spectator. He has coupled photographs taken at eye-level with photographs taken from below of sculptures known to have been originally placed well above eye-level. These photographs clearly show that Donatello practised a form of *skenographia* to compensate for the low position of the spectator. In a letter, Dr Munman has given me many valuable criticisms of an earlier version of this chapter.

19. For the idea that we do not just interpret a work of art but that we do so under a certain description, see Michael Baxandall, *Patterns of Intention: On the Historical Explanation of Pictures*, New Haven 1985, pp. 1–5.

20. Papyrus Oxyrhynchus 2162 published in Egypt Exploration Society 26: *The Oxyrhynchus Papyri*, part 18, edited by E. Lobel, C. H. Roberts and E. P. Wegener, London 1941, pp. 14–22.

21. 3.10.6–7.

22. Herodes, *Mime* 4.32–34.

23. *Satyricon,* 52, translated by Michael Heseltine in the Loeb Classical Library edition, London 1969.

24. 9.774, translated by W. R. Paton in the Loeb Classical Library edition, London 1958. See also Callistratus' description of the same sculpture: 'On the statue of a bacchante', K.423.23–24: '[T]hough void of the faculty of life, it neverless had vitality' (translated by Arthur Fairbanks in the Loeb Classical Library edition of Philostratus, *Imagines* and Callistratus, *Descriptions*, London 1960.

25. *Greek Anthology*, 9.826.

26. 6.7.22, translated by A. H. Armstrong in the Loeb Classical Library edition, vol. 7, London 1988.

27. Some anecdotes are understood in the same way. Note, for instance, Pliny's anecdote on the competition between Zeuxis and Parrhasius (35.65): Zeuxis made a picture which caused birds to believe the grapes he had painted were real, whereas Parrhasius made a curtain which Zeuxis himself believed to be real. When Norman Bryson finds it 'hard to imagine a more revealing story about painting in the West' (*Vision and Painting: the Logic of the Gaze*, London 1983, p. 1) he is, I believe, on the wrong track.

28. Aristotle, *De anima*, 402a7–8. See also, for instance, 412a20–21: 'So the soul must be substance in the sense of being the form of a natural body, which potentially has life' (translated by W. S. Hett in The Loeb Classical Library edition of Aristotle *On the Soul, Parva Naturalia, On Breath*, London 1964).

29. 'Xenophon's Socrates on the Greek art revolution', in *The Philosophy of Socrates*, edited by K. J. Boudouris, Athens 1991, pp. 339–49, and 'Gombrich on the Greek Art Revolution', *Nordisk Estetisk Tidskrift*, 12 (1994), pp. 63–77.

30. *Memorabilia*, 3.10.1–8.

31. *Art and Illusion*, p. 99.

32. This point was stressed by Thomas Hård af Segerstad in a seminar discussion of my photographic material.

33. A gestalt psychologist would claim that the square is a 'better' gestalt than the oblique figure.

34. See Killerich, *Græsk skulptur*, p. 5.
35. It may be mentioned here that in none of the pediments of the temple of Athena Aphaia at Aigina does this particular skill seem to have been applied by the sculptors.
36. Translated by S. H. Butcher in *Aristotle's Theory of Poetry and Fine Art*, New York 1951. This is certainly also true of sculpture.

Figure 10.1 Cornelis van Haarlem, *The Fall of Man*, 1592.

10

From normal to supranormal: observations on realism and idealism from a biological perspective

Jan Baptist Bedaux

WHILE going around the exhibition *Dawn of the Golden Age. Northern Netherlandish Art 1580–1620* in the Rijksmuseum in Amsterdam, I was asked by one of my students, who had been examining work by Goltzius, Wtewael and Cornelis van Haarlem (Figure 10.1), whether I could explain why some of their figures had such outlandish proportions. This would not have been the first time that an art history student asked that question, and I am convinced that it would also have occurred to many non-specialist visitors as well. The standard answer is usually that this formal vocabulary is typical of Mannerism, which adopted a highly idealised view of the human figure. This explanation is mere tautology, and I fear it would not satisfy a good student, who would immediately wonder how such an idealisation originated.

Now in the past few decades there have been many worthwhile publications on Mannerism, but a discussion of one of its key traits, this use of extreme proportions, seems to be studiously avoided. It is also in vain that one combs the 717-page catalogue of the *Dawn of the Golden Age* for an answer. Worse than that, the question is not even addressed. All that one learns from one of the introductory essays is that 'the figures [are] better proportioned than average children of men'.[1] The title of the catalogue also displays the usual disdain for Mannerist art, which may have taken silver but will never win gold.

Although this kind of extravagant formal vocabulary is usually identified with Mannerism, it is by no means restricted to it. For example, the extremely elongated fingers of the apostle Matthew in a drawing of *c.* 1585–90 by Jacques de Gheyn (Figure 10.2) are very comparable to those of the Majestas giving the blessing on a fourteenth-century antependium from Navarra (Figure 10.3), while the extreme proportions of the angels in the tympanum with the *Last Judgement* of *c.* 1130–35 in the cathedral at Autun are essentially no different from those which El Greco gave to the angel Gabriel in his *Annunciation* of

1596–1600 in the Prado. Picasso's *Woman with a Crow* of 1904 and Giacometti's *Headless Woman* of the 1930s in the Peggy Guggenheim Collection are examples of works demonstrating that the excessive elongation of limbs is also part of the vocabulary of modern artists.

Figure 10.2 Jacques de Gheyn, *Saint Matthias*.

We know from Pliny that the Greek sculptor Lysippus altered the standard proportions of the human figure by making his statues nine heads high instead of eight, so that they would appear taller:

> Lysippus is said to have contributed greatly to the art of bronze statuary by representing the details of the hair and by making his heads smaller than the old sculptors used to do, and his bodies more slender and firm, to give his statues the appearance of greater height.[2]

Figure 10.3 *Majestas Domini*, antependium from Navarra (detail).

And his sculptures do indeed appear taller than those by previous artists, and they have a more convincing lightness and liveliness. As has been noted, like the modern spectator, Lysippus may well have felt that the proportions of the statues by his predecessor Polyclitus, among others, however correct, made statues of marble and bronze look embarrassingly heavy.[3]

In his article 'The Renaissance conception of artistic progress and its consequences', Ernst Gombrich put forward the convincing hypothesis that Lorenzo Ghiberti elongated the figures for his revolutionary second door for the baptistery of San Giovanni in Florence in response to the above passage in Pliny.[4] However, the proportions of Ghiberti's figures are not extreme.

Figure 10.4 Parri Spinelli, *The Risen Christ.*

For that we have to turn to one of his pupils, the painter Parri Spinelli, who incidentally had been closely involved in the execution of his master's bronze door. Parri's hyperbolic figures (Figure 10.4) won plaudits from none other than Vasari:

Parri made his figures much more slender and tall than any painter who had preceded him, and where others made them at most ten heads high, he made his eleven and even twelve; nor were they ungraceful, for they were always supple and arched either to the left or to the right, to give them more spirit, as he expressed it.[5]

It will come as little surprise to learn that it was Lysippus who attracted the admiration of the 'theorist of Mannerism', Gian Paolo Lomazzo. In his *Idea del Tempio della Pittura* of 1590, he cites Pliny on Lysippus, adding that 'this improvement is regarded by the greatest masters as the most beautiful discovery ever made'.[6]

The penchant for long or elongated

limbs is not confined to the arts, but is also found in real life. Fashion models are generally selected for their height, and the surfeit of fashion designs constructed around extremely elongated, S-shaped figures that confronts us daily in the media demonstrates the incredible staying-power of Parri's formula. It is known that the management of the Folies Bergère in Paris meets its patrons' demands for the supranormal by only hiring dancers with long legs. Moreover, those legs are made to look even longer by dressing the girls in outfits cut to the hip, and having them dance in high heels. We learn from El Greco that women of past ages knew that footwear made them look more elegant. This artist, who had a preference for tall, shapely figures, once wrote that women wore high heels to make themselves look taller.[7]

In the *Madonna in the Garland* in Munich, a joint work by Rubens and Jan Brueghel the Elder (the former providing the fauna and the latter the flora), we find another sort of supranormal being: the putto (Figure 10.5).[8]

Figure 10.5 Peter Paul Rubens and Jan Breughel the Elder, *Madonna in the Garland*.

Although there is plenty to say in this particular context about Brueghel's speciality, the stunning garland, I will concentrate here on Rubens's contribution. He presents his Virgin and Child as isolated figures, as a painting within the painting, held aloft by a swarm of no less skilfully painted putti. It is their proportions that strike us as supranormal, certainly in comparison to those of the Christ Child, which are far more naturalistic. One wonders why these putti have been given such a supranormal look. More particularly, what prompted the striking difference in proportions between the Christ Child and the putti?

The reason why art history has never really got to grips with the phenomenon of the supranormal is because we have had no good explanatory model. Gombrich, however, long ago directed our attention to psychology and ethology at an early stage, and has demonstrated how valuable they can be for art historians, not just for solving problems but also for posing new questions and gaining new insights. Ethology, for instance, which has now been absorbed into the wider discipline of sociobiology, offers an explanatory model for this attachment to the supranormal. I am aware that sociobiology, the study of the biological basis for all forms of social behaviour among humans and animals, with a special emphasis on the evolutionary aspects, has run into considerable opposition, and quite understandably so. One justifiable criticism is that the importance of environmental factors is seriously underestimated in sociobiological theories of genetic and cultural evolution. At the same time, though, it has to be admitted that, certainly in the humanities and the social sciences, it is precisely that genetic side of human behaviour that has been seriously neglected. If we regard ourselves as a product of evolution in the animal kingdom, we cannot avoid the thought that human behaviour must also be based on an organisational structure determined by the genes. The ineluctable conclusion, then, is that human endeavours, including the creation of art, are the product of an interaction between the genes and the individual's environment. It is for that reason that, throughout his career, Gombrich has stressed the great importance of both psychology and ethology as ancillary disciplines for the history of art.

Many actions can be triggered by external stimuli, such that a specific form of behaviour often appears to be linked to a specific stimulus situation, such as dogs salivating when food is placed in front of them.[9] Needless to say, reacting to stimuli does not mean that all observable stimuli are employed when dealing with a particular situation. That is because the animal is equipped with detectors which are attuned to specific situations in which certain stimuli are at work. These mechanisms enable the animal to react adaptively in a biologically adequate manner upon its very first confrontation with a stimulus to which it has not been conditioned. This implies that a number of behaviour patterns or systems are preconditioned.

The detector that makes a selection and assesses the value of the elements in the stimulus situation is called a releasing mechanism. It enables supranormal stimuli situations to arise that result in exaggerated effective features, to which the animal responds more strongly than it would usually do. For example, if an oystercatcher's eggs are removed from the nest and dummies are placed beside the nest, some of which are larger than the real eggs, the bird will first roll the larger 'eggs' back into the nest, and only then the smaller ones. In other words, the man-made supranormal substitute elicits a specific but extreme response from the bird. One exclusively human characteristic is our ability to create extremely ingenious substitutes, such as pictures and statues, in which we ourselves can regulate the strength of a particular stimulus.

Trials have demonstrated that humans, too, have a similar, genetically-based organisational structure of behaviour. They confirm Konrad Lorenz's idea that innate releasing mechanisms underlie not only our observations but our thoughts as well, and although we do not know how much of our social life is determined by innate releasing mechanisms, there is evidence for their influence.

In 1943 Lorenz put forward the theory that the behaviour patterns associated with the care of small children and the affective responses that are aroused when one sees a baby can be released by a number of key stimuli which are associated with the child's shape. According to him, the following characteristics play a particularly important role in this process.

— Head large in proportion to the body.
— Protruding forehead large in proportion to the size of the rest of the face.
— Large eyes below the midline of the total head.
— Short, thick extremities.
— Rounded body shape.
— Soft, elastic body surfaces.
— Round, protruding cheeks.

If an object has some of these characteristics, it releases the affective and

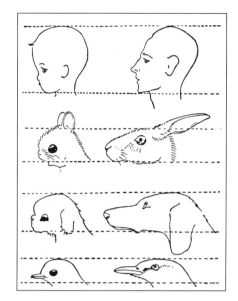

Figure 10.6 The releasing 'schema' for human parental care responses. Left: head proportions perceived as 'lovable' (child, gerbil, Pekinese dog, robin). Right: related heads which do not elicit the parental drive.

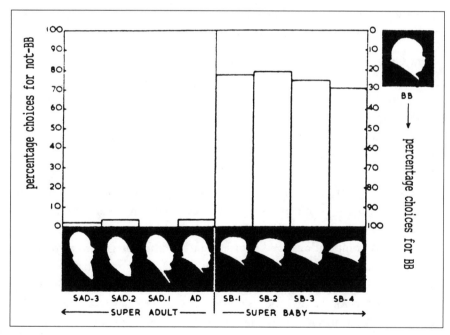

Figure 10.7. Results of experiments by Gardner and Wallach (1965) with relation to the Kindchenschema. The normal baby profile (BB) was offered opposite the profile of a normal adult (AD), the super-adult (SAD 1, 2, 3) and the super-baby profiles (SB 1, 2, 3, 4). The columns show, for every combination, the degree to which the profile deviating from BB was chosen.

behavioural patterns which are typical of the behaviour we display towards small children (Figure 10.6).[10]

Lorenz's hypothesis was confirmed by an experiment conducted by two psychologists, Gardner and Wallach. In order to test Lorenz's assertion they made a series of silhouettes of heads, ranging from the elongated to the compressed heads, and including the natural silhouette of a baby's head (Figure 10.7), and asked experimental subjects to choose the one they found most baby-like. The results showed that the respondents preferred not the natural baby's head (BB) but the supranormal ones (SB) with exaggerated babyish features.[11]

Lorenz's *Kindchenschema*, with all its implications for behavioural genetics, offers an explanation not only for the origin but also for the stubborn survival of the putto. The peak of its evolution is undoubtedly represented by the putti of François Duquesnoy (1597–1643), and especially the right-hand putto on his epitaph for Ferdinand van den Eynde in S. Maria dell'Anima in Rome, which must be dated between 1633 and 1640 (Figure 10.8).[12] That, anyway, was the view of the artist's biographer Gian Pietro Bellori, who outlined the following train of development in his *Vite* of 1672:

> The Greeks were excellent at sculpting and painting the Erotes and the Genii as young boys, and it seems that Callistratus gives a very good description of the putti around the statue of the Nile, and Philostratus does so in his account of the Erotes at play.
>
> Michelangelo made putti in both marble and paint, all of them resembling figures of Hercules, devoid of tenderness. Raphael is the first to give them grace and charm; he depicts them in a lively manner, growing in beauty in proportion to their age. Titian and Correggio depicted them more tenderly. Annibale Carracci belonged to that group, and Domenichino is considered excellent. He used them more than any other artist in his compositions, and shows them in different guises: as babes in swaddling clothes and as adults, with the movements and qualities corresponding to the age of each. Francesco the Fleming limited himself more to the tender forms of little children, and in creating this likeness he miraculously advanced the manner, which is now imitated by everyone . . .
>
> In Rome, in the Church of Santa Maria dell'Anima, he made two tombs which are built up against columns on either side. The one is of Ferdinand van den Eynde, a gentleman from Antwerp, and the other of Adriaen of the Vrijburgh family of Alkmaar. On the first are two putti which raise a cloth to reveal the inscription. One of them covers part of

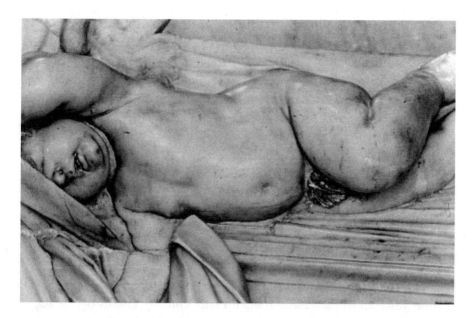

Figure 10.8 François Duquesnoy, *Epitaph for Ferdinand van den Eynde* (detail of the right-hand putto).

its head with a cloth as a token of sorrow, and it holds the hour–glass of death in its hand. This is without doubt the most beautiful little putto to which Francesco's chisel gave life, and sculptors and painters consider it exemplary, together with its companion, who is turned towards him and bows with him as he raises the cloth.[13]

Bellori was by no means alone in his admiration of Duquesnoy's putti. Rubens, whose putti can be regarded as the painterly pendant to Duquesnoy's, praises them fulsomely in a letter to the sculptor, in which he thanked him for the models after the putti on van den Eynde's epitaph:

I do not know how to express to you my obligation for the models you have sent me, and for the plaster casts of the two putti for the epitaph of van den Eynde in the Chiesa dell'Anima. Still less can I praise their beauty properly. It is nature, rather than art, that has formed them; the marble is softened into living flesh.[14]

Even Winckelmann, who shuddered at the corruptness of Baroque sculpture, fixated as he was by the art of antiquity, made an exception for Duquesnoy's putti:

Our artists resemble the classical sculptors in the sense that they too do not know how to make beautiful children, and I believe that they prefer to choose a Cupid by Fiammingo [Duquesnoy] to imitate than one by Praxiteles himself. The well-known story about a Cupid that Michelangelo made and then placed alongside one by an old master, in order to teach our generation how excellent the art of the ancients was, proves nothing here, for Michelangelo's children will never move us as deeply as nature itself does.

I do not believe that I am overstepping the mark when I say that Fiammingo acted like a new Prometheus, by modelling creatures that were rarely seen in art before him. If one can speak of art at all in the case of most of the figures of children on carved stones and in lofty works by the ancients, then one would wish that their children looked more child-like and chubby and less bony.

The children of Raphael and of the first great painters have exactly the same form, up to the moment when Franz Quenoy appears on the stage. The greater innocence and nature he gave his children make them exactly what Apollo and Antinous are for the youthful figure in the eyes of the artists who came after him.[15]

This passage has to be judged on its proper merits, since it comes from a publication in which Winckelmann attacked himself anonymously. In his reaction, which he published under his own name, and in which he admittedly does defend classical depictions of children, he nevertheless advises artists not to follow the antique too closely in this respect.[16]

Winckelmann's anonymous publication owes its importance mainly to his excellent analysis of the shortcomings of classical artists. But why, one wonders, did Winckelmann, despite Duquesnoy's merits, ultimately decide to defend the classical portrayal of the child? What it comes down to is that, according to Winckelmann, the artists of old idealised nature, and that included children, whereas contemporary artists got no further than literal imitation.[17] But surely, one would say, Duquesnoy's putto bears no relation to the children we see around us in the real world? It is an idealised, supranormal being to which our releasing mechanisms, and Winckelmann's, react in such a way that we pull out all our behavioural stops relating to cuddling and pampering children. Winckelmann's natural response to Duquesnoy's putto prevented him from seeing it as an idealised child, but on the contrary as a product of extreme naturalism. For after all, its 'tenerezza' releases affective behaviour, as does a real child. The classical child is unable to do this, because of its imperfect form. So what should be seen as an imperfection in classical sculpture becomes a virtue for Winckelmann, which he elevated to the level of 'edele Einfalt und stille Größe'.

The supranormal child evolved gradually in a process of schema and correction. I am, of course, referring to the evolutionary model postulated by Gombrich in *Art and Illusion*. There he demonstrated convincingly that the creation of images which satisfy certain specific demands of verisimilitude is achieved in a secular process of trial and error. The artists of antiquity and the Renaissance were groping their way towards a rendering of the motif by systematically eliminating mistakes. It was this critical attitude, according to Gombrich, that enabled these artists to overcome the technical and perceptual obstacles that stand in the way of a realistic imitation of the three-dimensional world.[18]

An examination of fourteenth- and fifteenth-century depictions of children in a random collection shows how difficult artists found it to make children look convincing. Leonardo, in his *Trattato della Pittura*, singles out two common mistakes in this area:

> That painting is most praiseworthy which conforms most to the object portrayed. I put this forward to embarrass those painters who would improve on the works of nature, such as those who represent a child a year old, whose head is a fifth of his height, while they make it an eighth; and the breadth of the shoulders is similar to that of his head, and they make it half the breadth of the shoulders; and thus they proceed reducing a small child a year old to the proportions of a man of thirty. They have so often made this error and seen it made that they have adopted it in practice, which has so penetrated and become established in their corrupt

Figure 10.9 Italian School, *Adoration of the Magi* (detail).

judgement that they make themselves believe that nature or whoever imitates nature commits a great error in not doing as they do.[19]

Leonardo's criticism is justified. Duccio's *Madonna of the Franciscans* is just one among many works that shows a child with a head that is too small in proportion to its body. The Christ Child in a fifteenth-century Italian

Figure 10.10 Michelangelo, *The Bruges Madonna*, 1505.

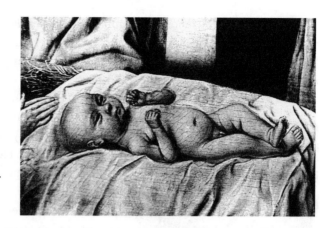

Figure 10.11 Master of Moulins, *Nativity of Cardinal Rolin* (detail).

Adoration of the Magi illustrates the other error noted by Leonardo, namely the disproportion between the widths of the head and the shoulders (Figure 10.9), which in this particular case makes the child look like an embryonic body-builder. In short, it was a process of trial and error, even leaving aside the lack of 'tenerezza' noted by Bellori in earlier depictions of children. According to him it is even missing from Michelangelo's children. This is best illustrated by his *Bruges Madonna* (Figure 10.10). There the Child displays the same harsh handling of the skin and stiffness in the hair as classical children, certainly in comparison with the children of Duquesnoy.

The Flemish Primitives were not at all bad in the faithful depiction of new-born infants, as witness the Christ Child in the *Nativity of Cardinal Rolin* of *c.* 1480 by the Master of Moulins (Figure 10.11). For a very long time, though, people were dissatisfied with this literal imitation. Children, too, were pressurised by the demands imposed by art theory on the rendering of the human form. In the course of the Renaissance the emphasis came to lie increasingly on the idealised depiction. But how were artists expected to put that idealisation into practice? If one consults art theory one discovers two means to this end: the Aristotelian and the Neoplatonic. In the former, idealisation was attained by selecting the most beautiful forms from nature. In the latter, the artist was led by the *idea* imbued in him by God. That is to say, in the Aristotelian theory, beauty is acquired a posteriori, while the Neoplatonic view held that beauty was present a priori as a conferred gift.[20] Now these two views are not as diametrically opposed as is usually suggested. I would even go so far as to say that in essence they do not differ all that much, for the Aristotelian art theory also presupposes an a priori knowledge of an ideal nature. How, otherwise, would the artist be able to make a selection?

The trial and error theory in Gombrich's *Art and Illusion* offers an excellent explanation for the evolution of the child from primitive creature to realistic being. But what happens if the natural appearances with which the artist matches his product are idealised? To put it another way, what was the artist to match if he wanted to surpass nature? Here Gombrich's theory in its

original form proves inadequate, which is why he found it necessary to expand it. He did so in his article 'Ideal and type', in which he postulates that during the process of trial and error the artist makes a match not only with natural appearances but also with the human ideal of beauty.[21] Here he closely approaches the two theoretical views outlined above. I thoroughly agree with Gombrich's formulation. However, the very general concept of the human ideal of beauty does need to be further defined, and to an extent this can be done with the aid of sociobiology. For example, as regards the idealisation of the child, it can be said that its modelling, as well as matching

Figure 10.12 Piat Sauvage, *Cortège in sculptural grisaille* (detail).

natural appearances, is also governed by specific key stimuli linked to innate releasing mechanisms, as described above.

To return to Bellori's biography of Duquesnoy, I would like to draw attention to a passage in which the author warns of the dangers that lie in wait for artists who think that they can emulate Francesco's putti:

> Those, however, who have imitated him have gone too far, and in the expectation of improving on his creations have laid bare the shortcoming by making the cheeks, hands and feet swell up, and by enlarging the head and the stomach in an ugly fashion – a bad habit which has taken possession of all painters.[22]

Although not contemporaneous with Bellori, one is reminded of creatures like those in paintings by a late Duquesnoy follower Piat Sauvage (Figure 10.12). We can deduce from this passage in Bellori that there is an upper limit to supranormal models. And indeed, if they become too far removed from reality they lose their credibility.

If we look at the Christ Child in Rubens's *Adoration of the Magi* in the Prado, we see that the realistic, new-born bag of bones known to us from the fifteenth century has now been completely overshadowed by the birth of the superbaby. The fact that it no longer looked like a new-born child was evidently considered acceptable. That makes it all the more remarkable that Rubens opted for a realistic Christ Child in the *Madonna in the Garland*, and not for a putto version, as in his *Virgin and Child surrounded by Children* in the Louvre (Figure 10.13). The answer cannot be that his son Albert, who was born in 1614, was the model for Jesus, for this is not a portrait. No, Rubens had another reason. The Virgin is displaying the Child in all his nakedness. Iconographically he was following a tradition that went back to the Renaissance, when it was felt necessary to emphasise the Incarnation of Christ rather than his divine nature, as had been done in the past. As Leo Steinberg has explained, the most extreme consequence of this was that artists began depicting Christ as the only child with bared genitals, in which, according to theologians, the sin of disobedience was implanted after the fall of man.[23] Rubens wanted to emphasise that Incarnation by depicting the Child naturalistically. Paradoxically enough, this naturalism is intricately bound up with the mystery of the Incarnation, which is stressed by fidelity to life. By isolating the Virgin and Child in a painting within a painting, Rubens created two distinct worlds: that of man, expressed in the painting of the Virgin with her Child, which has normal human proportions, and the supernatural world populated by supranormal beings.

I cannot refrain from a brief digression on the physical transformation which Mickey Mouse, the famous comic-strip figure, has undergone. In the course of the fifty years of his life he has gradually evolved into a national symbol. Under the pressure of public opinion his moral behaviour had to conform to his new status. As Stephen J. Gould has observed, the Disney studio made him politer, milder and friendlier. His appearance was modified, probably quite unconsciously, to fit his new character, by making his head, eyes and forehead larger (Figure 10.14).[24] It might be interesting to investigate whether there is a similar sort of relationship between the physical metamorphosis of the Christ Child and the contemporaneous and growing devotion to the infant Jesus.

Like other supranormal models, the putto has survived into the present day, not so much in modern art, although one does find it there, as in the

Figure 10.13 Peter Paul Rubens, *Madonna and Child surrounded by Children.*

advertising industry, which has quite understandably exploited it. *The Baby Made Me Buy It! A Treasury of Babies who sold Yesterday's Products* is the revealing title of a recent book. In order to market their product, the authors used a cover illustration of a 'putto' by Maud Tousey Fangel, which was used in the 1930s to promote Carter's infants' wear (Figure 10.15).[25]

Figure 10.14 Mickey Mouse's evolution over fifty years (left to right).

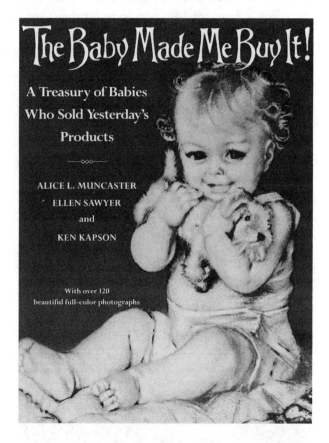

Figure 10.15 Cover of
the book *The Baby
Made Me Buy It*, 1991.

B. Rensch made a series of illustrations in which he quantitatively varied and exaggerated different combinations of various physical human features, and then asked experimental subjects to choose the ones they found the most beautiful. It turned out that, on average, people preferred models in which a feature was exaggerated beyond the normal. This study demonstrated that releasing mechanisms also underlie our preference for other supranormal figures, such as the extended figure discussed above. The same applies to the appreciation of body-builders in our culture and, by extension, of overly muscular figures in art. The incredible success of the *Laocoön* must largely be attributed to the brilliant handling of the exaggerated bundles of muscles, which brought about a true cult of musculature in art. It is not surprising, in the context of our desire for the supranormal, that the muscles are made even more prominent in imitations of the *Laocoön*. An excellent example of this is the copy commissioned by Pope Leo X from Baccio Bandinelli in 1520.[26] The same phenomenon is found in the arts of painting and drawing, such as the figure of Christ inspired by the *Laocoön* in a painting from the circle of Maarten van Heemskerck (Figure 10.16).

Leaving aside the highly developed musculature, it is not unimportant that there is usually a close approximation to the 'ideal' relation between the

Figure 10.16 Manner of Maarten van Heemskerck, *The Holy Trinity*.

widths of the shoulders and the hips in this kind of figure, such as Adam in the *Fall of Man* by Cornelis van Haarlem (Figure 10.1). Studies have demonstrated that in human courtship behaviour the relation between shoulders and waist in males (broad shoulders, small waist) and the hip–waist relation in females (small waist, large hips) is used among other cues to judge physical attractiveness. This seems to be a universal phenomenon, common to all cultures. These cues are directly related to reproductive success.[27] That also applies to fatness in women. The proverbial Rubens woman, for instance (although she is also found in the work of many other artists), belongs to the tradition that links fatness with feminine beauty, a connection that turns out to make biological sense. This is that a woman must store a reasonable amount of body fat to be capable of reproducing. The fat apparently has a regulatory role, and is important to the onset and the maintenance of normal menstrual cycles.[28] Here too an artist can increase fatness to make a woman look more attractive.

There are many indications that we judge the bodies of our fellow humans on the basis of innate information. This is strongly suggested by the fact that different cultures share some of the same ideals of female and male beauty. The appeal of dummies or models, in which certain of those characteristics are exaggerated, also points in this direction.

If the creative process is indeed controlled by biological processes, how does one account for the fact that the figure with extreme proportions, found so widely in Mannerism, was ousted by the less extremely proportioned figure of the Baroque? To put it another way, why does the intensity of the supranormal fluctuate throughout history? Probably quite simply because everything that repeats itself endlessly becomes extremely tedious, which is also, by the way, a biological fact. It was noted above that in the earlier theory of art the process of imitation swung between two poles, namely the exact and the ideal imitation. The thesis now could be that supranormal proportions are due to the effect of specific innate releasing mechanisms, which have a greater opportunity to influence the imitative process as the selective pressure on exact imitation decreases. Assuming that this is so, one would expect that tendency to have left some mark on sixteenth-century art theory, because it is in the art of that period that one is confronted with supranormal models in such large numbers. And that does appear to be the case. If one consults Lomazzo's theory of proportions in his *Idea del Tempio Della Pittura*, it turns out that he subordinated that theory to the metaphysical, Neoplatonic concept of the imbued *idea*.[29] If, on the other hand, one examines the theory that Bellori sets out in his *L'Idea del Pittore, dello Scultore e del'Architetto* (1664), it is immediately evident from the second part of the title, (*Scelta dalle Bellezze naturali superiore alla Natura*), that he was basing his theory on the Aristotelian principle of selection, namely that nature was once again the basis for imitation.[30] I have pointed out above that regarding imitation there is no essential difference between the Neoplatonic and Aristotelian theories of art, because both are in fact rooted in an a priori idea of beauty. However, there is also an important difference, which is that in the art theory inspired by Aristotle, beauty is always related to the world of phenomena. And although one also finds supranormal forms in nature, as in our modern-day fashion models, for instance, one rarely encounters extremes such as those that can arise from human releasing mechanisms.

The fact that one also finds credible supranormal figures in the course of the sixteenth century may also be connected with a new manner of drawing, described by Paul van den Akker as 'the interrupted, or broken drawing method', combined with the study of anatomy. This method, whereby the contour is divided into segments, left artists entirely free to concentrate on the expressiveness of the figural pose instead of on the mechanics of their own hand movements. As Vasari wrote in his treatise on learning the art of drawing:

> the best thing is to draw men and women from the nude and thus fix in the memory by constant exercise the muscles of the torso, back, legs, arms, and knees, with the bones underneath. Then one may be sure that through much study attitudes in any position can be drawn by help of the imagination without once having the living forms in view.[31]

One can imagine that this method, which made it possible to draw credible figures from the imagination, made supranormal figures more likely, partly because, as Vasari says, the artists did not have the living forms before them, and as a result the releasing mechanisms have more chance to operate.

Rubens's *Madonna in the Garland* shows how the two governing forces, the selective pressure on exact imitation and selective pressure on ideal imitation, can clash. Another good example of this is provided by El Greco's *Burial of the Count of Orgaz* of 1586–88 (Figure 10.17). The actual funeral of the count, which took place in the fourteenth century, is located in the earthly zone. The ritual, however, is being witnessed by men in sixteenth-century dress, and these are very probably portraits of men living in Toledo at the time. One, in any event, has been identified as El Greco's close friend Antonio de Covarrubias y Leiva.[32] Because portraits at that time demanded precise imitation, El Greco had to abandon his love of supranormal proportions in this zone. However, that does not apply to the upper zone, which appears to have been inspired by the hymn from the liturgy for the dead, *In Paradisum*, being sung by the priest down on earth: 'May the angels lead you into paradise; may the martyrs welcome you on your arrival and bring you into the city of Jerusalem. May the choir of angels receive you, and may you rest eternally with the once-poor man Lazarus.'[33] El Greco gives us a glimpse of the heavenly Jerusalem, where the count's soul, borne aloft by an angel, will soon be welcomed. The artist was free to populate this supernatural world with the supranormal figures to which he was so attached. An illuminating work in this context is the drawing of an eye in profile which El Greco made in the margin alongside a passage from the biography of Michelangelo in his own copy of Vasari's *Vite*.[34] This is where Vasari writes that Michelangelo:

used to make his figures of nine, ten or twelve heads, endeavouring to

Figure 10.17
El Greco, *Burial of the Count of Orgaz*, 1586–88.

realise a harmony and grace not found in Nature, saying that it was necessary to have the compasses in the eye, not in the hand, because while hands perform, the eye judges.[35]

It is important to realise that El Greco and Rubens were aware of the differences in the proportions of their figures, and had the opportunity of choosing realistic or idealised proportions. By contrasting them in a single painting, the relative difference in proportion takes on significance, in the sense that the normally proportioned figures allude to earthly reality, and those with supranormal proportions to the supernatural.

It seems that the human ideal of beauty can be defined more precisely in biological terms, or at least partly so. However, it should immediately be added that knowledge of the biological laws that generate that beauty can never guarantee the creation of a great work of art.

Notes

This article is based on my lecture, 'Sculpture from a biological perspective', given at the Rijksmuseum Vincent van Gogh in November 1987 at the invitation of the Society for Post-Graduate Art-Historical Research (SPKO).

1. G. Luijten *et al.* (eds), *Dawn of the Golden Age: Netherlandish Art 1580–1620* (exhibition catalogue), Amsterdam and Zwolle 1994, p. 15.
2. Pliny, *Natural History*, 34. bk. XXXIV, 65. For the translation use was made of The Loeb Classical Library, vol. 9.
3. J. Onions, *Art and Thought in the Hellenistic Age: The Greek World-View 350–50 BC*, London 1979, p. 42.
4. E. Gombrich, 'The Renaissance conception of artistic progress and its consequences' (*Norm and Form*, pp. 1–10).
5. Giorgio Vasari, *Le Vite dei più Eccellenti Pittori, Scultori e Architetti*, with an introduction by Maurizio Marini, Rome 1991, p. 315:

    Fece Parri le sue figure molto più svelte e lunghe, che niun pittore che fusse stato inanzi a lui; dove gl'altri le fanno il più di dieci teste, egli le fece d'undici e talvolta di dodici; né perciò avevano disgrazia, come che fossero sottile e facessero sempre arco o in sul lato destro o in sul manco, perciò che, sì come pareva a lui, avevano, e lo diceva egli stesso, più bravura.

    For the English translation use was made of the Everyman's Library edition, New York 1963, vol. 1, p. 257.

6. Giovan Paolo Lomazzo, *Idea del Tempio della Pittura*, edited with a commentary and translation by R. Klein, Florence 1974, vol. 1, p. 45 and vol. 2, pp. 659–60, note 4:

Scrisse Lisippo in suo trattato la via di osservare le quadrature dei membri dei corpi, e di fare le braccia e le mani lunghi, i piedi e la testa piccola, che dagli altri stati inanzi lui era fatta grossa sì come il naturale e catal picciolezza è stata riputata daì più grandi artifici la più bella invenzione che sia mai stata ritrovata.

7. F. Marías and A. Bustamente, *Las Ideas artísticas de El Greco: Commentarios a un Texto inédito*, Madrid 1981.

8. For the older literature about this picture see E. Kieser, 'Rubens' *Madonna im Blumenkranz'*, *Münchener Jahrbuch* (1950), pp. 215ff. and K. Ertz, *Jan Breugel der Ältere: Die Gemälde*, Cologne 1979, pp. 313, 611 and no. 326.

9. For the innate releasing mechanism see K. Lorenz, *The Foundation of Ethology: The Principal Ideas and Discoveries in Animal Behavior*, New York 1982, pp. 153–75, I. Eibl-Eibesfeldt, *Ethology. The Biology of Behavior*, New York 1975, pp. 65–103, 488–501, G.P. Baerends, 'De ethologische benadering van menselijk gedrag', in *Ethologie: De biologie van gedrag*, Wageningen 1973, pp. 288–324.

10. K. Lorenz, 'Die angeborenen Formen möglicher Erfahrung', *Zeitschrift für Tierpsychologie* 5 (1943), pp. 235–409.

11. B.F. Gardner and L. Wallach, 'Shapes of figures identified as a baby's head', *Perceptual and Motor Skills*, 20 (1965), pp. 135–42.

12. For the date of this epitaph see M. Fransolet, *François Duquesnoy sculpteur d'Urbain VIII*, Brussels 1942, pp. 118–20.

13. Li Greci scolperino e dipinsero eccellentissimante gli Amori e li Genii fanciulletti, e pare che molto a proposito li descriva Callistrato intorno la statua del Nilo, e Filostrato nell'immagine del giuoco de gli Amori. Michel Angelo in marmo ed in pittura li formò tutti risentiti come Ercoli, senza tenerezza alcuna. Rafaelle il primo conferì loro grazia e leggiadria, formandoli svelti e con le proporzioni dell'età crescente alla bellezza. Tiziano e'l Correggio più teneramente; Annibale Carracci si tenne fra costoro, ed il Domenichino è riputato eccellentissimo, il quale più d'ogni altro li usò ne' suoi componimenti, esprimendoli in varie forme, bambini in fasce ed adulti, con li moti e proprietà conformi all'età di ciascuno. Francesco Fiammingo si ristrinse più alle forme tenere de' bambini, ed in questa rassomiglianza si avanzò mirabilmente nella maniera che oggi è seguitata . . . In Roma nella Chiesa dell'Anima diede compimento alli due depositi murati di qua e di là in due pilastri; l'uno è di Ferdinando Van den [Eynden] gentiluomo d'Anversa, l'altro di Adriano, della famiglia Uryburgense d'Alcmaria. Nel primo sono accommodati due putti che nell'alzare un panno discoprono l'inscrizzione; nel qual panno si benda uno di loro parte della testa in contrasegno di mestizia, e tiene in mano l'oriuolo della morte. Questo certamente è il più bel puttino che animasse lo scarpello di Franceso, e che è tenuto avanti per essempio ed idea da scultori e da pittori, col suo compagno che si volge di rincontro e si piega insieme nell'alzare il panno (Giovan Pietro Bellori, *Le Vite de' Pittori, Scultori e Architetti Moderni*, edited by E. Borea, Turin 1976, pp. 294, 299–300).

14. Io non so come spiegare a V.S. il concetto delle mie obligazioni per li modelli mandatemi e per li gessi delli due putti della inscrizzione del [Van den Eynden] nella Chiesa dell'Anima, e molto meno so spiegare le lodi della loro bellezza: se li abbia scolpiti più tosto la natura che l'arte e 'l marmo si sia intenerito in vita..

This letter was reproduced by Bellori in his *Vite*, p. 302. For a commentary see Ruth Saunders Magurn, *The Letters of Peter Paul Rubens*, Cambridge, Mass. 1955, letter no. 248.1.22.

15. Unsere Künstler kommen darin überein, dass die alten Bildhauer nicht verstanden, schöne Kinder zu arbeiten, und ich glaube, sie würden zur Nachahmung viel lieber einen Cupido vom Fiammingo [Duquesnoy] als vom Praxiteles selbst wählen. Die bekannte Erzählung von einem Cupido, den Michelangelo gemacht, und den er neben einen Cupido eines altes Meisters gestellt, um unsere Zeiten dadurch zu lehren, wie vorzüglich die Kunst der Alten sei, beweist hier nichts: denn Kinder von Michelangelo werden uns niemals einen so nahen Weg führen, als die Natur selbst tut.

Ich glaube, es sei nicht zu viel gesagt, wenn man behauptet, Fiammingo habe, als ein neuer Prometheus, Geschöpfe gebildet, dergleichen die Kunst wenige vor ihm gesehen hat. Wenn man von den meisten Figuren von Kinderen auf geschnittenen Steinen und auf erhobenen Arbeiten der Alten auf die Kunst überhaupt schliessen darf, so wünschte man ihren Kindern mehr Kindsches, weniger ausgewachsene Formen, mehr Milchfleisch und weniger angedeutete Knochen. Eben dergleichen Bildung haben Raffaels Kinder und der ersten grossen Maler bis auf die Zeiten, da Franz Quenoy, genannt Fiammingo, erschien, dessen Kinder, weil er ihnen mehr Unschuld und Natur gegeben, den Künstlern nach ihm eben dasjenige geworden, was Apollo und Antinous demselben im Jugendlichen sind (J. J. Winckelmann, *Sendschreiben über die Gedanken von der Nachahmung der Griechischen Werke in der Malerei und Bildhauerkunst*, in *idem*, *Kleine Schriften und Briefe*, edited by W. Senff, Weimar 1960, pp. 66–7.)

16. J. J. Winckelman, *Erläuterung der Gedanken von der Nachahmung der Griechischen Werke und Beantwortung des Sendschreibens*, in *idem*, *Kleine Schriften und Briefe*, edited by W. Senff, Weimar 1960, p. 93.

17. *Ibid.*, p. 94.

18. *Art and Illusion.*

19. Leonardo da Vinci, *Treatise on painting*, translated and annotated by A. P. McMahon, Princeton 1956, vol. 1, p. 161 (433); see also p. 120 (290), 'How children's joints differ in size from those of men'.

20. For these concepts see E. Panofsky, *Idea: A Concept in Art Theory*, Columbia 1968; R. W. Lee, *Ut pictura poesis: The Humanistic Theory of Painting*, New York 1967, pp. 9–16.

21. E. H. Gombrich, 'Ideal and type in Italian Renaissance painting', in *New Light*, pp. 123–4.

22.   e colore nondimeno che l'hanno seguitato, come è facile alterare e dare nell'eccesso pensando di megliorare, hanno accresciutto e fatto sensibile il

difetto, enfiando gote, mani, piedi, ingrossando la testa e'l ventre bruttamente: il qual vizio si è insinuato insieme ne' pittori. (Bellori, *Vite*, p. 299).

23. Leo Steinberg, *The Sexuality of Christ in Renaissance Art and in Modern Oblivion*, New York 1983.

24. S. J. Gould, 'A biological homage to Mickey Mouse', *The Panda's Thumb: More Reflections in Natural History*, New York and London 1980, pp. 95–107.

25. A. L. Muncaster, E. Sawyer and Ken Kapson, *The Baby Made Me Buy It! A Treasury of Babies who sold Yesterday's Products*, New York 1991.

26. M. Bieber, *Laocoön: The Influence of the Group since its Discovery*, Detroit 1942.

27. T. Horvath, 'Correlates of physical beauty in men and women', *Social Behaviour and Personality*, 7 (1979), pp. 145–51; K. H. Skrzipek, 'Menschliche "Auslösermerkmale" beider Geschlechter, I: Attrappenwahluntersuchungen der Verhaltensentwicklung', *Homo* 29 (1981), pp. 75–88; *idem*, 'Menschliche "Auslösermerk- male" beider Geschlechter, II: Attrappenwahluntersuchungen des Geschlechtsspezifischen Erkennens bei Kindern und Erwachsenen', *Homo*, 32 (1982), pp. 105–19.

28. R. E. Frisch, 'Fatness and fertility', *Scientific American*, March 1988, pp. 70–7.

29. Lomazzo, *Idea*.

30. Gian Pietro Bellori, *L'Idea del Pittore, dello Scultore e del'Architetto: Scelta dalle Bellezze naturali Superiore alla Natura*, which was bound together with Bellori's *Vite*, pp. 3–25.

31. P. van den Akker, *Sporen van Vaardigheid: De Ontwerpmethode voor de Figuurhouding in de Italiaanse Tekenkunst van de Renaissance*, Abcoude 1991, and *idem*, '"Out of Disegno invention is born" – drawing a convincing figure in Renaissance Italian art', *Argumentation*, 7 (1993), pp. 45–66, G. Vasari, *Vasari on Technique*, translated be L. S. Maclehose, New York 1960, p. 210.

32. For this painting see J. Brown, 'El Greco and Toledo', in exhibition catalogue *El Greco of Toledo*, Toledo (The Toledo Museum of Art), Madrid (Museo del Prado), Washington (National Gallery of Art) and Dallas (Dallas Museum of Fine Arts), Boston 1982, pp. 123–8.

33. For this interpretation see, S. Schroth, 'The *Burial of the Count of Orgaz* by El Greco', in J. Brown (ed.), *Figures of Thought: El Greco as Interpreter of History, Tradition, and Ideas*, Washington 1982.

34. X. de Salas, *Miguel Angel y El Greco*, Madrid 1967, p. 37.

35. imperò egli usò le sue figure farle di nove e di dieci e di dodici teste, non cercando altro che col metterle tutte insieme ci fussi una certa concordanza di grazia nel tutto che non lo fa il naturale, dicendo che bisognava avere le seste negli occhi e non in mano, perché le mani operano e l'occhi giudica (Vasari, *Vite*, p. 1256).

For the translation use was made of the Everyman's Library edition, New York 1970, vol. 4, p. 171.

11

When skills become obtrusive: on E. H. Gombrich's contribution to the study of primitivism in art

Graham Birtwistle

THERE is obviously an element of risk involved in writing this essay before E. H. Gombrich's long-awaited book on *The Preference for the Primitive* has made its appearance.[1] But then, primitivism and issues related to it have long had a firm place in his writings. These researches constitute, as it were, the reverse side to the coin of themes presented in *Art and Illusion*, and they reveal Gombrich's deep fascination with the problems that arise when progress is questioned and skills in art become obtrusive. Material relevant to our theme is in fact spread over a half-century or more of publications, and by no means confined to those of his studies in which 'primitivism' or 'primitive' figure in the title.

As Gombrich himself has pointed out in one of those studies, historians can find themselves struggling to reconcile chronological and systematic approaches to their subject.[2] It will probably not surprise him to learn that such can also be the case when the subject in question is his own work. In what follows, I have not deliberately set out to trace the step-by-step development of Gombrich's thought on primitivism, even though I have found myself bearing some aspects of that evolutionary process in mind. Since my main concern has been to evaluate the significance of his researches (thus far), I have felt free to glean from studies written at different phases of his career, and in that respect something resembling a systematic approach prevails. Chronological factors do, however, have their own allotted place in this story. At the outset, and then again in the concluding remarks, we are reminded that the historiography of primitivism has its own history, and that developments which have occurred just in the past few years have given a new face to the study of primitivism.

A new debate and an older academic tradition

A generation of scholars has arisen for whom discussion of primitivism in art means discussion of the politics of culture. Ideological criticism of the concept 'primitive' and announcements of its obsolescence as an academic term were already in evidence in anthropological circles in the sixties,[3] but it was not until the eighties that the full force of such critique was felt in the fields of art history and art criticism. A good case can be made for locating the turning-point in 1984, the year in which William Rubin organized the spectacular exhibition *"Primitivism" in Twentieth-Century Art: Affinity of the Tribal and the Modern* at the Museum of Modern Art in New York.[4] For a sufficient number of critics in 1984, and for a growing body of critical opinion since then, Rubin's exhibition brought into the open much that was politically and culturally questionable in the history of modern art and its primitivist ideals. The great names of modernism were celebrated and elaborately researched, but the makers of 'tribal' art – works that had inspired the great names and that now spiced Rubin's exhibition and book – did not merit such attention. Their names and their concerns fell outside the scope of this Western history of art. In the post-colonialist and post-modernist eighties, it was judged, such a blatant continuation of colonialist and modernist prejudice was no longer acceptable.[5] Within a few years of Rubin's exhibition, 'primitivism' had become a term with just about as many dubious connotations as 'chauvinism'.[6]

How, then, was primitivism understood before Rubin entered the scene? Most of the signposts point back to pioneering work done in the thirties, first by the historians of ideas Arthur O. Lovejoy and George Boas and then by the art historian Robert Goldwater. In the 'Prolegomena to the history of primitivism' with which they opened their study of *Primitivism and Related Ideas in Antiquity* in 1935,[7] Lovejoy and Boas defined primitivism as a cluster of separate ideas, assumptions or attitudes, that in the course of history had sometimes interfused but sometimes contradicted one another. What made it possible to bracket these ideas under one term was their common tendency to reject the effects of progress and civilisation in favour of a natural or original state of things, though the many ways in which discontent manifested itself turned out to be matched by at least as many conceptions of nature and origins. Some of Lovejoy and Boas's distinctions, such as those between 'chronological' and 'cultural' kinds of primitivism and 'soft' and 'hard' variants, became a familiar feature in the vocabulary of scholars who followed them, and the Prolegomena contained a great many more. The definition of primitivism was not tied to any one particular symptom, nor was primitivism seen as a specifically European phenomenon; in their classic book of 1935 Lovejoy and Boas included chapters on primitivism in ancient western Asia and in Indian literature.[8] Needless to say, theirs was a rather different history of primitivism than the one the post-Rubin generation has come to know.

When Goldwater published his study *Primitivism in Modern Painting* in 1938,[9] it was evident that he had learned from Lovejoy and Boas. Goldwater rejected facile assertions about the 'primitiveness' of modern art and turned instead to the concept of primitivism, using it in much the same way as the historians of ideas to denote a collection of loosely related assumptions or attitudes. In Goldwater's case, the diversity within primitivism was closely tied to a typology of modern art as it was then understood, his argument took the reader from the Romantic Primitivism of Gauguin and the Fauves through Emotional Primitivism (German Expressionism) to Intellectual Primitivism (Cubism, Abstraction) and forms of primitivism associated with the subconscious and The Child Cult. As a prelude to the chapters on modern art he surveyed in some detail the rise of ethnological museums and the changing evaluations of 'primitive art' in nineteenth- and early twentieth-century ethnology, anthropology and art theory. But, significant though the Western fascination with tribal art may have been for Goldwater, it was not the definitive issue in the primitivism he discussed. Primitivism was about a variety of attitudes and assumptions and not just about a specific case or model.

It was Goldwater's book (subsequently revised in 1967) that remained the most frequently cited art-historical introduction to the subject right up to the time of Rubin's exhibition. Rubin has made it clear, in fact, that it was his desire to provide a replacement for Goldwater's venerable study that motivated his project in 1984.[10] Though he honoured Goldwater for his pioneering work, Rubin criticised him for having underrated the importance of formal borrowings by modern artists from tribal sources, and made it his own task to demonstrate the true extent of these. Indeed, Rubin and his fellow researchers successfully documented a host of such cases, carefully distinguishing possible sightings from impossible ones. But Rubin's fixation on the 'affinity of the tribal and the modern', and his conviction that only tribal art provided the definitive model for the primitivist, meant that he no longer dealt with the more complex kind of primitivism that had been the subject of Goldwater's book. Rubin's well-publicised 'ism' was in fact no longer the problem of primitivism as formulated by the historians of ideas and applied down the years to the history of art.

However, that older academic tradition has been continued and developed by other scholars – and none more than E. H. Gombrich. If Lovejoy and Boas wrote the Prolegomena for the study of primitivism, and Goldwater the primer for art historians, it is arguably Gombrich who has provided the advanced students' manual. More than any other scholar in the post-war era, Gombrich has used the resources of the history of ideas to elucidate assumptions and attitudes productive of artistic primitivism. But if he has followed the lead of Boas and Lovejoy, he has also transcended their methods.

Gombrich: primitivism ancient and modern, historical and systematic

When Gombrich's article on 'The debate on primitivism in ancient rhetoric' appeared in the *Journal of the Warburg and Courtauld Institutes* in 1966,[11] its analysis of primitivistic and anti-primitivistic themes in classical texts established the author firmly in the tradition of Boas and Lovejoy. In that same year, the Warburg Institute published George Boas's book *The Cult of Childhood*.[12] Of course, Gombrich's directorship of the Institute and the friendship between the two scholars removes much of the mystery, but the coincidence of their publications certainly heightens our awareness of the way their intellectual paths crossed at the time. While Boas was extending ancient primitivistic themes to include modern artists such as Klee, Miró and Dubuffet, Gombrich was taking the opposite course. His article announced a new series of studies on primitivism in modern art, but Gombrich began by returning to the world of classical antiquity.

Gombrich set out to examine the paradoxical possibility that arguments used in modern times to combat classicism and advance the cause of primitivism in art had been, as he put it, 'pre-figured and amply rehearsed in classical antiquity'.[13] Though he dealt with the ideas of orators such as Quintilian and Longinus, it was Cicero who most obviously drew Gombrich's attention:

> Cicero's meditations on the limits of effects and the unexpected vagaries of taste must rank among the most important reflections on the topic of primitivism – important precisely because they brush aside the argument between progress or corruption in which these debates normally become entangled.[14]

It was Cicero's awareness that over-indulgence in rhetorical effect can arouse distaste and that the true craftsman will know when to let go and when to use restraint that excited his enthusiasm, and Gombrich had no compunction in terming this a 'psychological theory'. It was for Gombrich a short step from Cicero's remarks to a formulation of psychological principles that trigger primitivistic impulses in art:

> The more the artist knows how to flatter the senses, the more he will mobilize defences against this flattery. The very progress of his skill will lead to a longing for less skill and more honesty. It is this subjective reaction, this contrast in effects, which will tend to surround earlier phases of art or of speech with an aura of moral superiority.[15]

Clearly, in 1966 Gombrich was finding more in the debate on primitivism in ancient rhetoric than simply the history of certain ideas. Though the 'rehearsal' of arguments about primitivism had significance for the study of the survival and transmission of classical themes into modern times, what had also come to light in Cicero's theory was a rationalised principle that could be redefined in the terms of modern psychology and used as an analytical tool. There were implications, therefore, for both historical and systematic perspectives on primitivism in art. And though the former linked him closely to Boas and Lovejoy, the latter added an extra dimension to the work of his predecessors.

It was most obviously the question of historical development that Gombrich took up in 1971 in his lecture for the Cooper Union on *Ideas of Progress and their Impact on Art*.[16] Under the heading 'From classicism to Primitivism', he looked briefly at ancient Greek notions of progess and decline in art before moving swiftly to his main theme: a discussion of the eighteenth-century ideas of the classicist J. J. Winckelmann, famed for his notion of *edle Einfalt*. In Winckelmann's schematic view of the way classical art developed, peaked and then declined, Gombrich found not only surviving classical ideas but also judgements that contained the seeds of a kind of primitivism that was yet to bloom:

> But though details are wrong Winckelmann certainly spotted the phe-nomenon of deliberately archaising sculpture and diagnosed correctly that the relief representing a libation at an altar must belong to this late phase since the archaic figures are displayed together with Corinithian columns. Winckelmann's speculations on the reasons for this deliberate primitivism are, of course, important for us. The earlier style is imitated, he thinks, because of the awe it inspires. Once more the ancient writers on rhetoric give him this important clue. For just as a certain harshness in the formation

and sound of words imparts grandeur to a speech, the harshness and severity of the early style exerts a similar effect.[17]

The psychological hint in that last remark was unmistakable, but Gombrich's main purpose was to establish a historical link between Winckelmann's ideas and the widespread growth of archaising and simplifying methods that characterised much European art at the close of the eighteenth century and the opening of the nineteenth. In art such as that of John Flaxman, the *barbus* in the studio of J. L. David, or the Nazarenes, Gombrich saw 'a natural transition from the cult of noble simplicity or *edle Einfalt* to that of pious simplicity or *fromme Einfalt*', and concluded: 'That great reversal of taste that led from classicism to primitivism had begun to have its impact on art.'[18]

The results of that reversal of taste were examined in Gombrich's four talks for BBC radio in 1979, under the general title *The Primitive and its Value in Art*.[19] The talks recapitulated the themes treated in 1966 and 1971 but also extended them to cover nineteenth-century developments and their consequences for twentieth-century artists such as Picasso, Henry Moore, Jean Dubuffet and Roy Lichtenstein. Not only did he scan back and forth across history from the ancients to the moderns, but his scanning picked out several different arguments for primitivism that can give rise to several different interpretations of the problem. There was the moral argument, which he linked with the name of Plato and typified as the condemnation of seductive techniques that can corrupt an honest mind. Then there was the powerful Aristotelian organic metaphor that could lend to the development of any art the aspect of a life-cycle and invest some of its products with the significance of youth and unspoilt potential. And, closely related to that, there was the physiognomic reaction to the outward signs of age, whereby something old becomes almost automatically revered. Paradox came into into play, however, when Gombrich conceded that 'such contrasts are too logical to be true to our real experience. It is the privilege of early art that it is not only heroic and idyllic, but also both old and venerable, young and endearing.'[20] Not only that, but he called once again on Cicero to give evidence that diminished the irrational power of the three previous arguments. This time, Cicero's insight into the mechanism of over-indulgence and consequent distaste was presented in terms of a theory of response: 'it is the beholder's sophistication that makes him reject an overdose of skill'.[21] And under the heading 'The priority of pattern', Gombrich opened a new perspective on modern primitivism. Much as in his major book *The Sense of Order*, which also appeared in 1979, he argued that decorative principles in art were not necessarily the same as illusory ones, and that nineteenth-century pioneers such as John Ruskin and Walter Crane had noted and embraced this possibility. As a result, the way was opened first for a recognition of the validity of non-classical pictorial methods and then, as the twentieth century got under way, for assertions of the superiority of non-European ones. All these different kinds of primitivism were carefully distinguished from one another, but for Gombrich the making of distinctions was not the end of the matter: 'Indeed, if we turn again to the historical sources of our modern preference for the primitive, we shall find them all stirred together in one heady brew.'[22]

Compared to Goldwater's account of primitivism in modern art, Gombrich's offered a more penetrating analysis of motivations and a much more convincing demonstration of how the history of art and the history of ideas intertwine. But at strategic junctures in the radio talks, Gombrich also turned to a more systematic, psychological discussion of his subject. Whereas in books such as *Art and Illusion* he had drawn on the work of J. J. Gibson in developing a psychology of perception to account for the development of artistic skills, in assessing what happened when skills became obtrusive he turned mainly to the depth-psychology of Sigmund Freud. Commenting in his first talk on Boas and Lovejoy's distinction between 'hard' and 'soft' primitivism, for example, he suggested: 'Both forms, of course, are reactions to what Freud calls the discontents of civilisation.'[23] In his fourth talk, the relevance of Freudian categories was made more explicit when Gombrich referred to his earlier collaboration with Ernst Kris on psychoanalytical approaches to caricature:

> Kris compared the stage of babbling in verbal humour with that of the scrawl in graphic wit. Both share the mechanism psychoanalysts call 'regression', the reversal to earlier phases of mental development; indeed, the surrender of rationality and control that characterise the adult mind.[24]

According to Gombrich, many twentieth-century art movements – he pointed to Fauvism, German Expressionism, Dada and Surrealism, and Abstract Expressionism – have valued regression out of 'a distaste for the skills developed by the Western tradition',[25] and though he found that the best modern artists know how to temper regressive leanings Gombrich also sounded a warning:

> Now this, to be frank, is the danger I see in the cult of the primitive. It is the cult of an extraneous negative virtue, the preference for the absence

of certain qualities which we have been taught to reject. But negation can never be enough. Nor can regression be.[26]

Discussion of negation and regression brought Gombrich to the climax and to the conclusion of his radio talks on primitivism in 1979. But these issues also brought him, and bring us, back to methods and conclusions established much earlier in his career. In studies made in the early fifties of 'Visual metaphors of value in art' and 'Psycho-analysis and the history of art' he had already laid substantial psychological foundations for his later analyses of the primitivism of Cicero, Winckelmann, and twentieth-century artists.

Meditations on negation

In the fifteenth century, Gombrich tells us in 'Visual metaphors of value in art'[27] Leone Battista Alberti rejected gold as a suitable means of decoration for a place of worship, and in doing so

> rejects the gratification of outward splendour in favour of something more 'dignified'. He values the white wall not only for what it is, but for what it is *not*. The terms 'pure' and 'unadorned' themselves imply this element of negation. Art now stands in a cultural context in which an expectation aroused and denied can by itself become expressive of ideas.[28]

Since then, Gombrich argues, Western culture has been marked by the process of sophistication which is largely driven by the principle of negation: 'There is always a strong negative element in what constitutes "good taste". It presupposes a mind not easily swayed by the appeal of immediate gratification which would be a lure to the "vulgar".'[29] But this is not the end of the story, since in the course of time sophisticates can arise who negate the negations of their predecessors.

> The use of gold which so shocked Renaissance writers as a sign of childish vulgarity now impresses us as pleasantly naive. We feel we can afford some indulgence in this simple pleasure. We are close to a sophistication of the second degree which welcomes the 'primitive' as a value, providing a metaphor for all that is strong, direct, forthright, and 'unsophisticated'.[30]

What can happen here, Gombrich goes on to explain in 'Psycho-analysis and the history of art',[31] is that our conviction that our taste is sufficiently advanced that it gives us the security to overcome some of our fear of revealing more elementary and childish longings. At one and the same

primitivistic moment, we can both demonstrate our superior level of sophistication and enjoy the rewards of regression.

There is much more to these arguments in Gombrich's articles from
1952–53, as well as in the reformulations he made for his radio talks in 1979.
But even in the short form in which I have presented them they offer the
student of primitivism in art plenty to think about. In a paradoxical way,
progress turns out to be a key to primitivism. Moreover, primitivistic values
turn out to have a chameleon-like quality: they change with their cultural
surroundings and in the light of whatever it is that we are concerned to
negate. It is not difficult to see implications here for an amplification of Boas
and Lovejoy's categorisations of primitivism and for an application of them
specifically to the history of art. 'Hard' and 'soft' variants – and many others
– can indeed be both distinct and yet related to one another through the
twists and turns of the sophisticating process. And the appeal to nature for
norms, which pervades the discussion of primitivism in the history of ideas,
is identified by Gombrich with biological responses which have psychological
consequences for taste and art: for example in the way regression and the
metaphorical values of the unsophisticated inject elements from man's 'nature'
into his culture. So if Gombrich has dealt with ideas in history more
thoroughly than Goldwater, he may be also be said to have supplied the
history of ideas with the kind of earthy roots that some critics have found
lacking in Lovejoy's methodology.[32]

Negation in action: Moore, Appel and Constant

Gombrich's insistence on asking not only what the primitivising artist wanted,
but also what he or she apparently did not want, must be one of the most
useful hints ever given to the student of primitivism. Once one has become
accustomed to looking for it, the significance of a pattern of sophistication
and negation emerges time and time again in art-historical researches into
primitivism, and it is often in artists' statements and critical reactions to their
work that the best clues are to be found.

Henry Moore, for example, has told us how as a student at the Royal
College of Art in the early twenties he was taught less by following college
classes than by visiting the British Museum and by reading Roger Fry – a
great advocate of the superiority of carved African sculpture over the Renaissance tradition of modelling.[33] Moore's negation of the academic tradition
certainly did not go unnoticed, however, as we know from his vivid account

of how the arch-conservative Professor Beresford Pite and the liberal but circumspect Sir William Rothenstein reacted to his work during a monthly critique:

> Rothenstein was in the front row when Pite said, "This student has been feeding on garbage – anyone can see that." There was a bit of Etruscan or Negro influence in it – I forget which. Anyway, he really let himself go, and the next day Rothenstein called me into his office and said, "I hope you weren't too upset – these things are bound to happen, you know."[34]

An even more public clash with authority and tradition overcame Dutch experimental artists such as Karel Appel and Constant in the heyday of their Cobra movement (1948–51). In 1949, Appel's mural for the canteen of the Amsterdam Town Hall was the subject of a press campaign which finally saw the painting covered up (Figures 11.1, 11.2), and in November of that year the major Cobra exhibition at Amsterdam's Stedelijk Museum – in which Appel and Constant were prominent participants – was pilloried by the leading Dutch art critics and gave cartoonists a field-day. It was Cobra's spontaneity and manifest interest in the simple figuration found in children's art that drew the critics' wrath: 'Monstrosities in a city museum. "World-

Figure 11.1 Karel Appel, *Questioning Children* (mural), 1949.

Figure 11.2 'The controversial Appel', 1949.

changing" artists show their lack of skill. Whim of museum authorities opens door to barbarians', ran one of the headlines,[35] while a critic cynically illustrated a drawing by his three-year-old daughter along with the Cobra works and challenged his readers to spot the difference. But these reactions were perhaps no less bound to happen than Pite's critique of the young Moore had been in the twenties. It was, after all, the intention of Cobra artists to overturn the existing artistic and social order and replace it with something more primitive and more honest. They looked for the victory of the 'counter-culture' over the established, classically-oriented 'culture', as Constant's articulate and aggressive theories in the experimental journal *Reflex* made clear.[36] But it is important to note that Constant did not see Cobra primitivism as a goal in itself but rather as a necessary step in a new development: 'That is to say, out of our experience in this state of unfettered freedom will come the laws for a new kind of creativity.'[37] What emerges here is Constant's own awareness not only of the role of negation in his primitivism but also of how that negation is part of a process of cultural change.

These case-histories gain in poignancy when we go on to look at the changes that did indeed occur in the course of time. The commissions given in the mid-fifties for the prestigious new UNESCO Building in Paris (1958) are in that respect quite revealing. Henry Moore made a colossal sculpture for the forecourt – the latest in a long line of reclining figures that had begun in the twenties with works based on archaic Mexican religious statuary – while Karel Appel provided a large, primitively expressionist painting for the restaurant. Those who had formerly clashed with authority and tradition had in fact become the acknowledged masters of the day – and this was not because they had denied their primitivism. Both artists had certainly developed their work, and Moore had arrived at a kind of synthesis of Renaissance and modern primitivist values. In Appel's case, however, the direction of change was to an even more 'barbaric' art (the term was Appel's own). But the 'tradition' had itself changed, sufficiently at least to embrace the primitivism of Moore and Appel. What had previously been an unacceptable negation of taste and values had turned into an acceptable polarity. When Appel's 'barbaric' painting was placed as a backdrop to the clean lines and civilised white tablecloths of the UNESCO restaurant, perhaps no clearer sign could have been given that mainstream modern culture not only had a place for Dionysus as well as Apollo but was revelling in the contrast between the two.[38]

However, if Appel's primitivistic painting was welcomed by UNESCO and the art world of the day, it was not to the taste of his former Cobra colleague, Constant. By the mid-fifties, Constant had rejected his earlier primitivistic methods and turned first to geometrical abstraction and then to the making of constructions that were pregnant with technological metaphor (Figures 11.3, 11.4). Constant stayed, as it were, ahead of the game, negating his own former primitivism just as his primitivism had once negated classical artistic values. In Constant's eyes, Appel had simply exploited the 'old' primitivism of Cobra, and that was not the thing to do.[39]

Gombrich's preference

On the face of it, these case-histories do seem to confirm the relevance for primitivism of the sophisticating process and its negations that Gombrich has sketched for us. At the same time, however, I have some doubts about Gombrich's explanation of the problem in terms of depth-psychology. For one thing, it strikes me as significant that Constant, whose shifts of style both towards and away from primitivism seem to tally so remarkably well with Gombrich's diagnosis, has given his own explanation of what happened. Constant was – and still is – a Marxian theorist, and has always accounted for his negations in dialectical terms.[40] For Constant, the dynamics of social change are even more fundamental for artistic development than is the psychology of taste. But Constant's alternative explanation helps to remind us that Gombrich's theory also implies collective cultural change, even though the terms used are overtly those of the psychology of individual taste. Indeed, in a certain light, something rather like a dialectical theory of cultural development can show up in Gombrich's psychological account of primitivism. It is not simply

Figure 11.3
Constant, *War*, 1950.

Figure 11.4 Constant, *Construction*, 1958.

that he relies heavily on the dialectician's principle of negation, but what he calls a 'sophistication of the second degree' bears a certain resemblance to the well-known dialectical pattern of negation and spiralling ascent, whereby something once negated is taken up again on a 'higher' plane. In pointing this out, I realise that talk of dialectics can mean entry into a morass of often idiosyncratic and largely discredited ideas, and I realise too that Gombrich has spent most of his working life battling against the influence of the Hegelian tradition of thought. Nevertheless, my suspicion is aroused by the very ease with which Gombrich's theory fits the most self-consciously dialectical of primitivist art movements.[41] And there is something more.

Whether or not the dialectical undertones are there, Gombrich's discussion of negation in primitivism seems to me to open a Pandora's Box; more implications and possibilities spring out than simply the psychological ones he prefers to deal with. Granted, discussion of taste in relation to art can be particularly well served by the psychological explanation, and the thought is irresistible that for many an international cultural official dining at the UNESCO restaurant, Appel's painting has provided a supremely piquant moment of sophisticated ego-regression. But then, I wonder if Gombrich really does think that the motivation for Appel's primitivistic art or for a movement such as Cobra can be reduced to biological-psychological mechanisms of taste. I must confess to finding Gombrich ambivalent on this point. Though he wisely warns against 'the fallacy of the single cause' and demonstrates the complexity of strands that interweave to produce modern primitivism, and though he often points out that discussing taste is not the same as discussing art, there are crucial moments in his argumentation when he seems to ignore both warnings. At the core, his discussion of primitivism does revolve around issues of taste, and these are the issues he finds most amenable to analysis in Freudian terms. Here I would want to suggest that while these issues can be of strategic importance in bringing the production and reception of art into close focus, there can also be other motivations for primitivism – ideological-political, philosophical or religious ones, for example – that bring into play other kinds of negation and progression, with their concomitant 'regressions'. Since the artist of modern times is not only a craftsman but by turns philosopher, political agitator or self-proclaimed shaman, discussion of his or her primitivism only in terms of skills and psychological mechanisms of taste will inevitably leave some questions unanswered.

Questioning the basic metaphor

> Every user meant something different when talking about the primitive, but the word itself, like other terms, had acquired what Lovejoy liked to call a 'metaphysical pathos'; it had become a word of power which offered itself to thinking men as a basic metaphor which no one wished to question.[42]

Many memorable sentences have come from Gombrich's pen, and this – taken from his tribute to George Boas – is surely one of them. The situation sketched is of course that of the twenties and thirties, and the questioning of that word of power and its basic metaphor is precisely what Boas and Lovejoy, Goldwater, Gombrich and others have gone on to do in their studies of primitivism. Now, after years of usage as academic concepts, it would seem that both 'primitive' and 'primitivism' have once again become words of power, though the metaphor has changed.

What lends these words their metaphoric power today is a deep sense of Western guilt. In a text which has become a classic of its kind, Thomas McEvilley wrote of Rubin's exhibition in 1984:

Of course, you can find lots of little things wrong with any big project if you just feel argumentative. But I am motivated by the feeling that something important is at issue here, something deeply, even tragically wrong. In depressing starkness, "Primitivism" lays bare the way our cultural institutions relate to foreign cultures, revealing it as an ethnocentric subjectivity inflated to coopt such cultures and their objects into itself.[43]

In subsequent exhibitions such as *Magiciens de la Terre* (Centre G. Pompidou, Paris, 1989) and *Africa Explores* (The Center for African Art, New York, 1991), McEvilley and others have made deliberate attempts to right Rubin's political wrongs and assist contemporary non-Western artists out of their anonymity, while new and ideologically aware studies of modern primitivism have concentrated on exposing patterns of Western cultural appropriation and persistent fictions about the non-Western 'Other'. But if much of the recent discussion of primitivism finds its starting-point in the critique of Rubin's exhibition, few critics and scholars have bothered to question Rubin on grounds other than the politics of culture. In fact, by defining his theme as 'affinity of the tribal and the modern' Rubin ignored a more complex scholarly tradition and took no account of other important variants of primitivism, including some that did not look outside the West for their models and some that were not even Western. In basing his sumptuous exhibition and book on this tight definition, Rubin not only moved on to a collision course with an increasingly powerful political-cultural lobby but he presented a new generation of scholars with a shrunken concept of primitivism and its history.

For this new generation there is perhaps little reason to question Rubin's definition of primitivism. It has, after all, provided an eminently suitable target for current Western self-critique. But that does not mean that all is well with the historiography of primitivism – or, for that matter, with Western self-critique. Since the debate on primitivism came to focus specifically on West/non-West relations, political and anthropological judgements have tended to take precedence over careful historiography, but the issues at stake remain essentially historical ones. Critique may address the current situation, but in practice it usually blames the past – the primitivism of earlier decades.[44] There is an advantage to be gained by this ploy: that important factor of Western guilt can be shrugged off the present and on to the past. We can be post-modernist, post-primitivist – and post-guilty. But one of the dangers of this practice is that historical figures, whose only means of answering charges brought against them is through the reconstructive work of historians, can be at best marginalised and at worst made into scapegoats who are meant to carry our Western guilt away. Moreover, a generation of intercultural theorists can keep at arm's length the very real possibility that the genealogy of their thinking may relate closely to aspects of the history of primitivism. The danger here is that 'critical' theorists thereby cut themselves off from a significant means of self-critique.

It is not so much that thinking men and women nowadays are reluctant to question primitivism. It is more that the questioning has become narrowed in focus and often inquisitorial in character. As a result of some of his earlier formulations about the primitive, Gombrich himself has not escaped the attentions of contemporary ideologically-aware investigators.[45] But though his later writings by no means show him to be politicising the discussion of primitivism, their very humanism brings with it a sensitivity to the lot of the individual non-Western artist – which is, many would argue, the issue on which justice in an intercultural art world really turns.[46] Gombrich is unlikely to emerge as a paragon of political correctness. What he has to offer is of another order; his studies help to restore much of the lost historiographical breadth and complexity to the questioning of the primitive and its meta-phorical values in art. Indeed, one might ask if the current critique of primitivism does not in some ways continue and extend that pattern of sophistication and negation which Gombrich has identified in the history of primitivism. But then, could it really be possible that this post-modern ideological negation of primitivism is, at root, simply a matter of taste and a question of psychology?

Notes

1. See *Eribon*, p. 86.
2. E. H. Gombrich, 'Adam's house in Paradise', in *Reflections*, pp. 147–51: 'Any-body who has ever tried to write the history of an idea knows of this problem of reconciling an intelligible systematic exposition with the needs of a chrono-logical narrative' (pp. 149–50).
3. See, for example, Ashley Montague (ed.), *The Concept of the Primitive*, New York 1968.
4. New York and Boston 1984, two volumes.
5. Thomas McEvilley, 'Doctor, lawyer, Indian Chief: "Primitivism in Twentieth-Century Art" at the Museum of Modern Art in 1984', *Artforum* 23 (1984), pp. 54–60.
6. See, for example, Susan Hiller (ed.), *The Myth of Primitivism: Perspectives on Art*, London and New York 1991.

7. Baltimore 1935, reprints New York 1965, 1973.

8. Chapters contributed by W. F. Albright and P.-E. Dumont.

9. New York 1938; revised and enlarged edition, *Primitivism in Modern Art*, Cambridge, Mass. and London 1986.

10. Rubin, *"Primitivism"*, p. 1.

11. Vol. 29, pp. 24–38.

12. *Studies of the Warburg Institute* (E. H. Gombrich, ed.), University of London, vol. 29.

13. Gombrich, 'Debate on primitivism', p. 24.

14. *Ibid.*, p. 31.

15. *Ibid.*, p. 32.

16. New York 1971 (limited edition); reissued in German translation as *Kunst und Fortschritt: Wirkung und Wandlung einer Idee*, Cologne 1978.

17. Gombrich, *Ideas of Progress*, p. 30.

18. *Ibid.*, p. 40.

19. Published in 1979 in four issues of *The Listener*. 'The dread of corruption', 15 February 1979, pp. 242–5; 'The turn of the tide', 22 February 1979, pp. 279–81; 'The priority of pattern', 1 March 1979, pp. 311–14; 'The tree of knowledge', 8 March 1979, pp. 347–50.

20. 'The dread of corruption', p. 244.

21. *Ibid.*, p. 245.

22. *Ibid.*

23. *Ibid.*, p. 243.

24. 'The tree of knowledge', p. 348. Cf. E. H. Gombrich and E. Kris, *Caricature*, Harmondsworth 1940.

25. 'The tree of knowledge', p. 348.

26. *Ibid.*, p. 349.

27. In *Meditations*, pp. 12–29.

28. *Ibid.*, p. 17.

29. *Ibid.*, p. 18.

30. *Ibid.*, p. 21.

31. In *Meditations*, pp. 30–44.

32. For discussion of critique of Lovejoy's method, see, for example, Maurice Mandelbaum, 'The history of ideas, intellectual history, and the history of philosophy', in *History and Theory: Studies in the Philosophy of History, Beiheft 5: The Historiography of the History of Philosophy*, The Hague 1965, pp. 33–66.

33. Philip James (ed.), *Henry Moore on Sculpture*, London 1966.

34. *Ibid.*, p. 36.

35. Gabriel Smit, 'Wangedrochten in een Stedelijk Museum. "Wereldvernieuwende" kunstenaars tonen hun gebrek aan kunnen. Grillen van directie openen deur voor barbaren', *De Volkskrant*, November 1949.

36. Constant, 'Manifest', *Reflex* 1, 1948; Constant, 'Cultuur en contra-cultuur', *Reflex* 2, 1949 (unpaginated). Constant's use of the term 'contra-cultuur' represents an early variant of the term 'counter-culture' (Dutch: 'tegencultuur') popularised in the 1960s.

37. Constant, 'Manifest'. See Graham Birtwistle, 'Cobra and Primitivism', *Kunstlicht*, 20, Winter 1986–87, pp. 2–8.

38. See the exhibition and catalogue *Polariteit: Het apollinische en het dionysische in de Kunst*, Stedelijk Museum, Amsterdam, 22 July–18 September 1961.

39. Constant (and co-editors), 'Ce que sont les amis de "Cobra" et ce qu'ils représentent', *Internationale Situationniste*, 1 (1958), pp. 4–6. The relevant passage (pp. 4–5) reads:

> En 1951, l'Internationale des Artistes Expérimentaux mit fin à son existence. Les représentants de sa tendance avancée poursuivirent leurs recherches sous d'autres formes. Certains artistes, au contraire, abandonnant la préoccupation d'une activité expérimentale, usèrent de leur talent pour mettre à la mode ce style pictural particulier qui était le seul résultat tangible de la tentative Cobra (par exemple Appel, au Palais de l'U.N.E.S.C.O.).

40. Constant, 'Opkomst en ondergang van de avant-garde', and 'De dialektiek van het experiment', in his *Opstand van de Homo Ludens*, Bussum 1969, pp. 11–48, 142–8.

41. In some, though not all respects, a similar critique is to be found in Alan Colquhoun, 'Gombrich and cultural history', *Architectural Design*, 51 (1981), pp. 35–9:

> It is this tension between the diachronic and synchronic studies of artistic works which creates the dialectical quality of Gombrich's thought – a thought that seeks to accommodate historical continuity and change on the one hand, and a theory of signification independent of historical determination, on the other (p. 38).

> For a discussion of dialectics in mid-century primitivistic art theory see my *Living Art: Asger Jorn's Comprehensive Theory of Art between Helhesten and Cobra (1946–1949)*, Utrecht 1986. See also Peter Wollen, 'The Situationist International: on the passage of a few people through a rather brief period of time', in his *Raiding the Icebox: Reflections on Twentieth-Century Culture*, Bloomington and Indianapolis 1993, pp. 120–57.

42. E. H. Gombrich, 'The history of ideas: a personal tribute to George Boas (1891–1980)', in *Tributes*, pp. 165–83 (pp. 173–174).

43. McEvilley, 'Doctor, lawyer', p. 60.

44. See Thomas McEvilley, 'The selfhood of the other: reflections of a Westerner on the occasion of an exhibition of contemporary art from Africa', in his *Art and Otherness: Crisis in Cultural Identity*, Kingston, New York 1992, pp. 85–108:

> At the heart of Modernism was a myth of history designed to justify colonialism through an idea of progress . . . Post-Modernism in the visual arts is part of the global project of cultural decolonization. It involves (among other things) an attempt on the part of Western people to get beyond strictly European ideas of esthetics and its history – ideas heretofore integral to their sense of identity (pp. 85–86).

The text was first published in 1991.

See also Clementine Deliss, 'Lotte or the Transformation of the Object', *Durch*, 8/9 (1990), pp. 3–27:

It is not acceptable at the present time to refer to the debate on the art-object/ethnographic object/ethnic-art-object without taking a political stance. This does not mean involving oneself in Anti-Apartheid demonstrations (although it can), but it does imply the necessity to contextualize one's writings in view of a current living situation in cultures outside of the great Western power complex which are, moreover, sadly dependent on it even since decolonization. The duo art/anthropology can no longer be viewed from a literary plane. The Primitivist and Surrealist legacies are no longer justifiable unless they are analyzed in an exceptionally self-critical manner (pp. 16–17).

45. For example, Sally Price, *Primitive Art in Civilized Places*, Chicago and London 1989:

E. H. Gombrich's elaborations of the attributes of Tribal Society adds yet another example to those already cited in earlier chapters, authenticating for current and future generations of readers stereotypic images of the Third World as a land of ignorance, confusion, and childishness (p. 125).

Price refers to, and quotes, passages from *The Story of Art* (1966 edition).

46. See for example, E. H. Gombrich, 'Tribal styles', in *Reflections*, pp. 23–32:

Reading these and similar passages one suddenly realizes with a shock that individuals never figured in the two previous books. It used to be said in old-fashioned schools that geography was about maps and history about chaps. If we are to trust etymology, anthropology, the science of man, should also be about people, but an increasing number of anthropologists today see it as their task to make maps of a people's mental structure. Like the earlier doctrine of the *Volksgeist*, this approach implies a degree of collectivism that ultimately negates the humanist faith . . . After all, the incalculable eddies in this field of observation are human beings, unique and unrepeatable, whether their name is Michelangelo or Ahmad Batoul (pp. 31–32).

The text was first published in 1972.

12

Orders with sense:
sense of order and classical architecture

Joaquín Lorda

> on discovering vestiges of geometrical shapes, he cried:
> 'I spy human traces!' (Vitruvius, *De architectura*, 6, 1).

GOMBRICH said that he regarded *The Sense of Order* and *Art and Illusion* as fragments of an ambitious book on the function of images.[1] But if the question which *Art and Illusion* sought to answer was well defined, the same was not true for *The Sense of Order*; decoration is complex, and the traditions governing ornamentation are extremely varied. *The Sense of Order* is therefore a 'polyphonic' work;[2] and Gombrich himself believed that it might seem lengthy and somewhat difficult to read.[3] The work's difficulty, however, is a consequence of its greater strength; it abounds in ideas. In *The Sense of Order* we learn that decorating consists not of using a book of 'patterns', but of entering into a knot of relationships of a biological, psychological, sociological, historical, plastic and theoretical nature, which it is impossible to undo at one tug without unravelling the many threads which make it up.

His argument can easily be summarised. The sense of order underlies all human creations, but it can also be observed at lower stages of evolution;[4] our perception establishes regularities, which may or may not exist, at all levels, in the physiological and the psychological,[5] and, with a considerable saving, only pays attention to the irregularities ('Popperian asymmetry').[6] The sense of order is complemented by the sense of meaning: our perception discovers 'things' rather than 'shapes'; the two senses operate simultaneously. Various chapters study their mutual influence on the design of an ornament and our perception of it; appropriately, he adds a brief history of ideas about decoration and style.[7] The book offers a vast number of suggestions, convincing examples and curious anecdotes.

The Sense of Order contains ideas which hold good for every kind of ornament. My present objective is a modest one: to provide a brief account of those which shed light on aspects of classical architecture. As *The Sense of Order* deals with ornament in general, this involves a distortion, though not a preposterous one; Gombrich assures us that 'architecture must be the test case for any theory concerned with the decoration of man-made structures'.[8] I should like to corroborate something which has already been demonstrated in many fields: Gombrich regretted not being able to spend time discussing particular traditions such as those of the Far East or the Islamic world,[9] but Jessica Rawson affirms, speaking of Chinese art, that *The Sense of Order* offers 'a range of possibilities of which I had hardly dreamed',[10] and even a critical author like Oleg Grabar, in his study of Muslim decoration, gathers together (not without criticism) Gombrich's ideas, placing them among the classics of ornamentation alongside Owen Jones, William Morris, John Ruskin, Gottfried Semper, Viollet-le-Duc and Alois Riegl.[11]

The fascination of beauty

This litany of authors serves to introduce a premise. In vain do we seek for common characteristics ('Ruskin is rhetorical and rousing, Semper is pedantic and soporific,'[12] writes Gombrich); but all have an ambitious vision and a sincere love of ornamentation.

In Gombrich's study there is also a personal element: since childhood he had felt drawn to these objects, in an everyday context, in a society in which examples of decorative art were enjoyed in a natural, intuitive and light-hearted way;[13] perhaps his later research was spurred on by the fact that he found himself embroiled in an intellectual dispute which was ultimately to scorn such manifestations. None the less, Gombrich differed from the majority of the writers listed above in that he researched into what, historically, decoration was like, but pronounces no 'message for our time'.[14]

In any case, in order to understand ornamentation, affinity is required rather than intellectual detachment; the experience of fascination in the face of a master-work aids us in recognising the autonomy of the ornament. The necessary rational working-out follows in its wake. If the tables are turned, ornamentation will be interesting as a manifestation of social or cultural hierarchies, or of intriguing messages, but we shall fail to glimpse its core; objects and buildings were created by artists who enjoyed dreaming them up, for patrons who enjoyed possessing them and contemplating them, even though enjoyment may not have been the initial objective.

The man-made order

Like Huizinga, Gombrich loves to represent creation as a joyous game played by the artist:[15] '*homo faber* must also be associated with *homo ludens*, man who enjoys playing'.[16] But pleasure does not only belong to the artist: there is also 'the beholder's share'.[17] When the spectator makes an 'effort after meaning',[18] to perceive what the artist has done, he or she is re-creating that work and enjoying it:[19] 'the pleasure we experience in creating complex orders and in the exploration of such orders (whatever their origin) must be two sides of the same coin'.[20]

Years ago, when someone described a style of architecture as 'great fun', this obviously meant that it could be enjoyed.[21] Of course, not every building or object warrants the description 'great fun'. Perhaps we stretch this metaphor too far if we call to mind a genuine toy which Gombrich mentions as a (failed) example of the creation of orders: the kaleidoscope.

'I am myself a devotee of this instrument and I like to share my pleasure with others. They usually respond with delight, but after a few exclamations of "ah" and "oh" they put it aside and talk of other things.'[22] Around its centre the kaleidoscope produces infinite symmetrical patterns, which are evanescent and unrepeatable. That is why they are so boring; there are no

expectations: their shape is hard to identify, their variations are random. An architectural design, however, like a rose window, is not an accidental form: our sense of order and meaning indicate to us that this is a human organisation, capable of arousing interest and pleasure; in fact 'we cannot divorce the impression it makes from our knowledge of the craftsman's skill and from awareness of meaning'.[23]

Let us look at a similar example: snow crystals. In *The Sense of Order*, Gombrich discusses the photographs of W. Bentley, showing thousands

Figure 12.1 Snow crystal.

with no repetition.[24] In 1857 James Glaisher recommended snow crystals as a revealing ornament, demonstrating that they met the requirements set by Owen Jones in *The Grammar of Ornament*.[25] His simplified drawings show their hexagonal structure, even though they lose in brilliance and transparency. But when we look through his snow crystals, as in Figure 12.1, the same thing happens as with the Kaleidoscope: at first, they fascinate us, but 'after a few exclamations of "ah" and "oh"', we grow bored; a game of this kind does not have human rules; our sense of order can read little in this redundant glacial geometry; the sense of meaning becomes paralysed: there is nothing here to understand. Of course, were the forms sketched in greater detail they might become more interesting.[26]

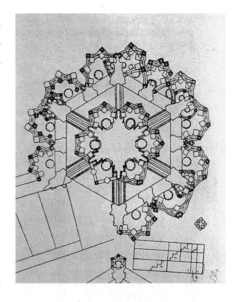

Figure 12.2 Hans Hamer, section of the pulpit in Strasbourg Cathedral

Figure 12.2 has a hexagonal design similar to the structure of Figures 12.1; but it hints at 'great fun': it represents the pulpit of Strasbourg Cathedral, designed and constructed by Hans Hamer in 1485.[27] Taking this 'crystal', an expert, like Hamer, would be able to guess at its architecture. The rest of us require Figure 12.3: our sense of order and meaning feel satisfied (even slightly satiated).

The complex order

The perception of Hamer's pulpit is different for each one of us, depending on how appropriate or refined our expectations are. We know that this is a pulpit; we may know of other, similar solutions, like that designed by Anton Pilgram for Vienna Cathedral, a quarter of a century later. We ought really to make an effort of mind to reconstruct, at least to some extent, the expectations of contemporary artists. Pilgram would have understood this perfectly, and would have been able to enjoy it (and criticise it with precision). If we lack his sensitivity, we must at least try to form our own sense of order by reading widely and looking at many examples.

If we have read a book like *The Sense of Order*, for example, we shall be more attuned to general questions: we shall be more conscious of 'The challenge of constraints',[28] enjoying the way they have been overcome, the

Figure 12.3 Hans Hamer front
elevation of the pulpit in Strasbourg

way stone has been transformed into something weightless and subtle ('Mastery of material');[29] how its hexagonal plan has managed to create a difficult coherence between balcony and pillar, and each canopy, which occupies some vertex or important position, by using angles of 60° ('Laws and orders'); how a method has been followed to achieve the greatest possible wealth of detail, *amor infiniti*, by means of 'graded complication',[30] by arranging frames with supports articulated by columnettes, entwined by mouldings and arches, filling the surfaces with a delicate detail of tracery: 'framing, filling, linking';[31] adding the lion of Saint Mark at the base ('Heraldic symbolism'); and reliefs on the principal mouldings which, though scarcely perceptible, were thought to be 'obscene' in the eighteenth century, and were removed ('A zone of licence'). To all this, add delicate sections, bases, small capitals, or finials, with tiny crockets, which will surely elude our gaze and interests ('Global Perception').

Of course, to create an object of this kind, Hamer did not start from scratch;[32] he would have been unable to reach such a degree of complexity ('The limits of foresight'). He and his clients knew what a pulpit was; and the function of preaching made it opportune to include a calvary, apostles and evangelists. But even for the parts which were left up to him, he had formulae at his disposal which he must have learnt from the context; the brief description given above bears witness to these: column, central plan, reliefs, leaves, etc. Just as the juggler practises by keeping first two objects in the air, gradually building up to a dozen, Hans Hamer had to master the 'tricks' of the tradition until he could sense their possibilities and their limitations, in order to incorporate them into his work, not by simple accumulation, but by interlocking them in more general orders. Hamer, as the 'first beholder and critic', would have weighed up each detail to check

that it caused the exact effect.[33] He was thus able to integrate rich ornamentation to improbable extremes in a solid structure, without the profusion
giving rise to confusion;[34] he created a 'complex order'.[35]

Gombrich puts this process on the same level as what engineers call *chunks*,
'the units of movements from which a larger skill is built in hierarchical
orders'.[36] The public, too, would grasp something of this, and would understand Hamer's aims and difficulties, as the stock-in-trades of his craft were
widely recognised and had established themselves as 'perceptual habits'.[37]

Tricks for articulation

In Gombrich's view, architecture perfectly exemplifies the force of habit.[38]
This can be seen, for example in the survival of the column: 'the Romanesque
column is a development of the ancient column and even the slender
columnettes and soaring piers of Gothic interiors betray this origin at first
sight'.[39] In fact, in the slimmest of vertical ribs which run through Hamer's
sketch, with its cylindrical shaft, moulded base and capitals, we can glimpse
columns, heirs to the classical tradition.

The persistence of such features is rooted in a phenomenon which Gombrich clearly perceived. 'We know that the force of habit is selective and
survivals are often capricious. Maybe motifs survive because they are easy to
remember and easy to apply in diverse contexts.' Yet Gombrich considered
that

> there are formal motifs which are not only inventions but also discoveries.
> By this I mean that they are found to fit certain psychological dispositions
> which had not been satisfied before. Medicine speaks of drugs which are
> 'habit-forming', and the history of such habit-forming drugs or spices is
> writ large over the face of the globe. No doubt it would be foolhardy to
> apply this idea uncritically to the history of art, but it is worth asking
> whether we may not speak of decorative motifs which, once invented,
> turn out to be habit-forming.[40]

Gombrich applied these words to the acanthus; but it is obvious that many
classical motifs, the column and its parts for example, respond to this notion:
they are 'discoveries'. In the tradition they have been purified in the hands
of successive artists, following 'the rhythm of trial and error, the Darwinian
process of mutation and the survival of the fittest'.[41] Their effectiveness makes
them into a foolproof trick, and they become addictive. One example suffices:

Figure 12.4 Top register: the astragal and its diffusion; middle register: the double-curved line and its diffusion; bottom register: the story of the double-curved line.

the astragal, the necklace-like moulding often found on columns beneath the capital, could be viewed as an 'explanatory accent',[42] to use Gombrich's expression: it separates the column from the fascia, in the form of a frieze, thus preparing the end of the element. The usefulness of this small device is immediately apparent. It makes its appearance in all objects where a join is necessary: in the classical column, in the column on Hamer's pulpit; in a door-knob, a candlestick, a table-leg, a baluster, a pedestal, a cannon, the funnel of a train, the cut-water of a bridge, a building. It has become *essential* (Figure 12.4, top register).

Tricks for movement

A classical building is highly *übersichtlich*,[43] easy to read: many of its elements facilitate an 'explanatory articulation',[44] and there are motifs, like the astragal, which are truly an 'explanatory accent'. Another, complementary quality exists, which is particularly developed in classical architecture: a refined sense of rhythm and movement. Although no one would deny that this quality is present, it proves extraordinarily elusive. Roughly speaking, it is found in the periods when artists had technical skills and were interested in representing the human body in a way that was as true to life as possible, and when great painters and sculptors worked with the elements of classicism, endowing them with a fullness of meaning.

Movement can, of course, be achieved in different ways, by superposing straight elements and varying the proportions between them. Many elements, however, make use of curves which elude all geometrical definition, as their course is dictated purely by feeling. One particularly fitting method, or trick, for creating movement, which certainly proved 'habit-forming', is the double-curved line: wave, ogee, bell-shaped, etc. Gombrich studies this as a basic resource for any ornamental tradition: the wavy line. Combined with the spiral, it is elemental, almost instinctive, as the flourish testifies.[45] We can recognise it in many classical elements: the mouldings of cyma recta and reversa, the console, the baluster, the calathus of the capital, the shaft of the column, and in almost all the decorative motifs of importance: the acanthus leaf, the acanthus scroll, and its myriad transformations (Figure 12.4, middle register).

Like a limb, the cyma and its derivations are under greater pressure when facing a gradient: from relaxation to tension. To get the tone exactly right requires the methods of drawing which Gombrich described in many studies for the paintings of Leonardo and Raphael (both architects): trial and error with drafts, and sometimes even *sfumato*. If there is no ability to adjust gradually, the arrangements appear tightly packed, as is the case with medieval styles, or else spaced-out, as in other classical traditions (Latin-American Baroque, for example) which compensate for this paralysis in other ways.

Gombrich expressly indicates the relationship between the rhythm and movement of figures and buildings, which he considers to be rooted in organic rhythms;[46] when we look at preparatory sketches, we acquire

an awareness of that free-flowing movement that pervades all Raphael's compositional drawings, where every figure and every group is envisaged in terms of melodious interaction. Whatever task a great artist is set, he will seek to attune it to his sense of rhythm and order, whether he is planning a building . . . or creating an image.[47]

The history of the spread and progressive mastery of these resources of articulation and movement would certainly bear scrutiny. Here too, the example of the cyma is revealing (almost to the point of ridicule), as we can easily see how it has been introduced everywhere, from the most minute objects to buildings, transforming them into progressively dynamic arrangements (Figure 12.4, bottom register).

The sense of decorum

The clarity of form and the ability to create a sense of movement which characterise classical elements account for their widespread usage, but fail to explain their nature: they endure because they prove to be suitable, fulfilling an essential function of the ornament. In Gombrich's words:

> Few civilizations were disposed to deny that inner worth should be acknowledged by an appropriate display of outward show. Not only the splendours of kings and princes, but also the power of the sacred has been universally proclaimed by pomp and circumstance.[48]

This relationship is known as the 'sense of decorum', and it is quite proper that *The Sense of Order* should handle this question.[49]

Gombrich points out 'the importance of the concept which shares its etymological root with decoration, that of decorum, which plays such a crucial part in the history of aesthetics'.[50] The sense of decorum is entwined in the very roots of a culture, and is an ultimate manifestation of the 'sense of order'. Today, it seems strangely alien, and its nature and power may easily escape us: 'the force and tyranny of that sense of order that ruled polite society'.[51]

A detail serves to illustrate this point: 'even I am old enough to remember a time when workers wore cloth caps and civil servants bowler hats, and when it would have been unthinkable for the two to swap headgears'.[52] Even in Spain it was apparently necessary for people of a certain standing to wear some kind of hat. In 1929, when Gombrich was twenty, an observant Spanish writer was amazed to see that a 'gentleman getting into a train at a tiny station, in the middle of Castile' was not wearing a hat; and concluded that he must be a follower of 'a system, a philosophical trend' propounded by a certain Maserling.[53] It would, of course, have been equally intriguing and significant to see such a man wearing a working-class cap.

Gombrich would also have remembered the time when a clear difference existed between a true column and any kind of pillar, when the two were not interchangeable (Figure 12.5).[54] Around this time, in 1931, a supporter of classicism expressed his view thus:

That certain buildings are for social reasons given the privilege of having columns, increases the significance of such buildings as have not. The Order . . . has a ceremonial quality with which civic architecture can ill dispense.[55]

In this field too, the formalities have dissolved, and today all supports are of the same class. In the past, however, the classical column was a support which was arrayed for grand occasions; according to the situation it could take on more or less emphasis: military or non-military uniform, 'full dress', 'levee dress' or 'alternative dress'[56] are echoed in Doric, Ionic and Corinthian columns, with their symbioses and variations.[57]

The obligation was more or less compelling. 'The more "formal" the occasion, the more emphasis is laid on the preservation of forms, both in the institutional and in the visual meaning of the term.'[58] A book like that of Vignola may well have some-

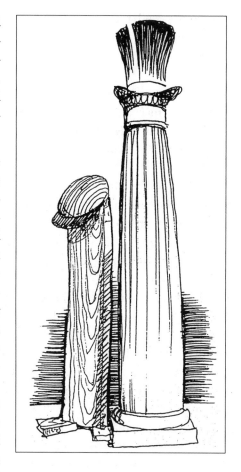

Figure 12.5 'Lordly column and vulgar pole'.

thing of the character of *Dress Worn at Court*, or at least of handbooks of etiquette such as *Il Cortegiano*, in which elegance is dictated by precept;[59] there are details like the astragal, a bow-tie, which are indispensable on any formal occasion.

Hidden meanings?

Such an interpretation of classical forms is, however, slightly misleading. An excellent book on classical architecture begins by stating that 'we should not think of the Classical orders primarily as elegant solutions to a problem of structural design', as 'buildings are as useful to our minds as they are to our bodies' and the classical orders 'were a material means of expression for communities, groups and individuals'.[60] There is no shortage of material drawing our attention towards deeper meanings.[61] Any reasonable study is enriching, even if its subject-matter is trifling; but Gombrich cautions us that 'there is no spell more potent than that cast by mysterious symbols of which the meaning has been forgotten'.[62] One runs the risk of under-valuing elegance as something obvious, and giving precedence to other aspects which, though generally of secondary importance, are attractively erudite.

'Generally' the elegance of these solutions makes them as useful to our minds as they are to our bodies; and this provides the best expression for communities, groups and individuals. It seems reasonable to think that history has selected and perfected columns or porticoes on the grounds of their elegance, even though they originally had other connotations. In the temple of Hera at Samos, it can be ascertained that the portico, 'perhaps the earliest one known . . . does not appear to have any structural value, and with a depth of only 1.30 m it could not provide much useful shelter for visiting pilgrims; nor could it have had much religious significance to an eighth-century Greek'; it can only be explained by 'a desire for monumental architecture'.[63] And in the very archaic temple of Apollo at Syracuse, two centuries later, the inscription can still be read: 'Cleomenes built this temple to Apollo, son of Cnidieidas, Epicles the columns, fine work.'[64] Whether Cleomenes or Cleosthenes should be read has been disputed; but there is no doubt that they were filled with pride at the beauty of the result (even though it was clumsy for its time). The columns are good solutions, par-ticularly because, in Alberti's words, 'gratiam habent, dignitatem afferunt', they possess grace and lend dignity.[65]

Sense of order and expression

Gombrich was always opposed to considering works of art as a manifestation of the spirit of the age, race, nation, mentalities or unconscious feelings of the artist, and he trimmed back the abuses in iconography.[66] A master-work has no need to shroud itself in mysteries in order to be attractive and to show itself to be profound and meaningful. Yet it should possess a refined, expressive quality. The same is naturally true for buildings.

We must beware, however, of 'graphological' or 'physiognomic' ex-pressions.[67] It is easy to glimpse a portrait of Philip II in El Escorial.[68] We project human characters onto anything which will allow us to: the summer skies are youthful and smiling; the mountain is stern. Such metaphors cannot be taken as a criterion for interpretation; El Escorial does not represent, and cannot represent, the melancholy of Philip II.[69] It is simply a question of decorum; it has the severe tone of a pantheon–monastery–residence for an austere court.

None the less, according to the requirements of decorum, it was right that Philip II should have demanded that his architect create a certain kind of expressiveness: 'simplicity of forms, severity in the overall impression, nobility without arrogance, majesty without ostentation'.[70] Curiously, Gombrich quotes a remark made by Hogarth on Saint Paul's Cathedral, using similar terms: 'There you may see the utmost variety without confusion, simplicity without nakedness, richness without tawdriness, distinctness without hardness and quantity without excess.'[71]

Gombrich showed that creating a complex order with contrasting qualities is an objective achievement: 'we speak of masterpieces precisely where we feel that this difficult feat has succeeded'.[72] To achieve a subtle quality such as 'majesty without ostentation', a balance must be established. Hogarth's commentary tells us that this result was achieved in Saint Paul's, and it was far from straightforward; in the initial designs it seems to have appeared 'not stately enough',[73] and only repeated trial and error yielded the right balance.[74] Hogarth's comments are not a poetic description, but a true critical judgement which Wren would have corroborated.

At this point we grasp the importance of the 'sense of order'. A notion of what is regular exists on many levels with regard to elements and arrangements proper to classicism, and these patterns have engendered perceptual habits in the public. Any deviation, any irregularity, is perceived as meaningful: 'It is here that the tenacity of traditions yields an unexpected advantage. It is only where expectations are formed that they can also be reassuringly confirmed, playfully disappointed or grandly surpassed.'[75]

The columns can be Doric or not, single or coupled, arranged in a 'giant order' or superposed, separated to a greater or lesser degree, or slender, with more or less entasis, etc. If they are more ornate than usual, they appear sumptuous; when simplified, they seem bare. If we overload them, however, they look ostentatiously vulgar, whereas if their simplicity appears to be self-imposed, they express a sober nobility.[76] We could go on almost *ad infinitum*, listing a vast range of associated qualities.

The number and complexity of the elements and arrangements has obviously grown between the 'fine' single columns of Epicles and Wren's complex façade (from the pan-pipe played by a shepherd to the church organ of Bach).[77] The artists, and their public, had incorporated 'chunks' consisting of more and more numerous and complex resources, and had applied them to create increasingly general and subtle effects.[78] The designer would play with the elements, with their proportion, their capacity for movement, integrating them into the overall composition like a composer; giving them timbre, volume and expressive accents, like a musician; thus, by emphasising or contrasting them carefully with each other, he or she would enable this enormous range of qualities to build a metaphor with its own individual meaning.

Sensitivity to nuance

The manifold conventions did not stifle the designer's freedom of expression; they served to further the refinement of the sense of order in artists and public alike, sharpening their sensitivity towards the meaning of the minutest of differences. The sense of order transformed classical architecture into an effective means of expression; as Gombrich reminds us with a masterly quotation from John Summerson, it is capable of 'magnificent rhetoric, calm pastoral beauty, lyrical charm or sustained epic grandeur'. Gombrich remarks that 'Such diversity in unity may only become possible where the designer works within strict alternatives which the public learns to appreciate.'[79]

In *The Sense of Order*, Geoffrey Scott's words on the classical tradition would not have gone amiss:

> It is present in the spectator's mind, sharpening his perception of what is new in the design; it gives relief and accent to the new intention, just as the common form of a poetical metre enables the poet to give full value to his modulations. So, in Renaissance architecture, a thickening of the diameter of a column, a sudden increase in the projection of a cornice, each subtlest change of ratio and proportion, was sure of its effect.[80]

Depending on the artist's calibre, the variations might turn out to be vulgar, but could also possess splendour. Recognition of this does not mean striking a compromise with a hazy aestheticism; it is reasonable that within the narrow margins of variation a point can be discovered by trial and error at which the solution seems that it could never be bettered. This is where the true mystery of the art lies. Gombrich taught us to apply rational arguments, to flee cheap sentimentalism and meaningless verbiage, yet he also always recognised the possibility of perfection in art.

Scott was writing in 1914, when Gombrich was perhaps beginning to familiarise himself with the buildings of Vienna (including Semper's famous museum façades). My initial premise, which is unprovable, was that in order to understand architecture and decoration, enthusiasm was necessary; but to explain it, we need to use our reason. Gombrich was never short of rational arguments, as his book amply shows. Nor did he lack enthusiasm; he had personal experience of the value of the nuance in architecture. But the Epilogue of *The Sense of Order* is dedicated to 'Some musical analogies', and this is no accident: Gombrich learnt much from music, including the wonderful effects that can be produced by some subtle variations, which he spoke of in an interview on *The Sense of Order*:

> You know the Hans Christian Andersen story about the princess and the pea? I think any great artist suffers if the stroke is just a *little* too strong or too weak. He has this immense feeling for every shade, which makes for the difference. My life was spent among musicians. My wife is a musician, my mother was a musician. I know, therefore, a little about this feeling for nuance, because if you perform a Beethoven sonata or whatever it is, the difference between various performances is, in a way, very small, but it is all-important. Therefore, I think that it is really this sensitivity to nuance which is one of the conditions of the great artist.[81]

Notes

1. *Symbolic Images* is also included: E. H. Gombrich, *The Sense of Order: A Study of Psychology of Decorative Arts*, second edition, London 1984, p. ix; E. H. Gombrich and D. Eribon, *Lo que nos cuentan las imágenes*, Madrid 1992, p. 87; and E. J. Sacca, 'An interview with Ernst Gombrich', *Canadian Review of Art Education Research*, 6–7 (1980–81), p. 16.
2. E. H. Gombrich and D. Eribon, *Lo que nos cuentan*, p. 109.
3. *Ibid.*, pp. 109–19: a history of motifs and theories at the same time, too many things, too long, it contains a theory which is somewhat complicated. In the preface to the second edition he admits there are 'certain difficulties . . . its length . . . the distance between general theories and the rich variety of individual creations' (*The Sense of Order*, p. xii).
4. *Ibid.*, p. 64, and see introduction, pp. 1–7.
5. *Ibid.*, p. 108, and see Part two: the perception of order', pp. 95–170.
6. *Ibid.*, p. 3; and see 'Popperian asymmetry' in the index, p. 408.

7. Despite its subtitle *Study in the Psychology of Decorative Art*, Gombrich knows that a purely psychological study would fail to take into account familiarity or taste; *ibid.*, p. 116. Hence the chapter 'Issues of taste' and those which follow; *ibid.*, pp. 17–32.

8. *Ibid.*, p. 164.

9. *Ibid.*, pp. ix, x.

10. *Chinese Ornament: the Lotus and the Dragon*, London 1984, p. 7.

11. *The Mediation of Ornament*, Princeton 1992, pp. 24–5; see also pp. 42, 190. Like *The Sense of Order*, it arose from the publication of the A. W. Mellon Lectures. See a favourable discussion in J. M. Rogers, *Islamic Art and Design, 1500–1700*, London 1983.

12. *The Sense of Order*, p. 47.

13. *Ibid.*, pp. vii–viii.

14. *Ibid.*, pp. xv, 73. *Art and Illusion* does not defend figurativism, either.

15. See the section 'Play and art' in *The Sense of Order*, pp. 12–16; and 'playing' in the index, p. 408.

16. *Ibid.*, p. 166.

17. *Ibid.*, pp. 107, 143.

18. *Ibid.*, pp. 102, 264.

19. He experiences some of the quivering excitement of 'making', he writes in *Art and Illusion*. When talking of music, he called this process 'generated creation', the highest degree of understanding; see *Tributes*, p. 24.

20. *The Sense of Order*, p. 12; for the link between ease of construction and ease of perception see pp. 9, 163, 288.

21. Cf. A. K. Porter, *Más allá de la arquitectura*, Madrid 1929, p. 23.

22. *The Sense of Order*, p. 149; and see the whole section on the kaleidoscope, pp. 149–51.

23. *Ibid.*, p. 150.

24. See 'snow crystals' in the index to *ibid.*, p. 410; Gombrich uses examples from W. A. Bentley and W. H. Humphreys, *Snow Crystals*, (New York, 1931); I have used the reprint, New York 1962.

25. J. Glaisher, 'On the crystal of snow as applied to the purposes of design', in *Art Studies from Nature as Applied to Design*, London 1872, pp. 133–75; see especially pp. 154–6. Partly published in 1855, his findings appeared in full first in *Art Journal* in 1857.

26. Glaisher compares them with Byzantine mosaics ('On the crystal of snow', pp. 158–63); they are in fact more like Roman designs. His 'stylised' drawings would prove appropriate as a secondary motif; the genuine crystals would be impossible to handle.

27. R. Recht, *La Cathédrale de Strasbourg*, Strasbourg 1993, p. 75.

28. Chapter III of *The Sense of Order*, pp. 63–94. Quoted below are the titles of the sections of chapters III, IX and IV.

29. Gombrich discusses the similar tabernacle of Saint Lorenz, Nuremberg, which postdates this work by eight years in *ibid.*, pp. 65–6.

30. *Ibid.*, 'graded complication' in the index, p. 405.

31. *Ibid.*, p. 75; and 'framing', 'filling' and 'linking' in the index, pp. 404, 404, 406.

32. *Ibid.*, pp. 83–9, 64, 209–13.

33. *Ibid.*, p. 92.

34. *Ibid.*, pp. 115–16, 209; and 'confusion' in the index, p. 402.

35. *Ibid.*, p. 84.

36. *Ibid.*, p. 163; and 'chunks' in the index, p. 402.

37. *Ibid.*, p. 180.

38. See the section entitled 'The language of architecture', in *ibid.*, chapter VII 'The force of habit', pp. 175–80.

39. *Ibid.*, p. 177.

40. *Ibid.*, p. 191.

41. *Ibid.*, p. 87.

42. *Ibid.*, p. 176.

43. *Ibid.*, pp. 145, 164.

44. *Ibid.*, pp. 165, 209. See also the section on 'Decoration', pp. 163–8; and 'articulation' in the index, p. 401. I do not concur with Gombrich's view that Gothic is 'the most important instance' (p. 209). The Renaissance made good use of the lesson.

45. See the sections 'Waves and vortices' and 'The transformation of the flourish' in *ibid.*, pp. 137–40, 241–3; the analysis by O. Jones, p. 53; and 'Hogarth', 'scrolls' and 'wavy line' in the index, pp. 405, 409, 411.

46. See the sections 'Order and movement' and 'Play and art' in *ibid.*, pp. 10–16; also 'Restlessness and repose', pp. 120–26. The preface to the second edition (p. xii) provides an important clarification.

47. *Ibid.*, p. 14.

48. *Ibid.*, p. 17.

49. See the sections 'The moral aspect', 'Classic simplicity' and 'Marks of distinction' in *ibid.*, pp. 17–20, 225–32; and 'decorum' in the index, p. 403.

50. *Ibid.*, p. 229.

51. *Ibid.*

52. *Ibid.*, p. 230.

53. Azorín, *Blanco en Azul*, fifth edition, Madrid 1968, p. 40.

54. Although a true column would not permit a bowler hat, nothing less than a top hat would do.

55. A. T. Edwards, 'Introduction' in A. Stratton, *The Orders of Architecture*, London 1931, p. 5.

56. Cf. A. Mansfield, *Ceremonial Costumes: Court, Civil, and Civic Costume*, London 1980, pp. 175–84.

57. This is a metaphor, although comparable gradations do exist. Strength: weak Corinthian–strong Doric (civilian–military); the Doric below, the Corinthian above. Richness: plain Doric–rich Corinthian; the Corinthian (first class) would occupy the centre, with the Doric or Ionic at the sides (second class). In *Art and Illusion*, orders are mentioned as a gradation of emphasis.

58. *The Sense of Order.*, p. 229.

59. A charming article on the Palazzo del Tè at Mantua relates rhetoric to architecture, mentioning the *sprezzatura* in *Il Cortegiano* 1.26 (*New Light*, pp. 161–3).

60. J. Onians, *Bearers of Meaning: the Classical Orders in Antiquity, the Middle Ages, and the Renaissance*, Princeton 1988, p. 3; Gombrich was acquainted with this work. It has been the best book on this subject for many years, and an interesting contribution, though Onians's vision may seem a little biased because of what he owes to literary sources. The orders are not classical architecture, and they cannot be reduced to the differences between Doric and Ionic, etc.; they admit of gradations which cannot be tabulated. Onians quotes *The Sense of Order*, but has not profited from it.

61. Cf. G. Hersey, *The Lost Meaning of Classical Architecture*, Cambridge, Mass. 1988, pp. 3–10, 148–52. This contains interesting contributions.

62. *The Sense of Order*, p. 218. See also the section 'Motifs and meanings', pp. 217–25.

63. J. J. Coulton, *Ancient Greek Architects at Work: Problems of Structure and Design*, second edition, Ithaca, NY 1985, p. 31.

64. R. Martin, *Grecia arcaica: el Universo de las Formas*, Madrid 1969, p. 16.

65. L. B. Alberti, *De Re Aedificatoria*, 6.13, Milano 1966, p. 521; the entire commentary is very revealing; Gombrich quotes Cicero: the columns are as dignified as they are useful (*The Sense of Order*, p. 20).

66. Era and nation: *The Sense of Order*, p. 225; race: *ibid.*, p. 184; mentalities: pp. 201–4; iconography: pp. 86, 217–25.

67. *Ibid.*, pp. 43, 62, 201.

68. S. Alvarez Turienzo, *El Escorial en las letras españolas*, second edition, Madrid 1985, pp. 77–100, 265–92. I also remember an English gentleman who, when talking to Queen Alexandra, felt that he was standing face to face with Saint Paul's Cathedral.

69. See comparison between the 'rationalist' Frederick the Great at Rococo Potsdam, and the 'flighty' Marie Antoinette at neo-classical Petit Trianon; *The Sense of Order*, p. 215. For metaphors, see *ibid.*, pp. 118–20, 129, 173–5; and index, p. 407.

70. P. Murray, *Arquitectura del Renacimiento*, second edition, Madrid 1989, p. 176. He does not mention the source of his quotation, which seems to have been a letter; it is not to be found in the bibliography of Spanish architecture which he gives, or in the usual bibliography of this subject; Philip II generally used a different tone: cf. J. Zarco de las Cuevas, *Documentos para la Historia del Monasterio de San Lorenzo el Real de El Escorial, III: Instrucciones de Felipe II para la fábrica y obra de San Lorenzo el Real*, second edition, Madrid 1990.

71. *The Sense of Order*, p. 23. The quotation is from W. Hogarth, *The Analysis of Beauty*, London 1753, p. 46.

72. *The Sense of Order*, p. 209.

73. K. Downes, *Sir Christopher Wren: The Design of St Paul's Cathedral*, London 1988, p. 15.

74. T. Friedman, '"Behold the proud stupendous pile": eighteenth century reflec-

tions of St Paul's Cathedral' in J. Bold and E. Chaney (eds), *English Architecture, Public and Private: Essays for Kerry Downes*, London 1993, pp. 135–46.

75. *The Sense of Order*, p. 177.

76. See the section 'Classic simplicity' in *ibid.*, pp. 18–20.

77. See the excellent section 'The logic of situations' in *ibid.*, pp. 209–13. It is not the place to discuss this here, but see 'Evolución' and 'Creación' in J. Lorda, *Gombrich: una Teoría del Arte*, Barcelona 1991, pp. 309–66.

78. Although there would be a certain loss, as in Baalbek's simplifications (*The Sense of Order*, p. 208).

79. *Ibid.*, pp. 177–8. The quotation is taken from J. Summerson, *The Classical Language of Architecture*, London 1963, p. 3.

80. G. Scott, *The Architecture of Humanism*, second edition, London 1924, pp. 202–3.

81. E. J. Sacca, 'An interview', pp. 20–1.

13

The Vienna School's hundred and sixty-eighth graduate: The Vienna School's ideas revised by E. H. Gombrich

Ján Bakoš

> I can say that I am a member of the Vienna School of art history[1]

IN Hans Hahnloser's list of graduates from the 'Vienna school' of art history, published in 1934, Ernst Hans Gombrich is numbered 168.[2] He studied art history and archaeology at Vienna University in the years 1928–33. Besides Julius von Schlosser and his assistants K. M. Swoboda and H. Hahnloser, his teachers were Hans Tietze and the archaeologist Emanuel Löwy.[3] Gombrich is not only a graduate of Vienna University, but also regards himself as a representative of the Vienna School of art history. Irrespective of whether it can be understood as a system[4] or a pluralistic succession of critical reflections on art-historical method resulting in quite different ideas,[5] Gombrich identified its common denominator as the belief in art history as a science.[6] Describing that idea as an 'overriding ambition',[7] he sees himself as continuing the traditions of the Vienna School.

'An overriding ambition'

The first draft of the Viennese doctrine was formulated as early as 1884 by Moriz Thausing.[8] He argued in support of an independent scientific discipline, defending it against interventions from artists, and separated it strictly from aesthetics. The 'manifesto' of art history as an exact science, rejecting all amateurism and '*belles lettres*', was formulated by his pupil Franz Wickhoff.[9] He was convinced that art history could acquire the status of an exact science, first, by applying the methods of the critical analysis of historical documents, philological critique, to the analysis of styles, and, second, by using Morelli's

method of connoisseurship, based on the analysis of morphological details.[10]

Alois Riegl, following the model of the natural sciences, regarded art as
an autonomous phenomenon, having a history of immanent and uninter-
rupted evolution. Thus art-historical research was conceived of as an impartial
or 'objective' rational procedure aiming at a causal explanation and discovery
of historical laws. In addition, aesthetics was replaced by psychology, and
normativism by historical relativism; all periods in the history of art were
regarded as equally valuable and governed by their own incommensurable
standards. Consequently, many marginalised artistic styles were rehabilitated.[11]

As a result of the cultural, mental and political crisis in Europe in the
second decade of this century, Riegl's pupil and successor, Max Dvořák,
relinquished his teacher's epistemological optimism.

He acknowledged the unique and, in a sense, irrational nature of historical
phenomena and, following Wilhelm Dilthey,[12] replaced the idea of causal
explanation with that of understanding. In spite of that, he did not lose his
belief in the extraordinary role art history played within human knowledge.
He restored its importance by means of a neo-Kantian conception of the
specific cognitive status of the humanities.[13]

The younger generation of art historians around 1930, represented by Hans
Sedlmayr and Otto Pächt, rejected Dvořák's irrationalism and criticised its
consequence, 'art history without art'. They returned to Riegl and concentrated on the work of art and the analysis of its structure and, with ideas
drawn from psychology, promoted the doctrine of art history as 'a strict
science' (strenge Kunstwissenschaft).[14]

Gombrich's teacher, Julius von Schlosser, who was under the influence
of Benedetto Croce at the time, was highly sceptical of all interpretations
which underestimated the individual nature of art.[15] So despite his pride in
the Vienna School,[16] he had serious reservations about Riegl's psychological
account of artistic change. He was also sceptical about Dvořák's spiritual
interpretation of the history of art as a history of world-views or ideas. He
also had doubts about the applicability of gestalt psychology and psychoanalysis
to the history of art, pursued by his disciples H. Sedlmayr and E. Kris, in
spite of the fact that his own conception implied 'a psychological problem
of formulae or "similes"'.[17]

Gombrich's choice

Gombrich's own motivations to study the history of art initially were not brought about by the disputes within the Vienna School; he would only come to them through his research. His motives have much more to do with the cultural and mental atmosphere in Vienna after World War I. The old 'liberal culture of law'[18] based on Enlightenment ideals was being replaced by irrationalism, or subjectivism and spiritualism. That deep cultural and mental change reached the general public after the war. Gombrich as a young boy saw it reflected in a totally new approach to art, which made him interested in the study of art history.[19] Dvořák's famous book *Kunstgeschichte als Geistesgeschichte*,[20] which was very significant in the post-war Viennese atmosphere, played an important role in his decision in favour of art history. Gombrich also had to choose between two institutes of art history existing together at the university at the same time. The first was led by Joseph Strzygowski, who was 'a fanatical opponent to the classical tradition', regarding it as a 'hegemonic art',[21] the second by Dvořák's successor in the chair of art history, Julius von Schlosser, who 'was interested only in the Classics'.[22] Consequently, Gombrich had to make a choice not only between two opposing human characters, an arrogant showman and an introvert scholar, but also between two approaches to the method of art history:[23] one rather imaginative and less pedantic, the other strictly rational and critical. He also had to choose between two value systems. Strzygowski contributed a great deal to the rehabilitation of many underestimated artistic cultures and to the idea of a global history of art.[24] Despite the fact that he 'was never an anti-Semite',[25] his inclination to interpret the history of art in terms of 'people, soil and blood',[26] as well as a hastening anti-Semitism in Vienna, made Gombrich decide in favour of the arch-humanist von Schlosser.

His antipathy towards all forms of nationalism and chauvinism also led to Gombrich's scepticism towards Wölfflin's lectures on *German and Italian Feeling of Form*[27] during his visit to Berlin. Given the traumas of anti-Semitism, it is unsurprising that Gombrich's generation of Jewish intellectuals should be concerned with the causes and consequences of racialism and nationalism. Gombrich's work should be seen in that context.

'A doubting Thomas' at the Vienna School

In Schlosser's seminar Gombrich was assigned some tasks that had a major effect on the subsequent development of his research. Schlosser had never criticised Riegl or Dvořák openly and was absolutely loyal to his predecessors. At the same time, his philosophical commitments led him to 'an implicit protest against Riegl'.[28] If the choice of a medieval pyxis as one of Gombrich's first seminar topics was probably accidental, assigning him to talk about Riegl's *Stilfragen* can be understood in terms of Schlosser's polemical strategy. Interestingly enough, in both cases Gombrich took the same principled approach as a 'doubting Thomas'.[29] He trusted no authority, nor Riegl, and very carefully checked all the views which were taken for granted. Deeply disappointed, he came to the conclusion that the study of medieval art history should be regarded rather as 'a learned guessing-game'.[30] As far as *Stilfragen* was concerned, he aired doubts about Riegl's evolutionary interpretation of the palmette to acanthus as a linear continuity.[31] Showing that Riegl's interpretation was speculative rather than strictly rational and objective, Gombrich launched his lifelong career of overturning idols. He had done it despite Riegl's intention of using the idea of continuity to prove that art history was accessible to rational analysis and that its objects were plural and equal. Gombrich, then and always, has preferred rational and critical verification to an empathic understanding. Such enormous courage in a young apprentice can be understood only as a result of a long intellectual tradition and a token of a highly educated milieu, free of taboos and dogmas. The 'doubting Thomas' position found its philosophical formulation in K. R. Popper's 'critical rationalism'[32] and his method of 'falsification', that later became the epistemological base of Gombrich's attacks on mythological explanations.[33]

'The second crisis of confidence'

The germs of many of Gombrich's ideas were already present in his earliest art-historical essays, and he returned to their themes later. Not just the doubts caused by his work on the medieval pyxis and *Stilfragen*, also his *Gymnasium* graduation essay on changes in art appreciation since Winckelmann[34] and the seminar work on a fourteenth-century legal manuscript (Sachsenspiegel) dealing with the problem of 'communication through gesture'[35] also continued to interest him. Furthermore, his dissertation on Giulio Romano's Palazzo del Tè at Mantua,[36] intended originally as an exploration of Dvořák's conception of Mannerism as an all-embracing style and a symptom of the spiritual crisis of the age, resulted in Gombrich's 'second crisis of confidence'[37] as far as the credibility of art-historical research was concerned. It is true that Gombrich identified the Palazzo del Tè as having a Mannerist architectural style,[38] but at the same time he came to the conclusion that Giulio Romano worked in two different styles at the same time. As a consequence, Gombrich lost confidence in the idea of style as an expression of age and instead began to accept Schlosser's concept of language allowing him to explain the simultaneous usage of two 'different modes of expression'[39] as two idioms. Working in the Mantuan archive, Gombrich became aware of the importance of the social determinants of style, i.e. the role played by the patron or the artist's status.[40] It was not only Schlosser's dualist model, differentiating between history of style and history of language,[41] which helped Gombrich to get rid of Dvořák's metaphysical idea. It was also the unconscious impact of Picasso[42] that led him to doubt the idea that style was a homogenous expression of its time.

Art history and contemporary art

The question of the relationship between art history and contemporary art became very important in the Vienna School.[43] It had been thematised by Franz Wickhoff in his *Wiener Genesis*.[44] Projecting Impressionism back on to late Roman art he succeeded in the mutual rehabilitation of both phenomena by taking away 'the stigma of decline'.[45] Dvořák discovered Mannerism as a particular style by means of Expressionism. According to Schlosser, Riegl proceeded in an opposite way: trying in vain to be independent of contemporary art, he projected the past on to the present and, consequently, he became a 'backward-looking prophet of Expressionism'.[46] In contrast to Wickhoff and Dvořák or Riegl, Schlosser kept his distance from modern art.[47] Losing confidence in the expressionist interpretation of styles, Gombrich appreciated Tietze's very early ability to transcend imprisonment in the expressionist doctrine.[48] He also originally admired Sedlmayr's structuralist attempt at using gestalt psychology for art-historical purposes,[49] which had its parallel in the contemporary art of 'die Neue Sachlichkeit'.[50] Nevertheless, at that time Gombrich preferred E. Kris's application of psychoanalysis to art history, combined with directions suggested by Schlosser and Löwy.[51]

Transition from apprenticeship to mastership

Gombrich's review of Ernst Garger's paper on the problems of evaluation in medieval art,[52] written shortly after finishing his university studies,[53] played a crucial role in his tackling Vienna School ideas and in crystallising his own point of view. Dvořák's pupil Garger tried to overcome the difficulties and consequences of the Vienna School's empathic conception of historical pluralism by replacing ability by intention, which resulted in an equalisation which justifies everything as intentional. Gombrich was not satisfied with Garger's solution, distinguishing between intention and achievement, by means of which he tried to rescue relativism. He criticised Garger for remaining imprisoned within a suprahistorical concept of artistic intention. Following Schlosser's analysis of the role of 'similes', Gombrich came to the conclusion that medieval art cannot be regarded as a conceptual variant of illusionist art, but has to be regarded as a particular conception of art. Thus it cannot be explained as an expression of transcendental metaphysics, but rather as a particular 'mode' that has close affinity with the 'primitive mode of image making'.[54]

Here we are confronted with the first draft of Gombrich's new concept of art as well as with his philosophy of art history that was formulated later in his essay 'Meditations on a hobby horse'[55] and fully developed in his famous book *Art and Illusion*.[56] It can be briefly and simply described as follows: 'All art is "image making" and all image making is rooted in creation of substitutes'.[57] There are two basic modes of art: the primitive and the imitative. The first is based on a principle of functional affinity and its limits are given by 'the minimum image' that has a biological basis. The second aims at external similarity; its extreme form is represented by naturalistic imitation, though it is also limited by the power of tradition (by artistic schemes or patterns). Nevertheless, the difference betweeen the two modes is, according to Gombrich, 'more a difference of degree, a spectrum'.[58] So the history of art can be regarded as a story taking place within a space defined by two sets: historical conventions on the one hand, and a biologically rooted anthropological constant on the other.[59] The particular shape of the history of art was then formed by artistic traditions in the first line, interrupted from time to time only by rare revolutions in concepts of art that followed changes in its social function. Needless to say, the review of Garger's paper contributed to unmasking the suprahistorical nature of Riegl's idea of artistic intention, and was the first step towards Gombrich's replacing Riegl's pluralist relativism by an anthropologically-based bipolar conventionalism.

A compensatory patricide

Without explicitly focusing on Riegl, it is quite obvious that Gombrich's Garger review aimed intentionally, even if indirectly, at an attempt at a value-free historical relativism. The critical analysis of Riegl's ideas represents a kind of a refrain running through all Gombrich's works. Riegl's theories not only fulfil the function of a trampoline for Gombrich's own ideas, but represent a fortress that has to be repeatedly attacked. Gombrich's relation to Riegl is very similar to Schlosser's ambivalent one; he is fascinated but provoked into refusal. He sums up his dialectical admiration for Riegl in a Popperian way: 'one can pay no greater tribute to a scholar or scientist than to take his theories seriously and to examine them with the care they deserve'.[60] Does Gombrich's lasting attraction to Riegl's ideas mean that he has not succeeded in falsifying them properly until now?

Riegl's writings can be regarded as the most comprehensive attempt to create a modern art history. According to Henri Zerner, Riegl 'attacked all the fundamental convictions of traditional art history', namely 'factual positivist history', 'an iconographic point of view', 'biographical criticism', 'the primacy of the individual artist's consciousness and will', 'the materialistic . . . explanation of stylistic evolution', 'any aesthetic theory that severs art from history', 'any normative system that attempts to reach a definitive . . . judgement' and 'hierarchical distinction between the applied . . . and the higher art'.[61] If Zerner is right to claim that 'these convictions have by no means disappeared today',[62] and we can add that the latest reception of Riegl's writings seems to confirm that claim;[63] in other words, if Riegl did not succeed in his systematic effort to replace traditional views on art history by a new set of oppositional ideas,[64] what legitimised Gombrich's persistent criticism? No doubt, Gombrich acknowledged that 'Riegl was one source'[65] of his interest in psychology, and 'it was Riegl who attempted to ground the history of art in the science of psychology'.[66] Despite that, his permanent criticism cannot be explained by rivalry alone, since, as Gombrich put it, 'it is surely evident that the psychology of perception, current today, differs vastly from the simplistic ideas about vision and touch with which Riegl operated'.[67]

Gombrich acknowledged the heuristic value of Riegl's belief in the autonomy of the history of art. At the same time, however, he unmasked it as a fraud which has its origin in the transplantation of Hegel's concept of the Spirit.[68] According to Gombrich, Riegl understood the concept of the 'will-to-form' as an 'artistic genius of a nation'[69] and, consequently, resolved the contradiction between the autonomy of art and its relation to the 'spirit of an age' in a typically Hegelian, i.e. dialectical, way as a parallel movement. Confronted with the cataclysm of World War II, Gombrich considered

Riegl's elimination of decline, his notion of autonomy and his commitment to historical determinism to be generally very dangerous ideas. Later,[70] he conceded that Riegl's 'elimination of all subjective ideals of value' was intended as a means 'to make the history of art scientifically respectable'.[71] Nevertheless, under the influence of Hegel Riegl gave way to the temptation 'to account for all stylistic changes' 'by one unitary principle'.[72] As a consequence, the concept of the 'will-to-form' became an instrument of racialist interpretation, according to Gombrich. Thus Riegl's attempt to establish art history as a science changed into a 'mythological explanation'.[73]

From then on Gombrich has insisted that Riegl's belief in 'the synchronic unity of style' is a metaphysical postulate.[74] Nevertheless, he recognised that this idea, as well as the necessity of 'the diachronic unity of stylistic development' and 'the unity of high arts and applied arts' were not only stimulated by 'fin de siècle' art, but also played an active role in defending modern artistic movements, especially Art Nouveau.[75] Although Gombrich's confidence in Riegl's good intentions rose, he could not rid himself of the suspicion that Riegl's idea of the continuity of artistic evolution implied a hidden nationalism and hegemonism (in favour of the Greeks and Romans).[76] According to Gombrich, there was no place for multiculturality in Riegl's system. It is noteworthy that because of Strzygowski's rehabilitation of the multicultural nature of the history of art Gombrich was willing to turn a blind eye to Strzygowski's tendency to racialism.

Gombrich did not recognise that there are two further possible reasons for Riegl's notions of equality, continuity and causality in art-historical processes: his ideal of exact science on the one hand, and the cosmopolitan view supported by the official ideology of the Habsburg state on the other. O. Pächt argued that Riegl shared that cosmopolitan or multinational idea, interpreting the '*Kunstwollen* of a nation' as an organic part of an universal artistic evolution that was attained by great individual artists.[77] In addition, Pächt defended Riegl's historical determinism against Gombrich's attacks. Against Gombrich, he insisted that art represented a creation characterised by necessity rather than by a free choice between alternatives. It is apparent that Pächt regarded art as a transcendental creation, while Gombrich regarded it as a social creation. Furthermore, Pächt's position presupposed an empiricist or sensualist belief in an innocent eye,[78] while Gombrich advocated conventionalism, though in a moderate form in comparison with Nelson Goodman's.[79] What matters here is that Gombrich's understanding of Riegl is in a sense simplified. He completely ignores the Kantian element in Riegl's system, mediated by J. F. Herbart and particularly his pupil R. Zimmermann,[80] which resulted in Riegl's scientism and universalism, and balanced the historicism of Hegel and the German Romantics. The question is, what motivated such an interpretation by Gombrich? Was it induced by the suspicion that an indirect or half-hearted Hegelianism could be more dangerous than a strict one? Or might Gombrich's polemics against Riegl be rather regarded as an act of compensatory patricide?

The 'grandson'[81] Gombrich has been trying to kill his 'grandfather' Riegl as a compensation for the true trespasser and programmatic adherent to Hegel, the father-figure Dvořák, who escaped assassination by his sons thanks only to his premature death.[82] From that metaphorical point of view Gombrich can be characterised as an orphan who had been brought up by his uncle, Julius von Schlosser. In comparison with his elder 'brothers' H. Sedlmayr and O. Pächt he never personally knew the father, and because of that he never suffered from any remorse. Victor Skhlovsky's theory[83] that the generation delay in the history of art does not have the form of a direct and dialectical son–(father)–grandfather sequence, but follows in a zig-zag way from uncle to grandson[84] found, in a way, its materialisation in the Schlosser–Gombrich relationship. It is important to say that not only social or psychological relationships but also opinions are very important in the intellectual continuity. Schlosser cannot be regarded as Gombrich's teacher purely by accident; Gombrich was attracted to him by values he shared.

'Hegel's giants'

The shock caused by nationalism and racialism in the thirties stimulated Gombrich's generation to search painstakingly for an explanation of chauvinism in German intellectual history. The principal source of totalitarianism was surprisingly found in one of the main currents of German philosophical tradition called 'historicism' by Popper,[85] and particularly in Hegel's philosophy of history. Gombrich classified Hegel's interpretation of history as 'a mythology' that 'is not only hostile to reason . . . and to scholarship' because 'it puts an end to further research';[86] it is also dangerous because 'it weakens resistance to totalitarian habits of mind'.[87] Gombrich identified Hegel's five following 'real giants':[88] 'aesthetic transcendentalism', i.e. the belief in 'art as manifestation of transcendental values'; 'historical collectivism', i.e. the conviction that 'the true heroes' of history as well as art history are supra-individual entities such as 'ages', 'nations' or 'races'; 'historical determinism', i.e. the belief in the necessity and rationality of history or in identity of the real and the rational; 'metaphysical optimism', i.e. the notion that history represents a progress of self-liberating Spirit; and 'dialectical relativism', i.e. the belief in the equality and even incommensurability of all historical ages on the one hand, and at the same time the conviction that history is a progressive movement, on the other.

Hegel's belief in art as a vehicle for the self-creation of the World Spirit,[89] and artistic style as an expression of the particular spirit of an age or nation and race, was a mythological explanation inaccessible to any verification.[90] His belief in impersonal forces and abstractions taken for spiritual entities; his notion of 'art as a revealing of truth' and as an expression or symptom of the spirit of each respective entity; or his faith that 'the human spirit manifests itself in all aspects of an age',[91] all result in a 'circular argument'[92] and 'physiognomic fallacy',[93] or even agnosticism.[94] Despite that, Gombrich acknowledges Hegel's merit in establishing 'the universal history of art' and his right to be called 'the father of the history of art'.[95] Moreover, Gombrich does not reject the original positive role expressionism played in 'the trans-valuation of all values' and in offering a common denominator for a universal art history.[96] At the same time he regards the overwhelming influence of Hegelian heritage as a dangerous epidemic.[97] Because of its easy applicability the 'Hegelian paradigm'[98] hypnotised 'the leading champions of art history and cultural history in the German-speaking countries'.[99] Not only neo-Hegelians such as M. Dvořák came under the spell of Hegel, but also radical relativists like W. Worringer or O. Spengler, representatives of the 'Hegelian right' like A. Malraux, neo-Marxist sociologists such as A. Hauser, and even passionate opponents of Hegel like J. Burckhardt and J. Huizinga or neo-Kantians such as E. Panofsky.[100] Gombrich calls himself 'a run-away Hegelian'.[101] His critique of Hegelianism also touched his older schoolmates, whom he admired in his youth for their attempt at making art history an exact science by means of psychology. Later Gombrich revised his originally affirmative attitude to H. Sedlmayr; he realised that Sedlmayr belonged to the camp of metaphysical collectivists and unveiled his concept of the structure of a work of art as an essentialist notion.[102] Not only Riegl but also Sedlmayr was addressed when Gombrich regretted 'the misuse of psychology in its historicist form'.[103] Moreover, the relativism of Hegelian origin is, according to Gombrich, still 'the official dogma . . . of contemporary art-historical teaching'.[104] That is why 'the history of art should free itself of Hegel's authority'.[105]

It is true that Gombrich was not indifferent to the historical motivations that had initiated Hegel's philosophy of history. He sees that Hegel's idea of art as a 'Theophany'[106] and his historical relativism came into being as reactions against eighteenth-century Enlightenment universalism and the French Revolution.[107] He admits that a theory cannot be taken for the cause of a crime; at the same time he is convinced that theories can open the way for crimes. Thus he does not think it necessary to take into account the fact that German historicism or Hegel's teleological model of history as Providence originally played an apologetic role against French hegemonism and were instruments of German national unification. Not intentions, but consequences, even if unintended, are the judge of theories.[108] As he put it, 'Nobody and nothing can relieve us of the burden of moral responsibility for our judgment.'[109]

According to James Elkins, Gombrich failed to jump out of 'Hegel's wheel',[110] despite the explicit declaration of his allegiance to deductionism. Following Popper, Gombrich claims: 'Not even a chronicle of art, let alone a history of style, could ever be based on the collecting of uninterpreted data.' And he concludes: 'Thus what we need is new and better theories that can be tested against historical material as far as such tests are ever possible.'[111] Irrespective of whether Elkins is right or wrong, Gombrich insists that one replaces abstractions by individuals; essences by conventions; expression by communication; social determinism by the 'logic of situation'; style by language and fashion; spirit of an age by mental or intellectual climate; cultural unity by multicausality; symptom by function; and the transcendental connection of art by 'the law of artistic tradition'.[112]

Genealogical line

While Gombrich's criticism of Hegel is inspired by Popper's overriding critique of historicism,[113] his plea for individualism and conventionalism is anchored in one branch of the Vienna School of art history. Gombrich's model can, in a sense, be regarded as a comment on Julius von Schlosser's ideas. 'I learned enormously from Schlosser', he acknowledges explicitly.[114] It is known that Schlosser developed a dualist conception of art history in trying to reconcile the historical relativism of the Vienna school with the anti-historical individualism of Benedetto Croce as expressed in his 'insular conception' of art.[115] Gombrich's famous Story of Art begins with a sentence borrowed from Schlosser's essay on 'History of style and history of language':[116] 'There really is no such thing as Art. There are only artists.'[117] According to Werner Hofmann,[118] there were two conceptions of art and its history within the Vienna School. The first, represented by Wickhoff, Riegl and Sedlmayr, believed in 'ars una'[119] and a linear and closed or irreversible historical process. The second, developed by Dvořák or Schlosser and followed by Gombrich,[120] preferred a pluralist idea of art and conceived of its history as an open, reversible and heterogeneous process. It is significant for Gombrich's rejection of all kinds of essentialism that he displayed his indebtedness to Schlosser. The introduction to his *Story of Art* continues as follows: 'There is no harm in calling all these activities art as long as we keep in mind that such a word may mean very different things in different times and places, and as long as we realize that Art with a capital A has no existence.'[121] It is evident that there exists a connection with Dvořák's idea that not only forms and contents, but the concept of art itself is historically changing, as expressed in his *Idealism and Naturalism in Gothic Art*.[122] The reason that Gombrich stressed his indebtedness to Schlosser, instead of Dvořák, lies ready to hand; Dvořák did not distinguish clearly enough between changes in the nature or 'essence' of art and changes in its social status and function, and Gombrich prefers the idea of art as a social convention to the belief in the historically changing essence of art: 'There is no essence of art. We can decide what we call art or not art . . . the category of art is one which is culturally determined.'[123] Gombrich avoids extreme conventionalism, arguing that 'we have a right to speak of art when certain activities become ends in themselves' or 'when the performance becomes as important as the function'.[124] He makes a concession to social anthropology, coming, in such a way, very close to the solution offered by Jan Mukařovský.[125]

Gombrich avoids relativism once more when saying that we use the term 'art' also in its second meaning i.e. as 'value judgment'.[126] Herein he follows Schlosser's dualistic distinction between social conventions and the creation of values by great artists. Nevertheless, Gombrich significantly transformed Schlosser's contrast of 'the history of style' to 'the history of language'. While Schlosser assigned the authorship of style to great artists, regarding language as a spreading of their achievements,[127] Gombrich identified style with language, taking language in the sense of *parole*,[128] and saw artists working within its framework. It is just at this point that Gombrich departs from Schlosser's aristocratic individualism and leans towards Riegl's democratic equalisation of 'the high arts' with 'the applied arts'.[129] The difference between Riegl's and Gombrich's democratisation of the concept of art can be characterised as the equalisation from below by Riegl (i.e. the applied arts regarded as equally high as the high arts)[130] in contrast to the equalisation from above by Gombrich (i.e. the high arts regarded as equally bound by the demands of skill as the applied arts). In Gombrich's view, art is a part of visual communication and, as a consequence, his own work on the problem of artistic representation can be regarded as a contribution to the 'linguistics of the image'.[131]

Following Schlosser's analysis of medieval art and his discovery of the role of schemas as well as artistic tradition,[132] Gombrich not only replaces Riegl's concept of a linear evolution by the concept of tradition, but also revitalises the idea of art as craftsmanship. He refuses the Romantic notion of art as expression or transcendental creation and, leaning on E. Löwy and K. R. Popper, shows that even naturalistic art has been based on the principle of 'schema and correction'.[113] Irrespective of the question whether contemporary art helped to open Gombrich's eyes towards that problem and influenced his interpretation of naturalistic art or not,[134] Gombrich's *Art and Illusion* can be regarded as a fulfilment of Wickhoff's project of the history of naturalism.[135] Paradoxically, the materialisation of Wickhoff's dream means at the same time a fundamental revision of one of the basic ideas of the Vienna School, i.e. its relativistic idea of an equally valid plurality of artistic truths. Gombrich does not regard the history of art as Wickhoff or Riegl did (as the history of vision or of convictions),[136] but, on the contrary, as the history of skilful representation. He disconnects the form and content of a work of art and shows that there can exist disharmony between the two. As a consequence, art cannot be regarded as a true expression, but as an 'image making' or even a technique of 'illusionist devices'.[137] Thus not only the concept of 'mastery' and 'skill' has been rehabilitated, but also the true opposite to historical relativism has been restored, i.e. the idea of progress, even if in the sense of a technological progress, on the one hand, and limited to a conventional frame of reference, on the other.[138]

'The balance of optimism and resignation'[139]

With a certain licence it can be said that the Vienna School of art history held to an antinomy between historical relativism on the one hand and universalism on the other. Universalism and its tokens, scientism and psychologism, were put into the service of relativism. Gombrich inherited the antinomic design of art history and tried to overcome it throughout his life.

As a matter of fact, he succeeded only in replacing it by another antinomic set, i.e. the antinomy of social conventionalism versus anthropologism.[140] He constantly balanced two poles of that antinomy, acknowledging the social and conventional nature of art on the one hand and the belief in a common denominator of all art, in a constant human nature as its basis and, consequently, in universal artistic values on the other.[141] Nevertheless, Gombrich makes substantial changes in the Viennese project; first, he reverses the ratio of elements that take part in the antinomic plot and puts the conventionalist idea into the service of the belief in an anthropologic constant. Historically established conventions are regarded as based on an elastic but polarised human nature.[142] Then, while refusing an absolute universalism,[143] he conceives the 'universal human psyche' in the permanent effort to accumulate historical experience.[144] So art, as one of the vehicles of cumulating human experience, consists of universally valid and understandable values. Artistic values 'have been realised in history'[145] and are the materialisation of various social rituals.[146] But they are also based on 'constants of the psyche of man' and 'the universal human response' even if taken as a hypothesis.[147] Gombrich regards relativism as a dangerous idea that results not only in an agnosticism or 'in the destruction of all belief in communicability',[148] but also directly in racialism.[149] In spite of the fact that 'relativism grew out of the reaction against the belief of eighteenth-century aesthetics that our response to art is rooted in human nature and must therefore be universal',[150] the historical motivations and intentions of relativism (the plea for equality of diversity or the call for tolerance) do not represent a satisfactory justification of relativism. Though he is fully aware that we cannot 'identify our civilization with civilization as such', that is not a reason 'to isolate our culture from others' or to lose 'an awareness of the unity of civilization'.[151] The consequences of an extreme relativism prevent Gombrich from accepting the hypothesis that our occidental values are imbued not only with our ideals but also our interests,[152] and force him to refuse the idea that our belief in universal human values can be regarded as yet another example of our imprisonment in the occidental myth of universality.

'An uneasy humanist'

As mentioned above, scientism was used to support relativism within the Vienna School. Logically, Gombrich's critique of relativism was followed by his revision of the Vienna school doctrine of art history as a 'value-free' science;[153] against Riegl's maxim that the best art historian is the one without any taste[154] Gombrich stressed his conviction that the 'question concerning value . . . will remain vital to the art historian'[155] and that 'the subjective response must be and remain at the heart of the humanist enterprise'.[156] Gombrich presents himself as 'an uneasy humanist',[157] and we can add that he can be regarded also as an uneasy rationalist.[158] On the one hand, he relies upon rationality as a proper judge in all human affairs; on the other, he limits his belief in rationality by permanent scepticism and criticism. At the same time he also modifies his gamble on conventionalism by refusing arbitrariness and clearly distinguishing between 'true and false hypotheses':[159] 'Just as science can eliminate a wrong explanation, a false hypothesis, so the disciplined humanist can rule out a false reading, a misunderstanding.'[160] Hence there is 'a limited plurality of interpretations'.[161]

Following Popper's monistic idea of the single epistemological basis of all sciences, Gombrich believes that a limited applicability of the method of testing general theories by means of falsification of hypotheses[162] also applies to art-historical research. At the same time, starting from the conviction that 'individuum est ineffabile',[163] whose origin in historicism is obvious, Gombrich accepts the neo-Kantian idea of the different nature of natural sciences on the one hand and social sciences or humanities on the other.[164] He endorses the notion according to which art history has a particular status and plays a special function shared by humanities in contrast to sciences. In his view art history cannot be regarded as a science, but rather as scholarship.[165] The principal purpose of art history is not research, but knowledge and its main procedure does not consist in problem-solving and explanation but in understanding and interpretation.[166] As a consequence, art history as a part of humanities does not aim at discoveries, but rather at maintaining memory.[167] Regarding the art historian as a humanist, Gombrich demands that he or she should be in the first line as 'the guardian of memories'[168] and universal human values. The Viennese ideal of the art historian as an impartial scientist has been replaced by the idea of the art historian as a scholar guarding values. Consequently not only the Viennese doctrine of art history as a science, but also its fundamental buttress, i.e. its belief in method as the only way to reliable and objective knowledge, has been revised by Gombrich. The belief in only one right scientific method, as propagated by Wickhoff and Riegl or the young Dvořák, and later by Sedlmayr or Pächt, has been replaced by a pluralist and pragmatist view preferring the solution of the problem to the purity of method.[169]

In spite of all his merciless criticism and revisionist views addressed to many fundamental ideas of the Vienna School, Gombrich can justifiably be regarded as a member of that school. After all, he follows faithfully the tradition of *Kunstgeschichtliche Anzeigen* or *Kritische Berichte* in regarding art history as a critical or even self-critical procedure. He also shares the faith that art history represents an important social and cultural mission. It is known that it was just that belief which enabled Gombrich to bridge the Vienna School and the Warburg Library traditions.

Notes

1. *Eribon*, pp. 39–40.
2. Hans R. Hahnloser, 'Chronologisches Verzeichnis der aus der "Wiener Schule"', bzw. dem Österreichischen Institut für Geschichtsforschung hervorgegangenen oder ihr affilierten Kunsthistoriker, *Mitteilungen des Österreichischen Instituts für Geschichtsforschung*, Ergänzungsband 13, Heft 2, 1934, p. 226.
3. See Sir Ernst Hans Josef Gombrich, 'Wenn's euch Ernst ist, was zu sagen – Wandlungen in der Kunstbetrachtung', in Martina Sitt (ed.), *Kunsthistoriker in eigener Sache*, Berlin 1990, p. 70 (*E. Gombrich in M. Sitt*); E. H. Gombrich, 'An autobiographical sketch', in *Topics*, pp. 14–17; and *Eribon*, pp. 36–49.
4. Otto Pächt, 'Am Anfang war das Auge', in M. Sitt, *Kunsthistoriker*, pp. 32 and 52.
5. Thomas Zaunschirm, 'Kunstgeschichte als Geistesgeschichte: eine andere Wiener Schule', in Kristian Sotriffer (ed.), *Das grössere Österreich*, Wien 1982, p. 162; and Edwin Lachnit, 'Ansätze methodischer Evolution in der Wiener Schule der Kunstgeschichte', in *Révolution et évolution de l'histoire de l'art de Warburg à nos jours, L'Art et les Révolutions* (Actes du XXVIIe Congrès International d'Histoire de l'Art, Section 5, Strassbourg 1992, p. 43 (*Révolution et évolution*)).
6. *Eribon*, p. 39; and E. H. Gombrich, 'Approaches to the history of art: three points for discussion', in *Topics*, p. 64.
7. *Topics*, p. 64; *Eribon*, pp. 39–40.
8. Moriz Thausing, 'Die Stellung der Kunstgeschichte als Wissenschaft', reprinted in *Wiener Jahrbuch für Kunstgeschichte*, Bd.36, Wien–Köln–Graz 1983, pp. 140–50. On M. Thausing see Artur Rosenauer, 'Moriz Thausing und die Wiener Schule der Kunstgeschichte', *ibid.* pp. 135–9.
9. *Eribon*, p. 39.
10. See Julius von Schlosser, 'Die Wiener Schule der Kunstgeschichte: Rückblick auf ein Säkulum deutscher Gelehrtenarbeit in Österreich', in *Mitteilungen des Österreichischen Instituts für Geschichtsforschung*, Ergänzungsband 13, Heft 2, Innsbruck 1934, pp. 161–80; and Ioli Kalavrezou-Maxainer, 'Franz Wickhoff: Kunstgeschichte als Wissenschaft', in *Wien und die Entwicklung der kunsthistorischen Methode* 1 (Akten des XXV. Internationalen Kongresses für Kunstgeschichte, Wien–Köln–Graz 1984, pp. 17–22 (*Wien und die Entwicklung*)). On G. Morelli

see Henri Zerner, 'Giovanni Morelli et la science de l'art', *Revue de l'art*, 40–41 (1978), pp. 209–15; Giovanni Previtali, 'A propos de Morelli', *Revue de l'art*, 42 (l978), pp. 27–31; and Jaynie Anderson, 'Giovanni Morelli's Scientific Method of Attribution – Origins and Interpretations', in *Révolution et évolution*, pp. 135–9.

11. On Riegl see e.g. Henri Zerner, 'Alois Riegl: art, value, and historicism', *Daedalus*, 105 (1976), pp. 177–88; Willibald Sauerländer, 'Alois Riegl und die Entstehung der autonomen Kunstgeschichte am Fin de siècle', in *Fin de Siècle, Zur Literatur und Kunst der Jahrhudertwende*, Frankfurt a.M. 1977, pp. 125–39; Hans-Berthold Busse, *Kunst und Wissenschaft*, Mittenwald 1981, pp. 43–65; Margaret Iversen, 'Style as structure: Alois Riegl's historiography', *Art History*, 2 (1979), pp. 62–72; M. Iversen, *Alois Riegl: Art History and Theory*, Massachusetts 1993; Margaret Olin, 'Spätrömische Kunstindustrie: the crisis of knowledge in Fin de Siècle Vienna', in *Wien und die Entwicklung*, pp. 29–36; M.Olin, *Forms of Representation in Alois Riegl's Theory of Art*, Pennsylvania 1992; Jan Bažant, 'Alois Riegl, vytvarny znak a symbol', in *Symbol v lidském vnímání, myšlení a vyjádřování*, Praha 1992, pp. 144–58; and Wolfgang Kemp, 'Alois Riegl (1858–1905)', in Heinrich Dilly (ed.), *Altmeister moderner Kunstgeschichte*, Berlin 1990, pp. 37–60.

12. E. H. Gombrich, 'Kunstwissenschaft', in *Das Atlantisbuch der Kunst: eine Enzyklopädie der bildenden Künste*, Zürich 1952, p. 663 (*Kunstwissenschaft*); and J. von Schlosser, 'Die Wiener Schule der Kunstgeschichte', p. 199.

13. On Dvořák see e.g. Lech Kalinowski, *Max Dvořák i jego metoda badan nad sztuka*, Warszawa 1974; H. B. Busse, *Kunst und Wissenschaft*, pp. 85–108; Sandor Radnóti, 'Die Historisierung des Kunstbegriffs: Max Dvořák', *Acta historiae artium*, 26 (1980), pp. 125–42; Rudolf Chadraba, 'Max Dvořák a vídeòská škola dìjin umìní', in *Kapitoly z èeského dìjepisu umìní II*, Praha 1987, pp. 9–70; Mitchell Schwarzer, 'Cosmopolitan difference in Max Dvořák's art historiography', *The Art Bulletin*, 84 (1992), pp. 669–78.

14. See Meyer Schapiro, 'The New Viennese School', *The Art Bulletin*, 18 (1936), pp. 258–66; Artur Rosenauer, 'Zur Neuen Wiener Schule der Kunstgeschichte', in *Révolution et évolution*, pp. 73–83; and O. Pächt, 'Am anfang', pp. 32, 57–58.

15. Julius von Schlosser,'Die Wiener Schule der Kunstgeschichte', p. 201. J. von Schlosser, '"Stilgeschichte" und "Sprachgeschichte" der bildenden Kunst', in *Sitzungsberichte der Bayerischen Akademie der Wissenschaften, philosophisch-historische Abteilung* 1935, pp. 3–39. On J. von Schlosser, see Otto Kurz, 'Julius von Schlosser, Personalità–Metodo–Lavoro', *Critica d'Arte*, 11–12 (1955), pp. 402–19; Michael Podro, 'Against formalism: Schlosser on Stilgeschichte', in *Wien und die Entwicklung*, pp.37–43; Eva Frodl-Kraft, 'Eine Aporie und der Versuch ihrer Deutung: Josef Strzygowski – Julius v. Schlosser', *Wiener Jahrbuch für Kunstgeschichte*, 42 (1989), pp. 7–52; Edwin Lachnit, 'Julius von Schlosser (1866–1938)', in H.Dilly (ed.), *Altmeister*, pp. 151–62. See also a special issue of *Kritische Berichte*, 16 (1988), devoted to Schlosser, with contributions by E. H. Gombrich, A. Bayer, E. Lachnit, K. T. Johns and Th. Lersch.

16. *Eribon*, p. 39.

17. E. H. Gombrich, 'Kunstwissenschaft und Psychologie vor fünfzig Jahren', in Wien und die Entwicklung, pp. 100–1 (*Kunstwissenschaft und Psychologie*).

18. See Carl E. Schorske, 'Austrian aesthetic culture 1870–1914: a historian's reflection', in *Akten des XXV. Internationalen Kongresses für Kunstgeschichte, Eröffnungs- und Plenarvorträge*, Wien–Köln–Graz 1985, pp. 27–40. For more details see C.E. Schorske, *Fin-de-siècle Vienna: Politics and Culture*, New York 1981.

19. *Topics*, pp. 12–13; *E. Gombrich in M. Sitt*, p. 64.

20. *E. Gombrich in M. Sitt*, p.65; *Topics*, p. 14; and E. H. Gombrich, 'Focus on the arts and humanities', in *Tributes*, p. 13.

21. *Eribon*, p. 37; *E. Gombrich in M. Sitt*, pp. 92–3.

22. *Eribon*, pp. 37–8.

23. See Edwin Lachnit, *Kunstgeschichte und Zeitgenössische Kunst*, Dissertation, Universität Wien 1984, pp. 118–19. According to Lachnit, Strzygowski concentrated on system instead of on the method of art history research.

24. *Topics*, p. 14; E. H. Gombrich, 'The exploration of cultural contacts: the service to scholarship of Otto Kurz', in *Tributes*, p. 237; and *E. Gombrich in M. Sitt*, pp. 92–3.

25. *Eribon*, p. 37.

26. E. Frodl-Kraft, 'Eine Aporie', pp. 23, 27.

27. *E. Gombrich in M. Sitt*, p. 72.

28. Otto Pächt, 'Alois Riegl', in O. Pächt, *Methodisches zur kunsthistorischen Praxis*, München 1977, p. 151.

29. *Tributes*, p. 13.

30. *Ibid.*, p. 14; *E. Gombrich in M. Sitt*, p. 68. Gombrich's study was published in *Jahrbuch der Kunsthistorischen Sammlungen in Wien*, N.F. 7 (1993), pp. 1–14, under the title 'Eine verkannte karolingische Pyxis im Wiener Kunsthistorischen Museum'.

31. *E. Gombrich in M. Sitt*, p. 69; *Topics*, p. 16; *Eribon*, p. 38.

32. K. R. Popper, *The Logic of Scientific Discovery*, New York 1959.

33. Edwin Lachnit expressed very fittingly the ambiguous nature of Gombrich's point of view in the title of his article on Gombrich 'Traditionalist und Mythenzertrümmerer', *Falter*, 13 (1989), p. 14.

34. *E. Gombrich in M. Sitt*, p. 65; *Eribon*, p. 35; *Topics*, p. 13.

35. *E. Gombrich in M. Sitt*, p. 69; *Topics*, p. 16.

36. E. Gombrich, 'Zum Werke Giulio Romanos I.,II.', *Jahrbuch der Kunsthistorischen Sammlungen in Wien*, N.F. 8 (1934), pp. 79–104, N.F. 9 (1935), pp. 121–50; *Topics*, pp. 17–19; *E. Gombrich in M. Sitt*, p. 73; and Klaus Lepsky, *Ernst H. Gombrich, Theorie und Methode*, Wien–Köln 1991, pp. 27–33.

37. *Tributes*, p. 14.

38. *Eribon*, pp. 40–1.

39. *Ibid.*, p. 41.

40. *E. Gombrich in M. Sitt*, p. 73; *Topics*, p. 18; *Tributes*, p. 14; Lepsky, *Ernst H. Gombrich*, pp. 27–33.

41. Lepsky, *Ernst H. Gombrich*, p. 28.

42. *Eribon*, p. 41.

43. A study of that relationship was written by Edwin Lachnit in *Kunstgeschichte*.

44. Franz Wickhoff and Wilhelm Ritter von Hartel, *Die Wiener Genesis*, Wien 1895; J. von Schlosser, 'Die Wiener Schule der Kunstgeschichte', pp. 176–7; E. Gombrich, *Kunstwissenschaft*, pp. 658–9.

45. *Art and Illusion*, p. 15. See also *The Sense of Order*, pp. 195–6.

46. J. von Schlosser, *Die Wiener Schule der Kunstgeschichte*, p. 189. E. H. Gombrich, *Kunstwissenschaft*, p. 660, saw in Riegl a forerunner of Cubism; W. Sauerländer, in 'Alois Riegl', stressed the connection betweeen Riegl and the Fin de Siècle art. Werner Hofmann in *Gegenstimmen: Aufsätze zur Kunst des 20. Jahrhunderts*, Frankfurt a.M. 1979, and in his paper 'Was bleibt von der "Wiener Schule?"', *Kunsthistoriker: Mitteilungen des Österreichischen Kunsthistorikerverbandes*, 1 (1984), p. 4 and 2 (1985), p. 6 (*Was bleibt*) speaks of a parallel with the 'Jugendstil' or 'l'art pour l'art' movements. E. Lachnit, *Kunstgeschichte*, pp. 94–5, identifies Riegl's relationship to modern art as a parallel to Cézanne.

47. E. Lachnit, *Kunstgeschichte*, p. 195.

48. E. H. Gombrich, 'André Malraux and the crisis of Expressionism', in *Meditations*, p. 79; *E. Gombrich in M. Sitt*, p. 70. On Tietze's relationship to modern art see Dieter Bogner, 'Hans Tietze und die moderne Kunst', *Wiener Jahrbuch für Kunstgeschichte*, 33 (1980), Wien–Köln–Graz, p. 13.

49. *E. Gombrich in M. Sitt*, p. 73; E. Gombrich, *Kunstwissenschaft und Psychologie*, p. 101.

50. A. Rosenauer, 'Zur Neuen Wiener Schule', pp. 76–7.

51. *E. Gombrich in M. Sitt*, pp. 74–6; *Eribon*, pp. 103–4. At that time Gombrich was attracted by Schlosser's interest in 'the conceptual image' and Löwy's in 'the gradual modification of the schema'. Kris's impact on Gombrich resulted not only in their common study on caricature ('The principles of caricature', *British Journal of Medical Psychology*, 17 (1938), pp. 319–42) but also in Gombrich's application of some principles of psychoanalysis in his study on Giulio Romano. See K. Lepsky, *Ernst H. Gombrich*, pp. 30–1, 33–6.

52. Ernst von Garger, 'Über die Wertungschwierigkeiten bei mittelalterlicher Kunst', *Kritische Berichte*, 5 (1932–33).

53. E. Gombrich, 'Wertprobleme und die mittelalterliche Kunst', *Kritische Berichte*, 6 (1937), reprinted in English as 'Achievement in medieval art', in *Meditations*, pp. 70–7.

54. *Meditations*, p. 75.

55. E. Gombrich, 'Meditations on a hobby horse or The roots of artistic form', *Meditations*, pp. 1–11.

56. *Art and Illusion*, especially chapter III.

57. *Ibid.*, p. 9.

58. *Eribon*, p. 104.

59. Later, under the influence of Popper, Gombrich complements that structures distinguishing between the art of 'open societies' and closed ones. The first was based on the principle of competition, the second on the principle of repetition, according to Gombrich. See his 'The logic of Vanity Fair: alternatives to historicism in the study of fashions, style and taste', in *The Philosophy of Karl*

Popper, edited by P. A. Schilpp, The Library of Living Philosophers, Vol. 14, La Salle 1974, p. 935 (*Vanity Fair*), reprinted in *Ideals*, pp. 60–92.

60. *The Sense of Order*, p. viii.
61. H. Zerner, 'Alois Riegl', p. 179.
62. *Ibid*.
63. See W. Kemp, 'Alois Riegl'.
64. They can be enumerated as follows: (a) historical rules and causal explanation; (b) analysis of form; (c) the history of style; (d) an impersonal artistic intention (*Kunstwollen*); (e) an autonomous source of historical movement, even if with spiritualist or vitalist implications; (f) the historical nature of art (i.e. art = the history of art); (g) the relative nature of values and equality of all historical epochs; (h) an anti-aristocratic conception of the relation between the high arts and the applied arts.
65. *Eribon*, p. 103.
66. *Topics*, p. 64.
67. *Ibid*, p. 65.
68. *Kunstwissenschaft*, pp. 658–61.
69. We use here O. Pächt's expression; see O. Pächt, 'Alois Riegl', p. 149.
70. *Art and Illusion*, p. 14.
71. *Ibid*.
72. *Ibid*, p. 16.
73. *Ibid*.
74. *The Sense of Order*, p. 195.
75. *Ibid.*, p. 197.
76. *Ibid.*, pp. 195–7.
77. O. Pächt, 'Alois Riegl', p. 148.
78. See O. Pächt, *Am Anfang war das Auge*, in M. Sitt, *Kunsthistoriker*, pp. 25–61.
79. See E. Gombrich, 'Image and code: scope and limits of conventionalism in pictorial representation', in Wendy Steiner (ed.), *Image and Code*, Ann Arbor 1981, pp. 11–42; and Nelson Goodman, *Languages of Art: an Approach to a Theory of Symbols*, New York 1968.
80. See J. von Schlosser, 'Die Wiener Schule', pp. 181–93; and Karl Clausberg, 'Wiener Schule – Russischer Formalismus – Prager Strukturalismus', *Idea: Jahrbuch der Hamburger Kunsthalle*, 2 (1983), pp. 152–80.
81. W. Kemp, 'Alois Riegl', p. 46, calls E. H. Gombrich 'ein Enkelschüler von Riegl'.
82. A. Rosenauer, 'Zur neuen Wiener Schule', p. 73, characterises the return of the Sedlmayr–Pächt generation to Riegl as follows: 'Während man sich von den Vätern lossagt, wendet man sich zur Generation der Grossväter zurück'.
83. As Jurij Tynjanov believed; see Victor Erlich, *Russian Formalism, History, Doctrine*, 's-Gravenhage 1955, German translation, *Russischer Formalism*, München 1964, p. 290.
84. *Ibid.*, p. 291.
85. See, for example, K. R. Popper, *The Open Society and Its Enemies*, London 1945; and H. Arendt, *The Origins of Totalitarianisms*, New York 1951.

86. 'Art and scholarship', in *Meditations*, p. 114.

87. *Art and Illusion*, p. 17.

88. 'The father of art history', in *Tributes*, pp. 52–64.

89. *Tributes*, p. 55; E. H. Gombrich, *Art History and the Social Sciences*, Oxford 1975, p.10 (*Social Sciences*), reprinted in *Ideals and Idols*.

90. *Art and Illusion*, pp. 16–17; *Meditations*, p. 114.

91. 'Mannerism: the historiographic background', p. 103.

92. 'Relativism in the humanities: the debate about human nature', in *Topics*, p. 40.

93. *Meditations*, p. 108; *Topics*, p. 40.

94. 'André Malraux and the crisis of Expressionism', in *Meditations*, p. 80.

95. *Tributes*, p. 51.

96. *Meditations*, p. 80.

97. *Tributes*, p. 51; *Meditations*, p. 114.

98. *Tributes*, p. 63. It is worth mentioning that Gombrich's relationship to Hegel as well as to Riegl changed gradually from strict rejection to a kind of appreciation; compare his earlier expression 'Hegelian dogma' (*Norm and Form*, p. 103) with the later term 'Hegelian paradigm' ('A plea for pluralism', *Ideals*, p. 186).

99. *Tributes*, p. 62.

100. E. H. Gombrich, *In Search of Cultural History*, Oxford 1969 (*In Search*), reprinted in *Ideals*, pp. 24–59; *Meditations*, pp. x, 78–85, 86–94; *Art and Illusion*, pp. 16–17; *Vanity Fair*, p. 940; *Tributes*, p. 62.

101. *Tributes*, p. 51.

102. *Kunstwissenschaft*, p. 662; *Art and Illusion*, p. 17; *Meditations*, p. 112. *Kunstwissenschaft und Psychologie*, p. 101; E. H. Gombrich, review of *Kunstgeschichte und Kunsttheorie im 19. Jahrhundert*, *The Art Bulletin*, 46 (1964), pp. 418–20.

103. *Art and Illusion*, p. 17.

104. *Tributes*, p. 65.

105. *Ibid.*, p. 51.

106. *Ibid.*, p. 54.

107. *Ibid.*; *Social Sciences*, p. 46; and 'Relativism in the Humanities', in *Topics*, pp. 36–7.

108. *Vanity Fair*, p. 926; Gombrich followed here 'the genuinely sociological problem of the unintended social repercussions of intentional human actions' described by K. R. Popper.

109. *Tributes*, p. 69.

110. James Elkins, 'Art history without theory', *Critical Inquiry*, 14 (1988), pp. 354–78.

111. *Vanity Fair*, p. 926.

112. *Vanity Fair*, p. 927 'Expression and communication', in *Meditations*, pp. 56–69; *Social Sciences*, p. 22. *Tributes*, pp. 16, 24, 64. As far as Gombrich's dualism, tradition or convention versus individual history and mastership is concerned, see the comment by Svetlana Alpers, 'Is art history?', *Daedalus*, 1 (1977), pp. 9–10.

113. K. R. Popper, *The Poverty of Historicism*, London 1957.

114. *Eribon*, pp. 103–4; see also E. H. Gombrich, 'Einige Erinnerungen an Julius von Schlosser als Lehrer', *Kritische Berichte*, 16 (1988), pp. 3–64.
115. M. Podro, 'Against formalism'; E. Lachnit, 'Julius von Schlosser'; and W. E. Kleinbauer, *Modern Perspectives in Western Art History*, New York 1971, pp. 13–14.
116. J. von Schlosser, *'Stilgeschichte' und 'Sprachgeschichte'*.
117. E. H. Gombrich, *The Story of Art*, New York 1953, p.5.
118. W. Hofmann, *Was bleibt*, pp. 4–7.
119. According to Hans Belting in *Das Ende der Kunsgeschichte?*, München 1984, the premise of 'ars una' represents a common denominator of the whole Vienna school.
120. In Hofmann's view Gombrich combined impulses of both currents of the Vienna school (W. Hofmann, *Was bleibt*, p. 4).
121. *The Story of Art*, p. 5.
122. Max Dvořák, *Idealismus und Naturalismus in der gotischen Skulptur und Malerei* (originally published in 1918), in M. Dvořák, *Kunstgeschichte als Geistesgeschichte: Studien zur abendländischen Kunstentwicklung*, München 1924, pp. 120, 124–7:

> The belief in permanent principles of art is to be counted among the causes of the prevailing uncertainty and confusion in the critical examination of works of art from earlier periods, works which arose amid other general historical presuppositions. This belief was based upon the assumption that, no matter how often the goals and technical skills of art might change, the concept of a work of art can nevertheless be considered something which in principle is constant and immutable. Nothing, however, is more false and more unhistorical than such an assumption, for the concept of the work of art and of the artistic has in the course of its historical development undergone the most diverse transformations even with respect to its most fundamental presuppositions, and is at all times a temporally and culturally defined and variable result of the general evolution of mankind. What was understood by the term 'art' and what was sought in it and demanded of it varied in the old oriental, in the classical, in the medieval and in the contemporary European intellectual world – to say nothing of other cultural milieus – just as much did the conceptions of religion, morality, history or the sciences.

> The English translation above is by R. J. Klawiter (*Idealism and Naturalism in Gothic Art*, Notre Dame 1967, pp. 122–3). For more details on Dvořák's historical relativism see S. Radnóti, 'Die Historisierung'.

123. *Eribon*, p. 72.
124. *Ibid.*, p. 76.
125. Robert Kalivoda, 'Die Dialektik des Strukturalismus und die Dialektik der Ästhetik', in his *Der Marxismus und die moderne geistige Wirklichkeit*, Frankfurt a.M. 1970; Peter Steiner, 'The conceptual basis of Prague Structuralism' in Ladislav Matejka (ed.), *Sound, Sign and Meaning*, Ann Arbor 1976; Jiří Veltruský, 'Jan Mukařovský's structural poetics and aesthetics', in *Poetics Today*, 2 (1980–81); Květoslav Chvatík, *Tschechoslowakischer Strukturalismus*, München 1981; Lubomír

Doležel, *Semiotic Poetics: The Prague School Design*, Lincoln and London 1990; J. Bakoš, 'Der tschecho-slowakische Strukturalismus und die Kunstgeschichts-schreibung', *Zeitschrift für Ästhetik und allgemeine Kunstwissenschaft*, 36 (1991), pp. 53–103.

126. *Eribon*, pp. 71–2.

127. See the interpretations of Schlosser's differentiating between 'the history of style' and 'the history of language' by M. Podro, 'Against Formalism', p. 38, and E. Lachnit, 'Julius von Schlosser', pp. 157–8.

128. E. Lachnit, *Kunstgeschichte*, p. 96.

129. *The Sense of Order*, p. 197.

130. W. Hofmann, *Was bleibt*.

131. *Eribon*, p. 105.

132. Julius von Schlosser, 'Zur Kenntnis der künstlerischen Überlieferung im späten Mittelalter', *Jahrbuch der Kunsthistorischen Sammlungen in Wien*, 23 (1903); *Die Kunst des Mittelalters*, Berlin 1923.

133. *Art and Illusion*, pp. 24, 99; *Eribon*, pp. 103, 106.

134. E. Gombrich in M. Sitt, p. 86. Gombrich rejects any conscious and direct influence of modern art on his ideas, but admits many correspondences between them. And he continues:

> Ich würde auch von mir behaupten, ich hätte nicht so viel mit dem Darstellungsproblem beschäftigt, wenn es nicht damals auch eine abstrakte Kunst gegeben hätte. Man sieht ja etwas erst, wenn es im Kontrast zu etwas anderem steht.

135. W. Hofmann, *Was bleibt*, p. 5.

136. *Art and Illusion*, pp. 14–18.

137. *Social Sciences*, p. 36.

138. *Vanity Fair*, pp. 77–81; *Topics*, pp. 67–8; *Eribon*, p. 75; E. H. Gombrich, *The Ideas of Progress and their Impact on Art*, New York 1971 (German translation, *Kunst und Fortschritt: Wirkung und Wandlung einer Idee*, Köln 1978).

139. *Tributes*, p. 23.

140. *Vanity Fair*, p. 948.

141. *Ibid.*, p. 948. *Social Sciences*, p. 47; see also 'They were all human beings – so much is plain: reflections on cultural relativism in the humanities', *Critical Inquiry*, Summer 1987, pp. 686–99.

142. *Topics*, pp. 44–5.

143. *Ibid.*, p. 39.

144. *Social Sciences*, p. 47.

145. *Ibid.*, p. 58.

146. For more details see *Ideals and Idols*, pp. 60–92.

147. *Topics*, pp. 44–5. *Social Sciences*, pp. 42, 46.

148. *Meditations*, p. 80.

149. *Topics*, p. 7.

150. *Social Sciences*, p. 46.

151. *Tributes*, p. 12.

152. See James S. Ackermann, 'On judging art without absolutes', *Critical Inquiry*, 5 (1979), pp. 441–69, and his polemics with Gombrich, *ibid.*, pp. 794–9.

153. *Topics*, p. 55.

154. J. von Schlosser, *Die Wiener Schule*, p. 189.

155. *Social Sciences*, p. 42.

156. *Tributes*, p. 17; see also Gombrich's 'Reason and feeling in the study of art', in *Ideals*, pp. 205–7.

157. *Tributes*, p. 15.

158. See on Gombrich, K. Lepsky, *Ernst H. Gombrich*; L. D. Etlinger, *Art History Today*, London 1961, pp. 18–20; Carlo Ginsburg, 'Da A. Warburg a E. H. Gombrich', *Studi Medievali*, 1966, pp. 1045–65 (English translation in C. Ginsburg, *Myths, Emblems, Clues*, London 1990); Michael Podro, 'The importance of Ernst Gombrich', *The Listener*, 89, No. 2299, 19 April 1973, pp. 508–10; E. Lachnit, 'Traditionalist'; Josef Krása, 'Ernst H. Gombrich a dnešní dějiny umění', in E. H. Gombrich, *Umění a iluze*, Praha 1985, pp. 505–17; Joaquín Lorda, *Gombrich: Una teoria del arte*, Barcelona 1991; and Richard Woodfield, 'Gombrich, formalism and the description of works of art', *British Journal of Aesthetics*, 34 (1994), pp. 134–45.

159. *Eribon*, p. 98.

160. *Meditations*, p. 66; *Tributes*, p. 17.

161. *Tributes*, p. 20.

162. *Social Sciences*, p. 10; *Tributes*, pp. 17–18; *Eribon*, p. 98.

163. *Social Sciences*, p. 31.

164. See G. G. Iggers, *The German Conception of History: the National Tradition of Historical Thought from Herder to the Present*, Middletown, 1968, pp. 124–266.

165. *Tributes*, p. 17.

166. *Social Sciences*, p. 17.

167. *Ideals*, p. 57; *Tributes*, p. 11.

168. *Meditations*, p. 107.

169. 'A plea for pluralism', in *Ideals*, pp. 184–8.

Response from E. H. Gombrich

15.II.95

Dear Professor Bakos,

I have now read the revised version of your paper and I feel I must respond in some form. I am certainly impressed by the hard work you put into that project and by the 170 footnotes to your 17 pages. I am all the more struck by the fact how rarely it may be possible to reconstruct a sequence of historical events from a few scattered sources. For inevitably I know more about my intellectual development than you could possibly find out from my writings.

While I do not wish to minimise the impression which Dvořák's book made on me, I must tell you that my interest in art and art history developed much more organically. I have often told the story how I was first captivated by the stone axes in Vienna's Naturhistorische Museum and by a book which my sister owned on *Das alte Wunderland der Pyramiden*, which made me want to study Egyptology. Soon I discovered Greek art for myself, and I still happen to have an essay I wrote in the sixth form at about 15 on a Greek vase by Brygos in the Vienna Museum. At the same time I declared in another school essay, that Leonardo da Vinci was my favourite hero and I gave some practice talks (Redeübungen) at school on quattrocento art. I doubt if I had read Dvořák at that time.

As to my choice between the two Institutes, it was probably governed also by coincidence. The widow of Max Dvořák ran a 'club' for young historians which met, I think, once a month. I don't know anymore who introduced me in the first year at University in 1928/9, but I there met a number of colleagues whom I liked, Julius Held, for instance, now a famous specialist on Rubens, and the late Kurt Schwarz who later dealt in antiquarian books. I think it was they who persuaded me to apply to Schlosser's Institute. I had frequented many lectures by Strzygowski, but it is true that his vanity repelled me. To be admitted to Schlosser's Institute I had first to write a research paper on a church in Vienna, (Peterskirche) and had my first taste of archive work, which fascinated me. I was accepted by Swoboda on the ground of its results.

My 'doubts' you attribute to the whole history of mediaeval art were confined to studies of the 'dark ages', the seventh and eighth centuries where the evidence is indeed scanty.

I hope, by the way, that I am not the only art historian here in the West who does not worship 'idols', that is authority. The motto of the Royal Society, founded by Newton is still 'nullius in verba' (we swear no authority), and this attitude is an essential ingredient of intellectual freedom, which was so sadly absent in totalitarian regimes, and did not have to wait for Karl Popper.

My doctoral thesis was not intended as a confirmation of Dvořák's thesis on Mannerism, but as an examination of its applicability to architecture.

It was Garger also, who knocked down an idol, the worship of really 'primitive' late antique and early medieval art. I still like to quote his remark that 'gingerbread figures, even when they are made of stone, are not necessarily works of art'. But he therefore posed the question of values in mediaeval art which interested me and on which I wrote without wanting to contradict Garger. He had nothing to do with Riegl.

Now to your dramatic story of my 'patricide'. I am afraid that it leaves out an essential episode I must now tell: My friend and colleague Joseph Bodonyi had been assigned a paper in Schlosser's Seminar on the rivalling theories of the origins of the golden ground. Schlosser had liked it and suggested he should make this into his doctoral dissertation. Unhappily Bodonyi, who was a very nice man, but a neurotic, developed a 'block', he felt unable to write, and his father who had to support him, got increasingly worried. So he invited me to come to Budapest to help his son finishing this thesis. I spent a pleasant month there, which was almost entirely filled with discussions on late antique art etc. I managed to get the thesis written (which may well also have absorbed some of my own ideas), but when it was ready, we felt that it was still too short. So we decided to lengthen it, by adding an appendix, 'Kritik der Lehre Riegl's', which you can still read if you can get hold of that thesis. It was at that time that I read *Die spätrömische Kunstindustrie* with meticulous care, and having earlier studied *Stilfragen* for Schlosser's Seminar I still think I can claim to know those principal works by Riegl better than many of those who write about him. But it is wholly misleading to claim that I am obsessed with Riegl. If you look at my nine essay volumes and my main publications you will find that only in *The Sense of Order* do I take issue with him and for good reasons. Otherwise I rarely think of Riegl since my interests lie elsewhere.

It is true that I may have felt somewhat irritated by the way my elder colleagues Pächt and Sedlmayr made an 'idol' of him, because I am too

much aware of certain absurdities in his writings. Let me quote an example
and ask you, if you accept that view?:

> der Wandel in der spätantiken Weltanschauung war eine notwendige
> Durchgangsphase des menschlichen Geistes, um von der Vorstellung eines
> (im engeren Sinn) rein mechanischen reihenweise gleichsam in di Ebene
> projizierten Zusammenhanges der Dinge zu derjenigen eines allverbreiteten
> chemischen, gleichsam den Raum nach allen Richtungen durchmessenden
> Zusammenhanges zu gelangenwer in jener apätantiken Wendung einen
> Verfall erblicken möchte, vermisst sich, dem menschlichen Geiste den
> Weg vorzuschreiben, den er hätte nehmen sollen um von der antiken sur
> modernen Naturauffassung zu gelangen. (pp. 403–4 of *Spätrömische Kunst-*
> *industrie*), see also the footnote!

[The transformation of the late antique world-view was a necessary tran-
sitional phase for the human spirit in order to arrive from the idea of a
(in the narrower sense) purely mechanical, serial, connection of objects
projected on to a plane to that of an omnipresent chemical, space pervading
connection. Whoever wants to regard this late antique development as a
decline arrogates to himself the authority to prescribe today to the human
spirit the road it should have taken to come from the ancient to the modern
conception of Nature.]

One does not have to enjoy toppling idols to recognise this for what it
is – portentous nonsense.

Incidentally, I have in front of me Schlosser's essay on the *Wiener Schule*
and read on p. 186 how Riegl yielded to the tendency of seeking for an
amply mythological 'national spirit' and even to the highly suspect 'racial
psyche' ('eines reichlich mythologischen "Volksgeiste", ja sogar der höchst
bedenklichen "Rassen" psyche drängte.') I wholly endorse Schlosser's further
remarks on p. 190 on Riegl's 'Neo-vitalism'. I never thought I would have
to defend my views on these obsolete intellectual fashions, which have so
obviously contributed (and still contribute) to the horrors of this tragic
century. So, forget about the 'grandpa', I know what I am talking about.
The same applies to Hegel.

But frankly, I don't think it matters to what extent I belong to the Vienna
school or any other school, of course we all absorbed views and problems
from our teachers, but my present interests lie on a very different plane, as
any reader of my writings (and possibly of my future writings, if I live so
long) will be able to judge.

I am sorry I have had to be so outspoken, but while I happen still to be alive, I must put 'the record straight'.

> Noch is es Tag, da rühre sich der Mann,
> Die Nacht bricht ein, wenn niemand wirken kann.

With all good wishes,

Yours sincerely,

List of contributors

Ján Bakos is Director of the Institute for Art History, Slovak Academy of Sciences, Bratislava and Associate Professor at the Department of Art History, Comenius University, Bratislava. He has published a substantial number of books and articles in the Slovakian language on art history and art-historical methodology.

Jan Baptist Bedaux studied art history and archaeology at the universities of Louvain and Utrecht. At present he is Associate Professor of Art History at the Free University of Amsterdam. He is the author of several publications on the iconography of Netherlandish art, including the exhibition catalogue *Tot Lering en Vermaak* (1976, co-author and editor), his dissertation *The Reality of Symbols: Studies in the Iconology of Netherlandish Art 1400–1800* (1990) and 'Velázquez's Fable of Arachne (*Las Hilanderas*): a continuing story' (*Simiolus*, 1992). In 1992 he organised the first international conference on sociobiology and the arts, of which the papers are now being published (*Sociobiology and the Arts*, Amsterdam and Atlanta 1995). He is currently preparing a book on the biological foundations of art.

Dr Graham Birtwistle teaches modern art history at the Free University of Amsterdam. An authority on the Cobra movement, he has published *Living Art: Asger Jorn's Comprehensive Theory of Art between Helhesten and Cobra (1946–1949)*, Utrecht 1986, which is currently being translated into German, and texts in international editions such as *Corneille, The Complete Graphic Works, 1948–1975*, Amsterdam 1992, and *Asger Jorn 1914–1973/ Asger Jorn Retrospective*, Amsterdam and Frankfurt 1994. He has also written for the new encyclopaedia *Dutch Art from 1475 to 1990*, New York 1995, and his lectures and articles on theoretical problems in primitivism and intercultural art have contributed to current debate in Europe, North America and South Africa.

Menachem Brinker is Professor of Literature and Philosophy at the Hebrew University of Jerusalem. He has published five books in Hebrew, two of them devoted to a philosophical theory of literature and the interpretation of fiction. Sections from these books have been published in English and French in *Critical Inquiry, The Journal of Aesthetics and Art Criticism, Littérature, New Literary History, Poetics Today, Poetique, Revue International de Philosophie,* etc. He also contributed a critical essay to the Hebrew translation of *Art and Illusion*.

Ian Gordon, a Fellow of the British Psychological Society, is a Senior Lecturer in Psychology at the University of Exeter. He has taught and carried out research in universities in Australia, Canada and New Zealand and accounts of his experiments into visual and tactile phenomena have been published in a number of the world's leading scientific journals, including *The Journal of Experimental Psychology*, *Leonardo*, *Nature*, *Perception* and *Perception and Psychophysics*. His book, *Theories of Visual Perception*, has been adopted as a standard text in several countries. He is the co-inventor of an aid for the visually handicapped.

John M. Kennedy is a psychologist, interested in perception and representation. He is the author of *Drawing and the Blind*, New Haven 1993. In 1992–93 he was the President of 'Psychology and the Arts', Division 10 of the American Psychological Association. He has written extensively on outline, figure-ground, perspective, chiaroscuro and metaphor in pictures. Chang Hong Liu, now at McMaster University, Ontario, was a doctoral student of Kennedy's at Toronto in the field of the psychology of symbolism.

Klaus Lepsky studied Art History, History of Architecture and Philosophy in Aachen and London and received his Ph.D. in 1989. He is now a science librarian at the University and State Library of Dusselfdorf. He has published a book on E. H. Gombrich's theory of art, *Ernst H. Gombrich, Theorie und Methode* (1991) and articles on philosophical and psychological issues in art theory: 'Perspektive – Symbol, Konvention, Wirklichkeit' (*Zeitschrift für Ästhetik und allgemeine Kunstwissenschaft*, Bd. 31/2 (1986), pp. 214–230); 'Bild und Wirklichkeit – Die Wirklichkeit im Bild' (*Natur und Kunst: Kunsthistorisches Jahrbuch Graz*, 23 (1987), pp. 166–173).

Joaquín Lorda is an architect and teaches the history of art and architecture in the School of Architecture at the University of Navarra. He wrote his doctoral dissertation on the ideas of E. H. Gombrich and has published a number of articles on the theory of architecture, classical architecture and ornament. He is the co-author, with Carlos Montes, of *E. H. Gombrich: Marco conceptual y Bibliografía*, Pamplona 1985 and the author of *Gombrich: Una teoría del arte*, Barcelona 1991.

Göran Sörbom has been chairman of the Department of Aesthetics at the University of Uppsala in Sweden since 1979. He has also been Chairman of

KING ALFRED'S COLLEGE
LIBRARY

the Scandinavian Society of Aesthetics from its foundation in 1983. He received his doctoral degree for his dissertation *Mimesis and art: Studies in the Origin and Early Development of an Aesthetic Vocabulary*, Uppsala 1966. He has published books and papers in Swedish on the theory of value, the theory of art and the history of aesthetics. In English he has mainly published papers on the ancient theory of art: 'What is in the mind of the image-maker? Some views on pictorial representation in antiquity' (*Journal of Comparative Literature and Aesthetics*, 10 (1987), pp. 1–41); 'Imitations, images and similarity: some views from antiquity', *Aesthetic Distinction: Essays presented to Göran Hermerén on his fiftieth birthday*, edited by T. Anderberg, T. Nilstun and I. Persson, Lund 1988; 'Xenophon's Socrates on the Greek art revolution', in *The Philosophy of Socrates*, edited by K. J. Boudouris, Athens 1991; 'The theory of imitation is not a theory of art', in *Understanding the Arts: Contemporary Scandinavian Aesthetics*, edited by J. Emt and G. Hermerén, Lund 1992; and 'Aristotle on music as representation' (*Journal of Aesthetics and Art Criticism*, 52 (1994), pp. 37–46).

B. R. Tilghman was Professor of Philosophy at Kansas State University until his retirement in 1994. He is the author of *The Expression of Emotion in the Visual Arts*, The Hague 1970; *But is it Art?* Oxford 1984; *Wittgenstein, Ethics and Aesthetics*, London 1991 and is the editor of *Language and Aesthetics*, Kansas 1973.

David Topper is Professor of History at the University of Winnipeg, where he teaches both History of Art and History of Science. He was the recipient of two teaching awards: the Robson Memorial Award for Excellence in Teaching at the University of Winnipeg (1981), and the National 3M Teaching Fellowship (1987). Since 1982 he has been an international co-editor of *Leonardo: Journal of the International Society for the Arts, Sciences, and Technology*. His research and publications reflect the eclectic nature of his interests, covering facets of the art/science interface: philosophical matters and historical case-studies on the nature of and interaction between art and science, the role of perception in science and in art, and the realm of scientific illustration. Some of his recent publications include 'Newton on the colors of the spectrum' (*Studies in the History and Philosophy of Science* (1990)); 'The parallel fallacy: on comparing art and science' (*British Journal of Aesthetics* (1990)); 'Towards an epistemology of scientific illustration', in *Picturing Knowledge: Historical and Philosophical Essays Concerning the Use of Art as Science*, edited by B. Baigrie, Toronto 1995; and 'Trajectories of blood: Artemisia Gentileschi and Galileo's parabolic path' (*Women's Art Journal*, in press).

Richard Woodfield, the editor, teaches art theory in the Department of Visual and Performing Arts at The Nottingham Trent University; he is also a visiting professor at the Central European University's Department of the History and Philosophy of Art and Architecture in Prague. He was trained as a philosopher, has published articles on the history of aesthetics, edited a series of eighteenth-century art theoretical texts and E. H. Gombrich's *Reflections on the History of Art* and *The Essential Gombrich* for Phaidon Press. He is currently working on a variety of projects, including a book on Gombrich's work, and is also Secretary of the British Society of Aesthetics.

Edmond Wright holds degrees in English and Philosophy, and a doctorate in Philosophy. He has recently been a Fellow at the Swedish College for the Advanced Study of the Social Sciences, Uppsala. He has edited *The Ironic Discourse, Poetics Today*, 4 (1983); *New Representationalisms: Essays in the Philosophy of Perception*, Avebury 1993; and is currently an advisory editor of *The Blackwell Encyclopaedic Dictionary of Psychology*. He has published over thirty articles on language, perception and the philosophy of science in *Mind, Philosophy, Philosophy and Phenomenological Research, Philosophy of Science, Synthèse*, and other journals. He has also published two volumes of poetry.

Index

KING ALFRED'S COLLEGE
LIBRARY